ANGEL &FAITH™

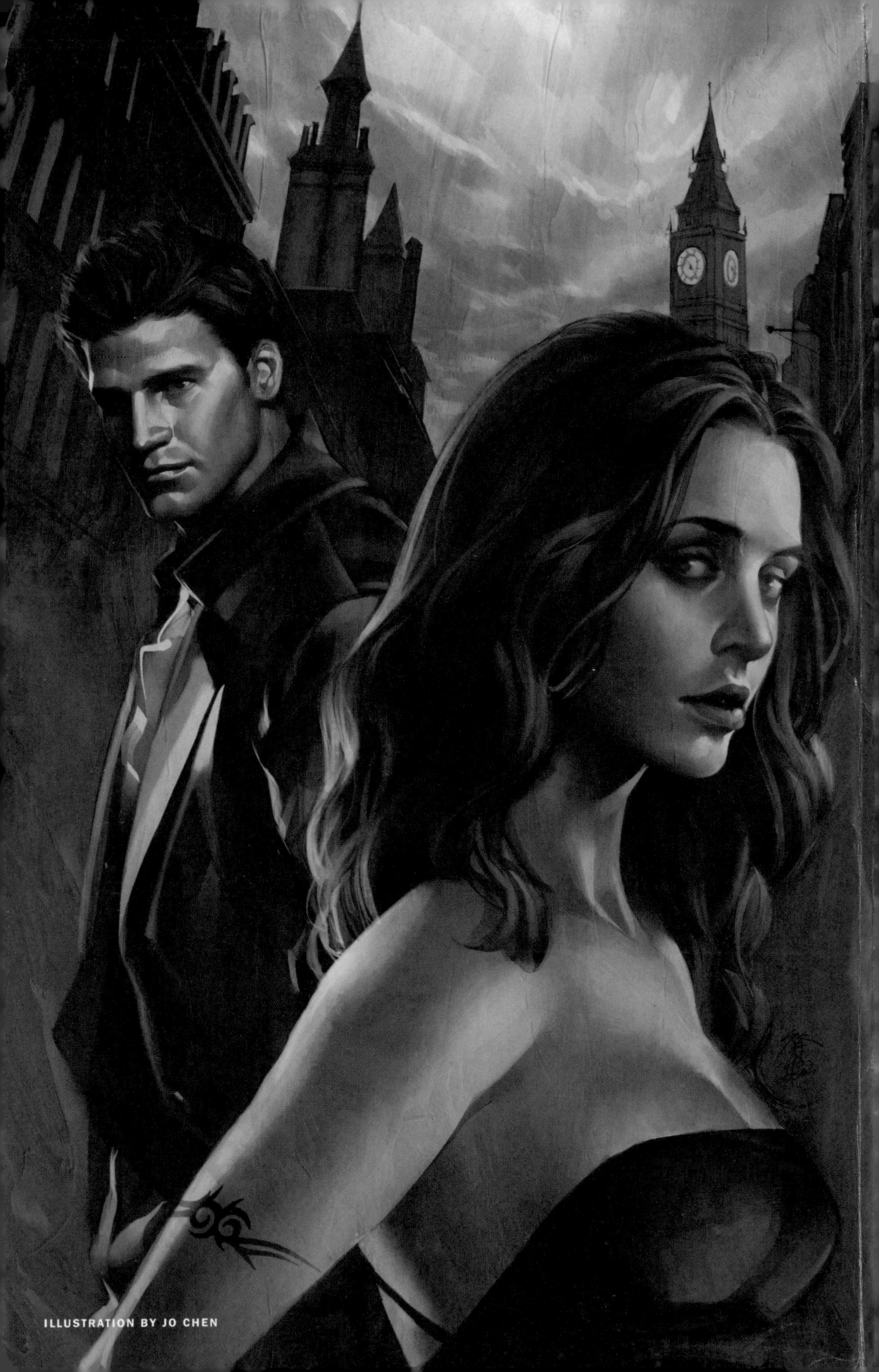

ILLUSTRATION BY JO CHEN

ANGEL &FAITH

SEASON 9 · VOLUME 1

SCRIPT
CHRISTOS GAGE

LIVE THROUGH THIS

ART
REBEKAH ISAACS

IN PERFECT HARMONY

ART
PHIL NOTO

COLORS
DAN JACKSON

LETTERS
RICHARD STARKINGS & *Comicraft's*
JIMMY BETANCOURT

COVER ART
STEVE MORRIS

EXECUTIVE PRODUCER
JOSS WHEDON

DARK HORSE BOOKS

PRESIDENT & PUBLISHER
MIKE RICHARDSON

EDITORS
SCOTT ALLIE & SIERRA HAHN

ASSISTANT EDITOR
FREDDYE LINS

COLLECTION DESIGNER
JUSTIN COUCH

Published by Dark Horse Books
A division of Dark Horse Comics, Inc.
10956 SE Main Street
Milwaukie, OR 97222

DarkHorse.com

To find a comics shop in your area, call the
Comic Shop Locator Service toll-free at
(888) 266-4226.

First edition: June 2012
ISBN 978-1-59582-887-3

10 9 8 7 6 5 4 3 2 1

This story takes place during *Buffy the Vampire Slayer* Season 9, created by Joss Whedon.

Special thanks to Debbie Olshan at Twentieth Century Fox and Daniel Kaminsky.

NEIL HANKERSON Executive Vice President • TOM WEDDLE Chief Financial Officer • RANDY STRADLEY Vice President of Publishing • MICHAEL MARTENS Vice President of Book Trade Sales • ANITA NELSON Vice President of Business Affairs • DAVID SCROGGY Vice President of Product Development • DALE LAFOUNTAIN Vice President of Information Technology • DARLENE VOGEL Senior Director of Print, Design, and Production • KEN LIZZI General Counsel • MATT PARKINSON Senior Director of Marketing • DAVEY ESTRADA Editorial Director • SCOTT ALLIE Senior Managing Editor • CHRIS WARNER Senior Books Editor • DIANA SCHUTZ Executive Editor • CARY GRAZZINI Director of Print and Development • LIA RIBACCHI Art Director CARA NIECE Director of Scheduling

This volume reprints the comic-book series *Angel & Faith* #1–#5 from Dark Horse Comics.

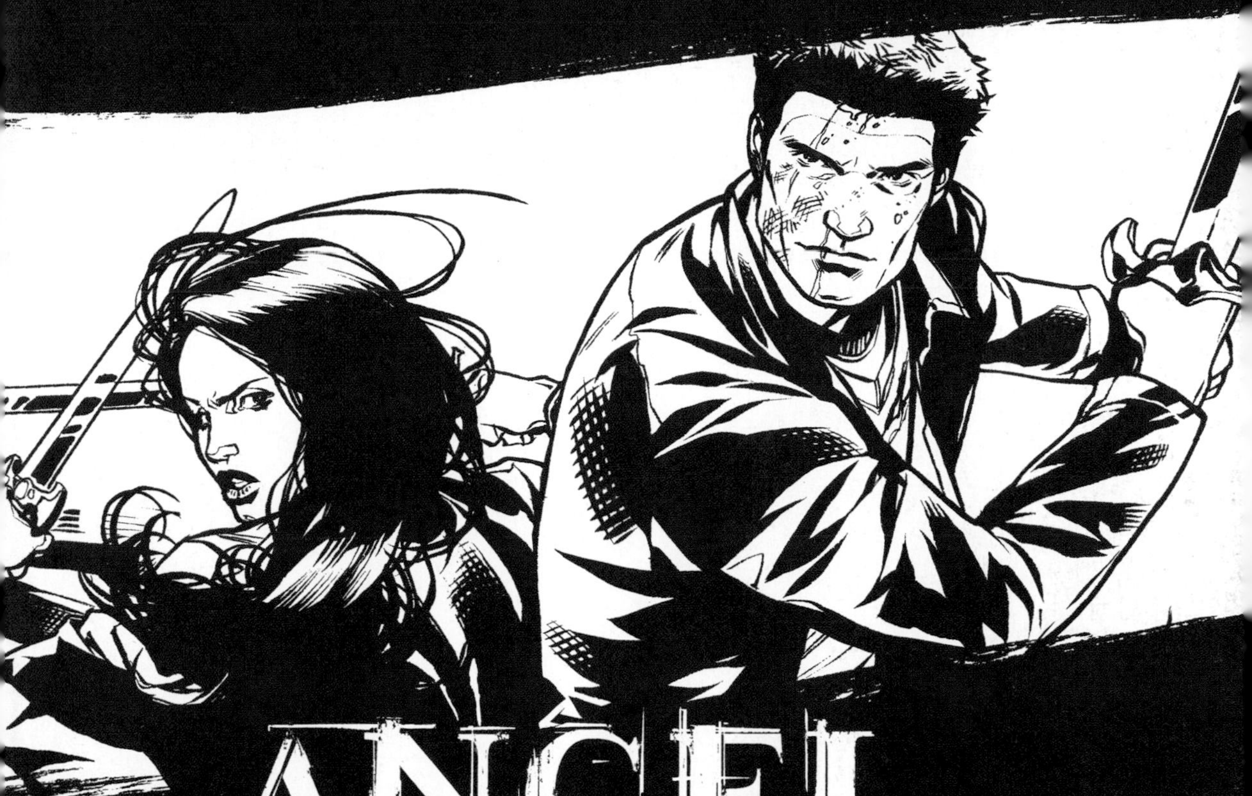

ANGEL & FAITH™

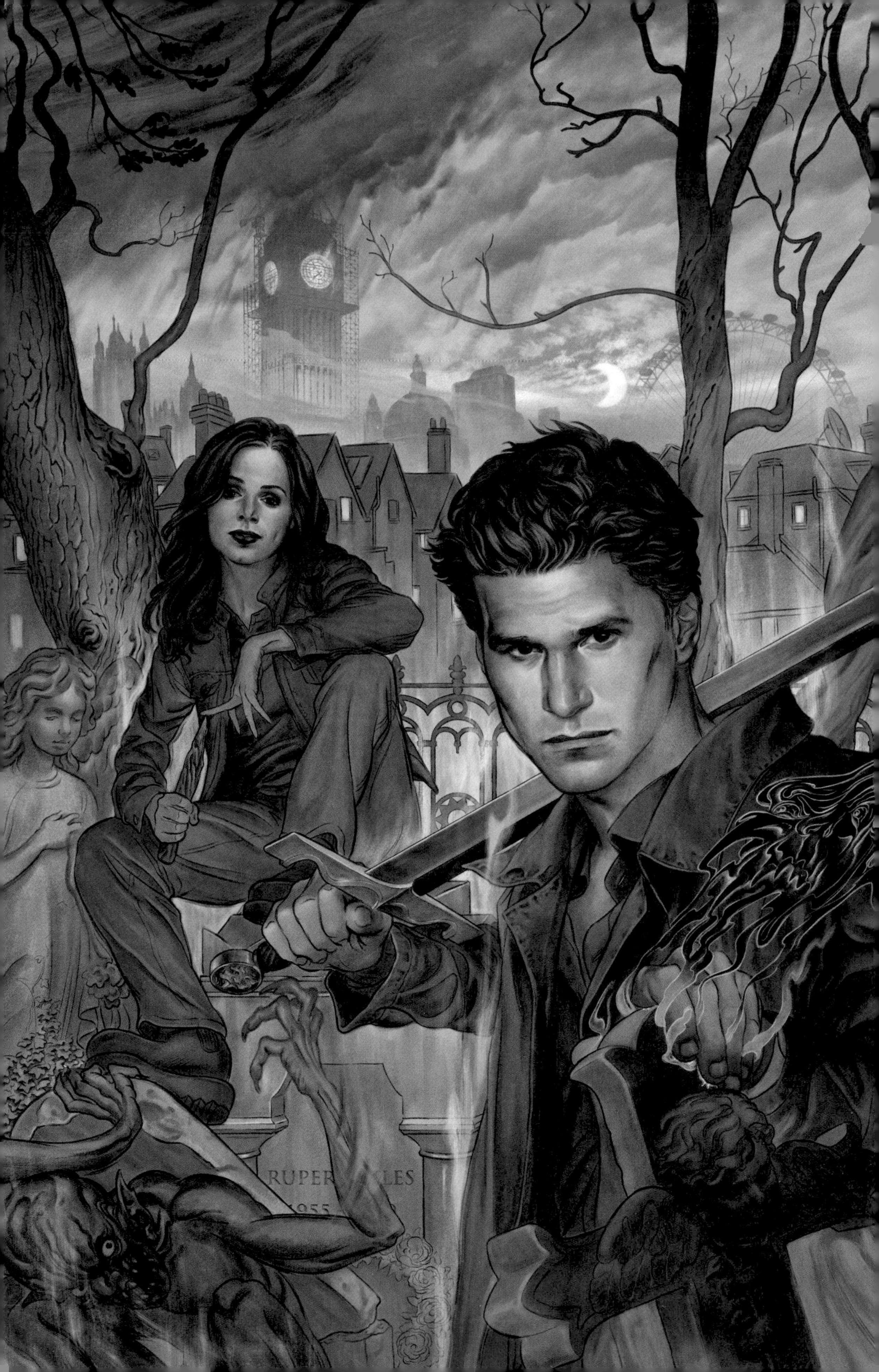
RUPER LES
1955

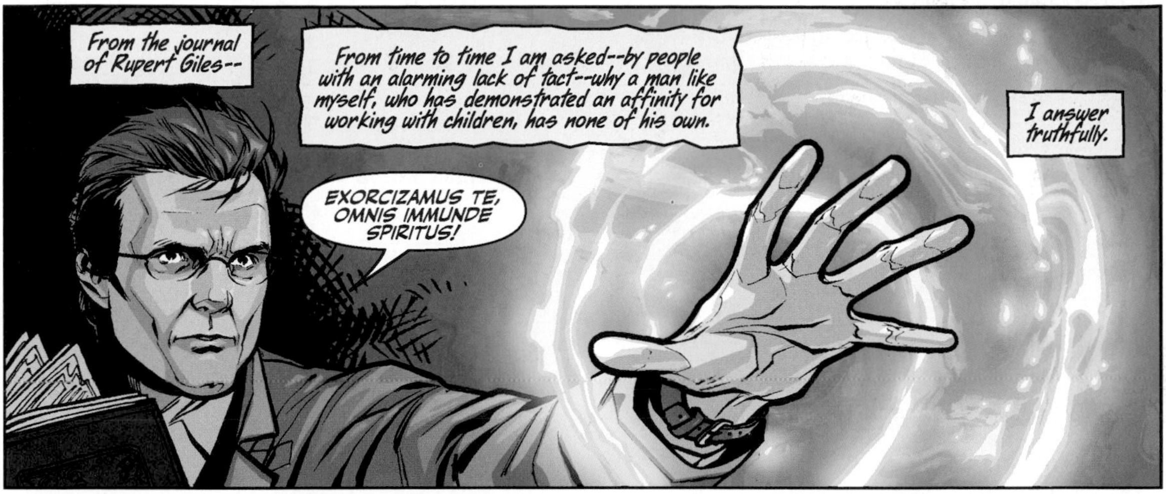
From the journal of Rupert Giles--
From time to time I am asked--by people with an alarming lack of tact--why a man like myself, who has demonstrated an affinity for working with children, has none of his own.
EXORCIZAMUS TE, OMNIS IMMUNDE SPIRITUS!
I answer truthfully.

LIVE THROUGH THIS PART ONE

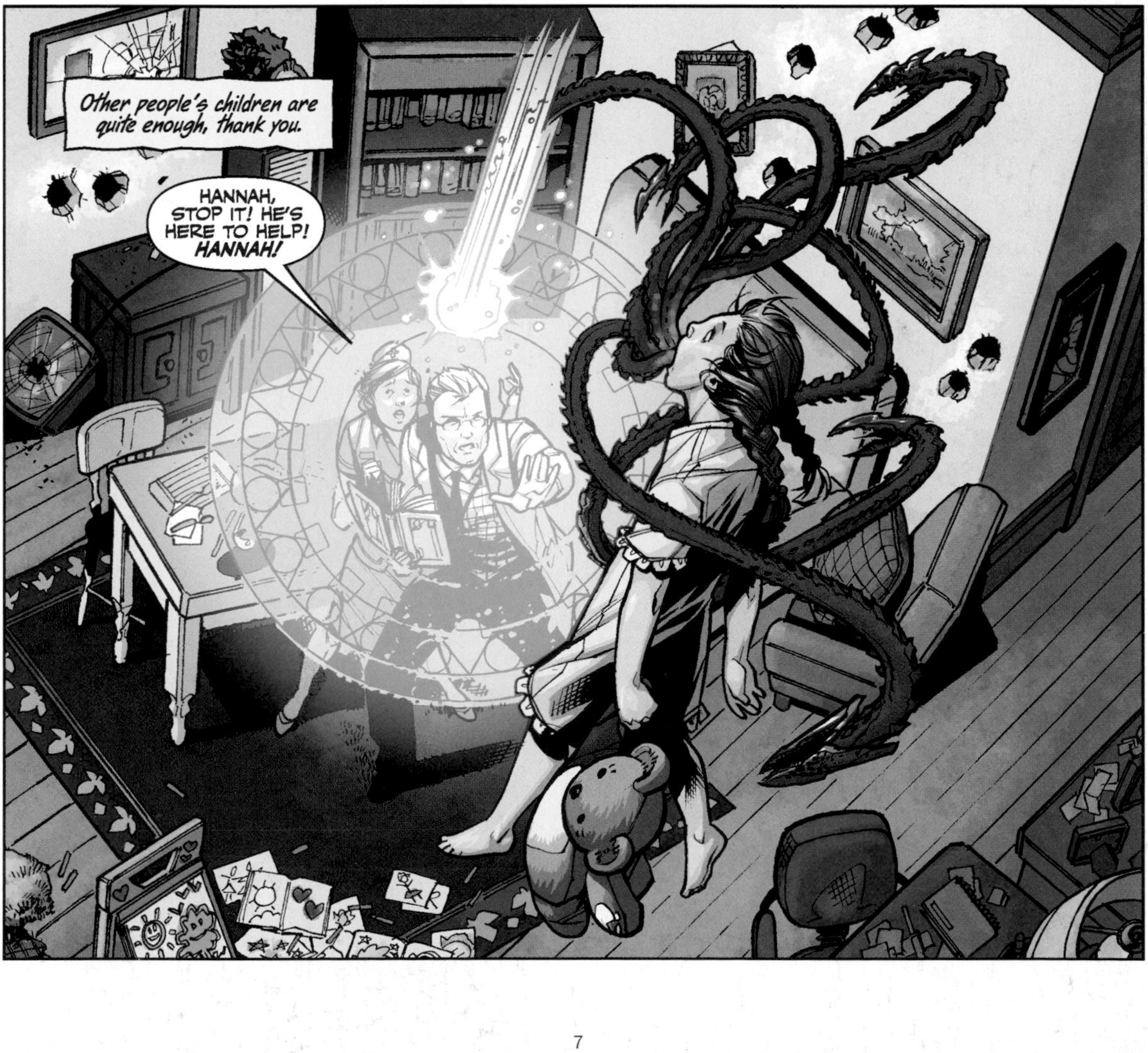
Other people's children are quite enough, thank you.
HANNAH, STOP IT! HE'S HERE TO HELP! HANNAH!

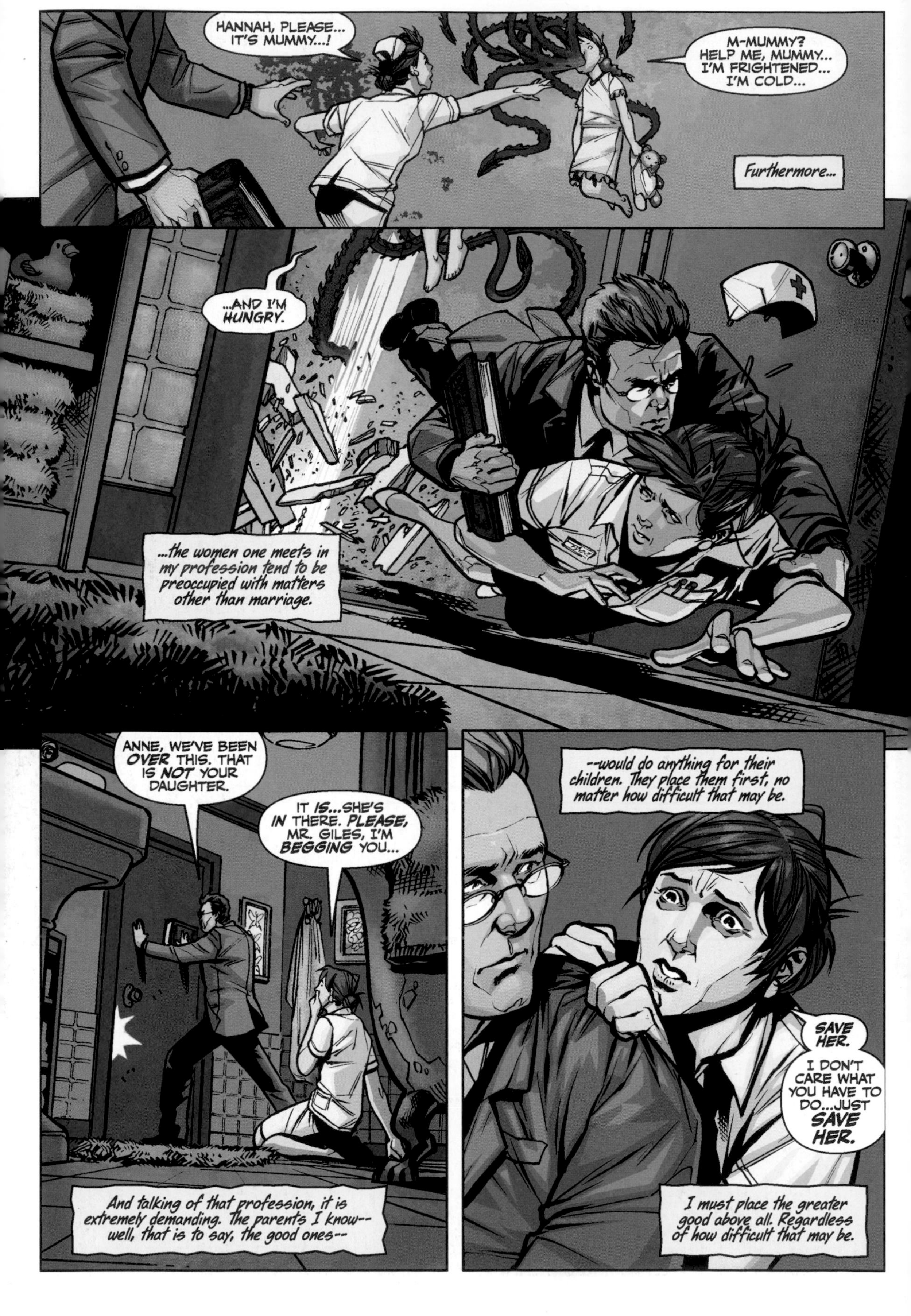
HANNAH, PLEASE... IT'S MUMMY...!
M-MUMMY? HELP ME, MUMMY... I'M FRIGHTENED... I'M COLD...
Furthermore...
...AND I'M HUNGRY.
...the women one meets in my profession tend to be preoccupied with matters other than marriage.
ANNE, WE'VE BEEN OVER THIS. THAT IS NOT YOUR DAUGHTER.
IT IS...SHE'S IN THERE. PLEASE, MR. GILES, I'M BEGGING YOU...
And talking of that profession, it is extremely demanding. The parents I know--well, that is to say, the good ones--
--would do anything for their children. They place them first, no matter how difficult that may be.
SAVE HER.
I DON'T CARE WHAT YOU HAVE TO DO...JUST SAVE HER.
I must place the greater good above all. Regardless of how difficult that may be.

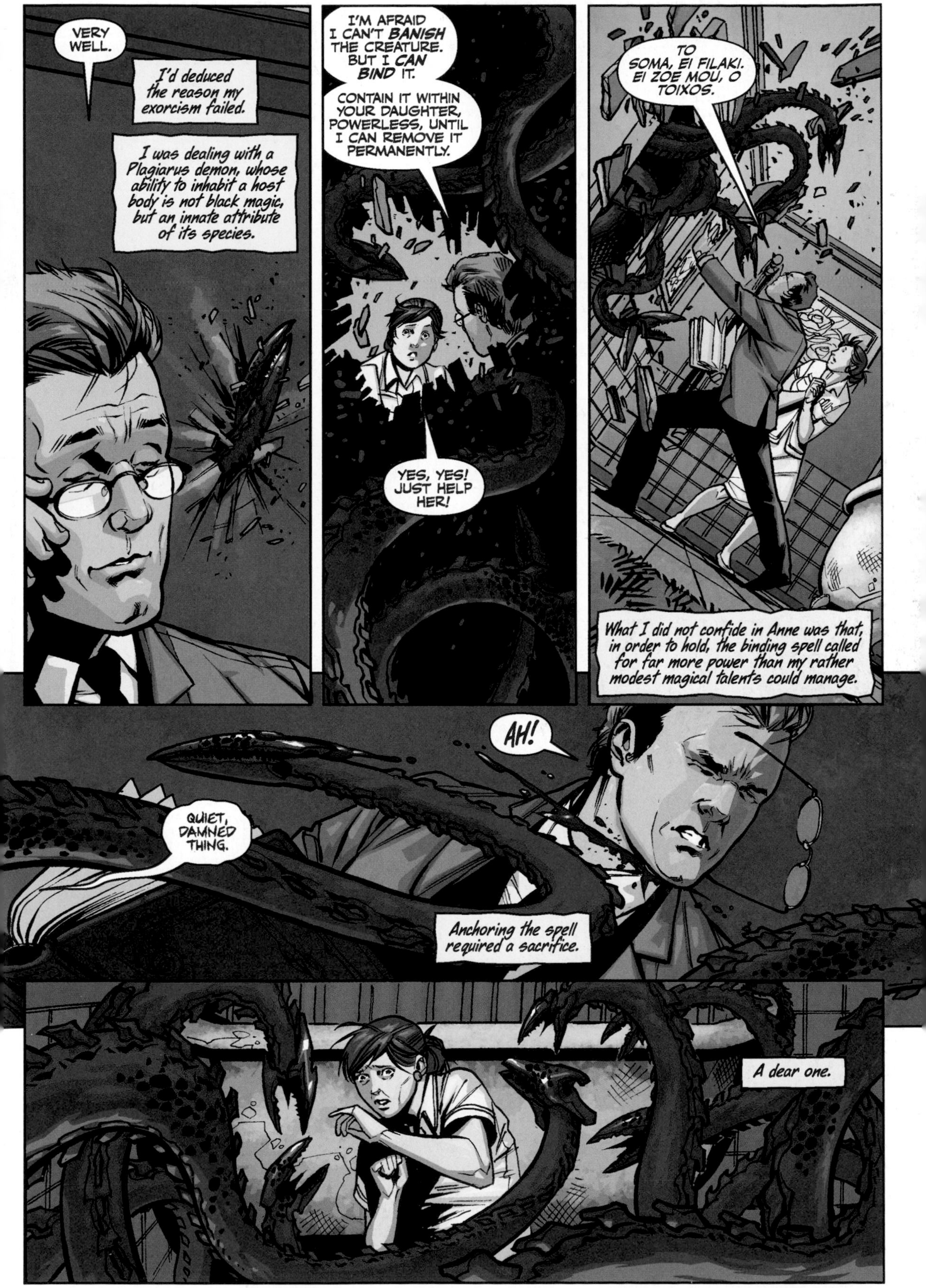
VERY WELL.
I'd deduced the reason my exorcism failed.
I was dealing with a Plagiarus demon, whose ability to inhabit a host body is not black magic, but an innate attribute of its species.
I'M AFRAID I CAN'T BANISH THE CREATURE. BUT I CAN BIND IT.
CONTAIN IT WITHIN YOUR DAUGHTER, POWERLESS, UNTIL I CAN REMOVE IT PERMANENTLY.
YES, YES! JUST HELP HER!
TO SOMA, EI FILAKI. EI ZOE MOU, O TOIXOS.
What I did not confide in Anne was that, in order to hold, the binding spell called for far more power than my rather modest magical talents could manage.
AH!
QUIET, DAMNED THING.
Anchoring the spell required a sacrifice.
A dear one.

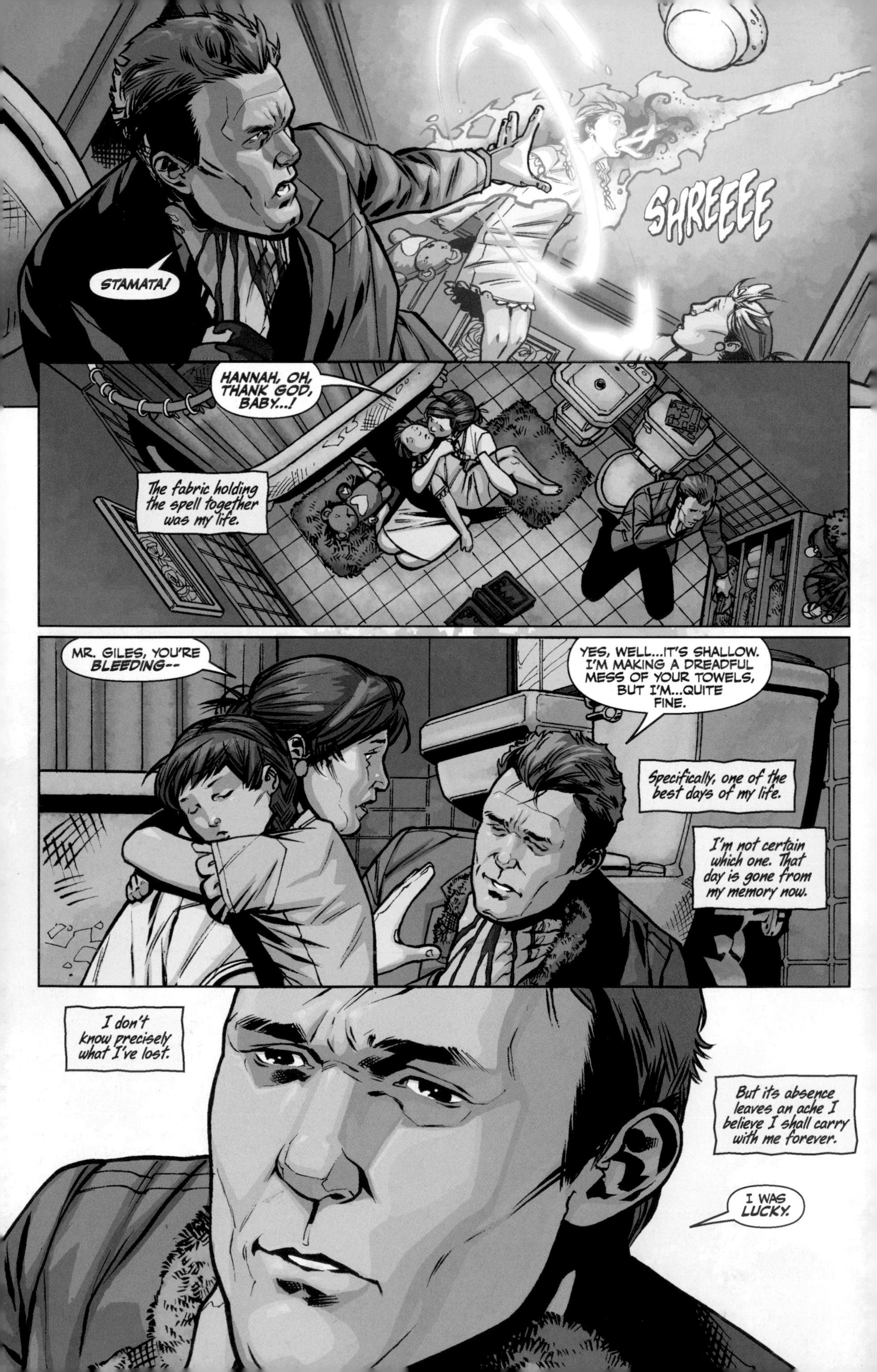
STAMATA!
SHREEEE
HANNAH, OH, THANK GOD, BABY...!
The fabric holding the spell together was my life.
MR. GILES, YOU'RE BLEEDING--
YES, WELL...IT'S SHALLOW. I'M MAKING A DREADFUL MESS OF YOUR TOWELS, BUT I'M...QUITE FINE.
Specifically, one of the best days of my life.
I'm not certain which one. That day is gone from my memory now.
I don't know precisely what I've lost.
But its absence leaves an ache I believe I shall carry with me forever.
I WAS LUCKY.

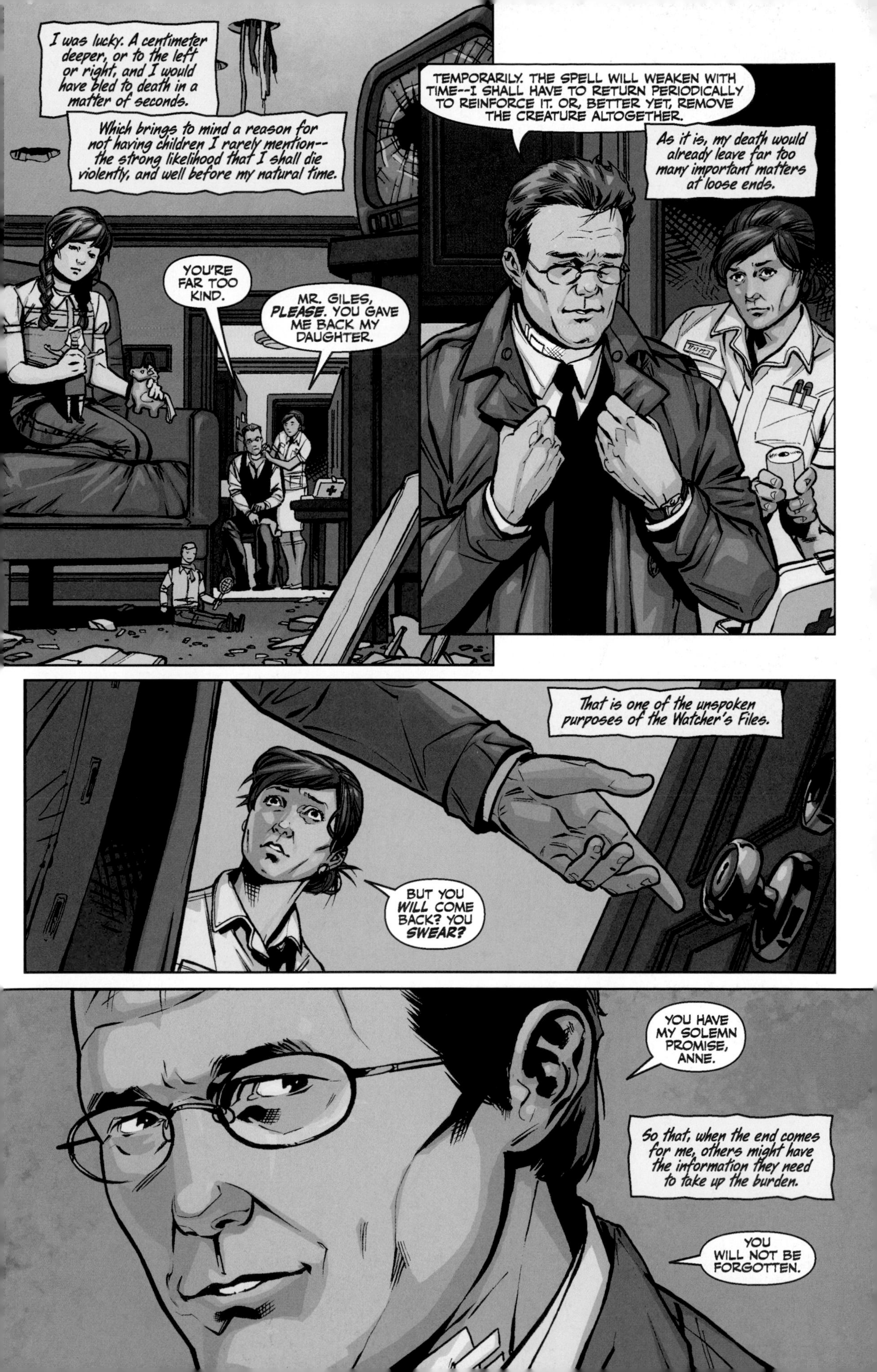
I was lucky. A centimeter deeper, or to the left or right, and I would have bled to death in a matter of seconds.
Which brings to mind a reason for not having children I rarely mention--the strong likelihood that I shall die violently, and well before my natural time.
YOU'RE FAR TOO KIND.
MR. GILES, PLEASE. YOU GAVE ME BACK MY DAUGHTER.
TEMPORARILY. THE SPELL WILL WEAKEN WITH TIME--I SHALL HAVE TO RETURN PERIODICALLY TO REINFORCE IT. OR, BETTER YET, REMOVE THE CREATURE ALTOGETHER.
As it is, my death would already leave far too many important matters at loose ends.
That is one of the unspoken purposes of the Watcher's Files.
BUT YOU WILL COME BACK? YOU SWEAR?
YOU HAVE MY SOLEMN PROMISE, ANNE.
So that, when the end comes for me, others might have the information they need to take up the burden.
YOU WILL NOT BE FORGOTTEN.

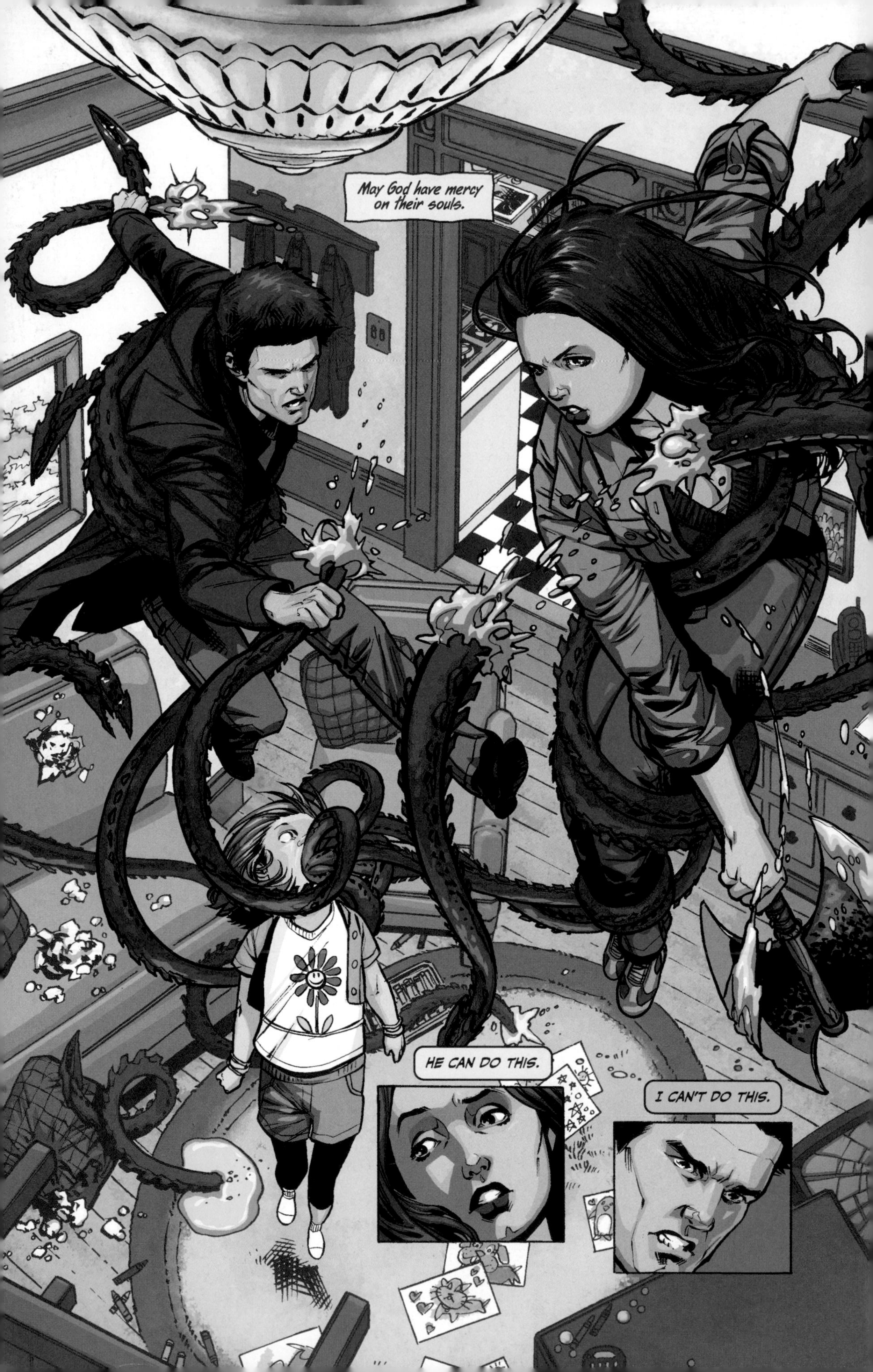
May God have mercy on their souls.
HE CAN DO THIS.
I CAN'T DO THIS.

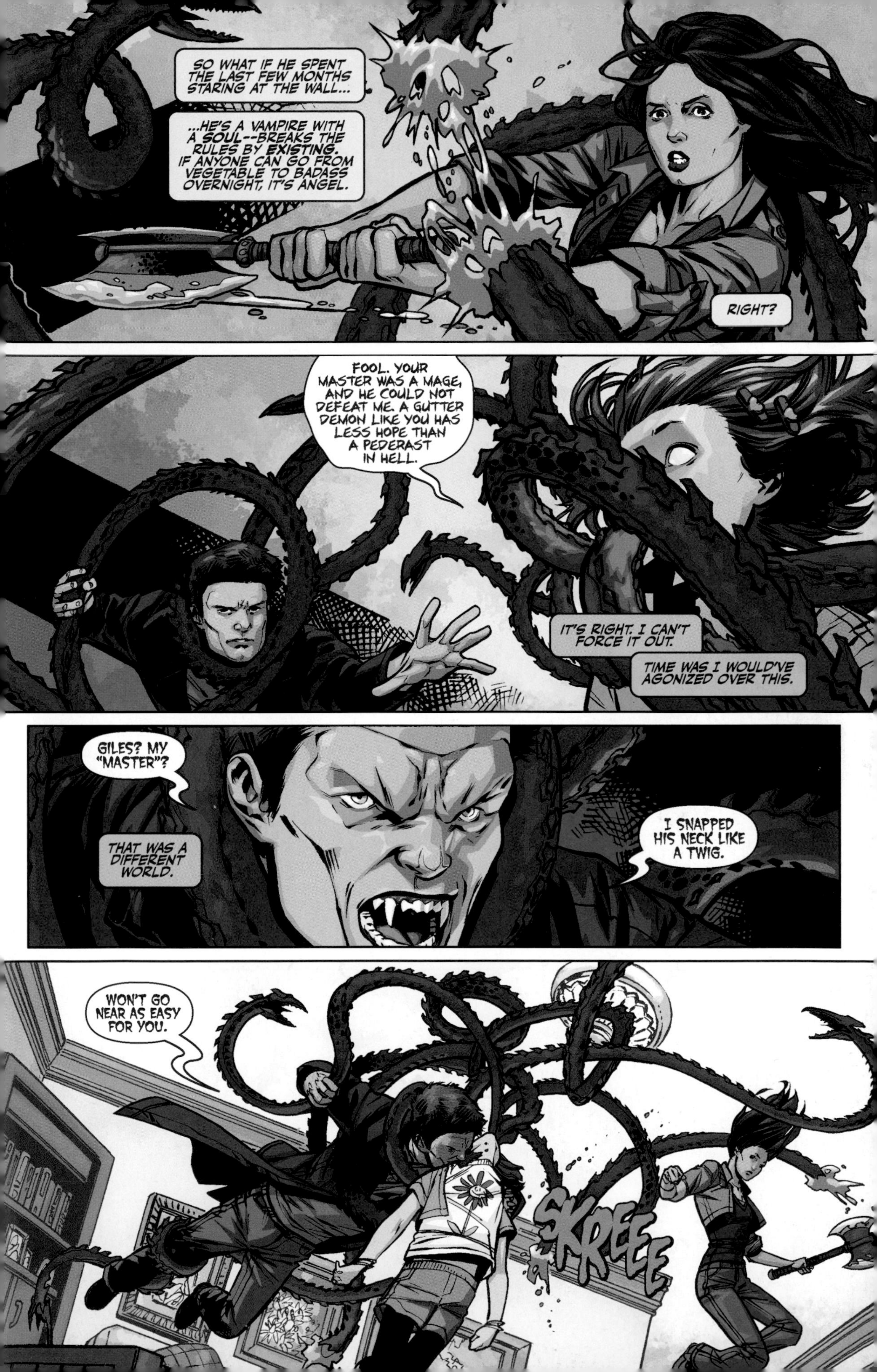
SO WHAT IF HE SPENT THE LAST FEW MONTHS STARING AT THE WALL...
...HE'S A VAMPIRE WITH A SOUL--BREAKS THE RULES BY EXISTING. IF ANYONE CAN GO FROM VEGETABLE TO BADASS OVERNIGHT, IT'S ANGEL.
RIGHT?
FOOL. YOUR MASTER WAS A MAGE, AND HE COULD NOT DEFEAT ME. A GUTTER DEMON LIKE YOU HAS LESS HOPE THAN A PEDERAST IN HELL.
IT'S RIGHT. I CAN'T FORCE IT OUT.
TIME WAS I WOULD'VE AGONIZED OVER THIS.
GILES? MY "MASTER"?
THAT WAS A DIFFERENT WORLD.
I SNAPPED HIS NECK LIKE A TWIG.
WON'T GO NEAR AS EASY FOR YOU.
SKREEE

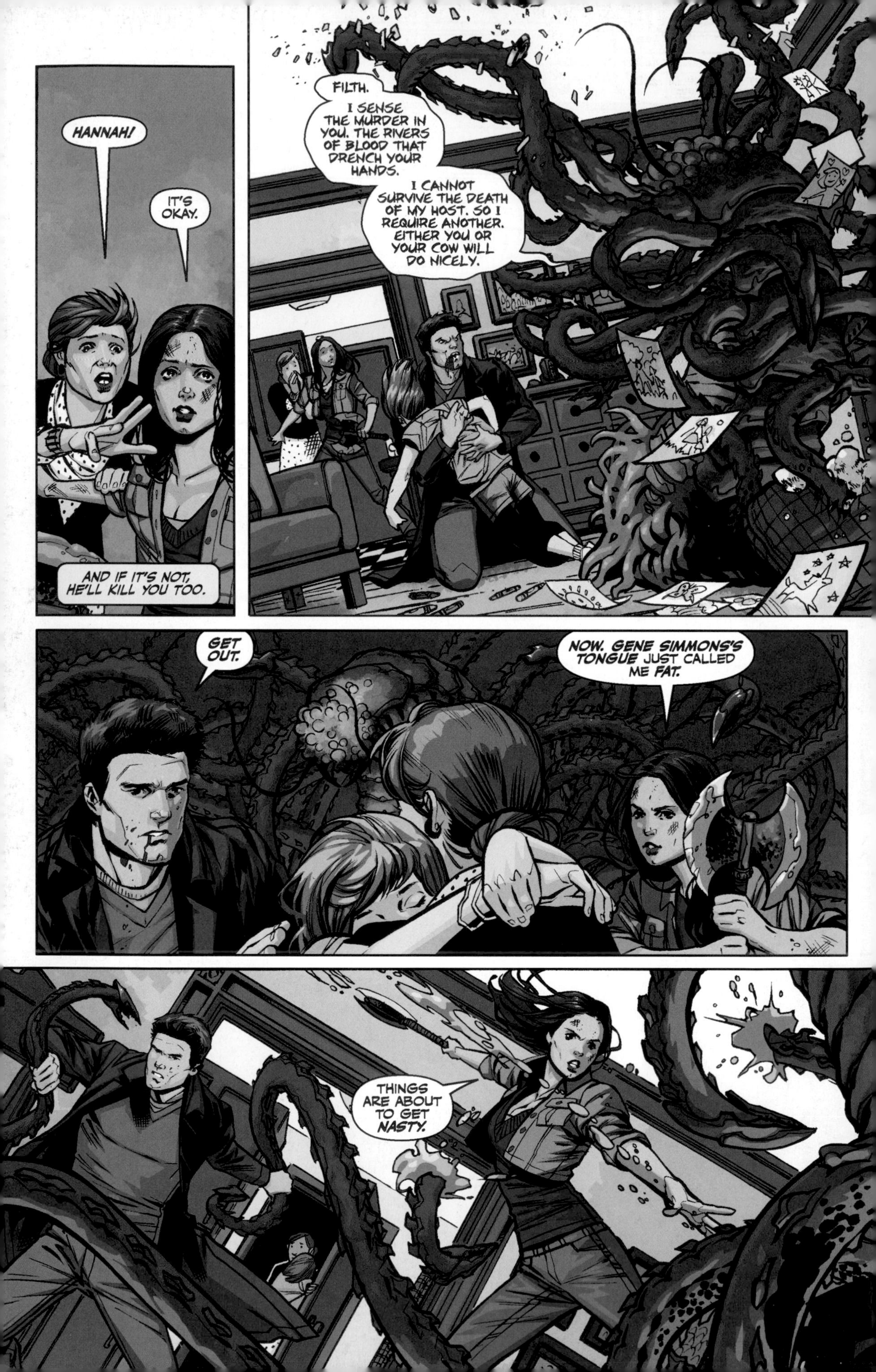
HANNAH!
IT'S OKAY.
AND IF IT'S NOT, HE'LL KILL YOU TOO.
FILTH.
I SENSE THE MURDER IN YOU. THE RIVERS OF BLOOD THAT DRENCH YOUR HANDS.
I CANNOT SURVIVE THE DEATH OF MY HOST. SO I REQUIRE ANOTHER. EITHER YOU OR YOUR COW WILL DO NICELY.
GET OUT.
NOW. GENE SIMMONS'S TONGUE JUST CALLED ME FAT.
THINGS ARE ABOUT TO GET NASTY.

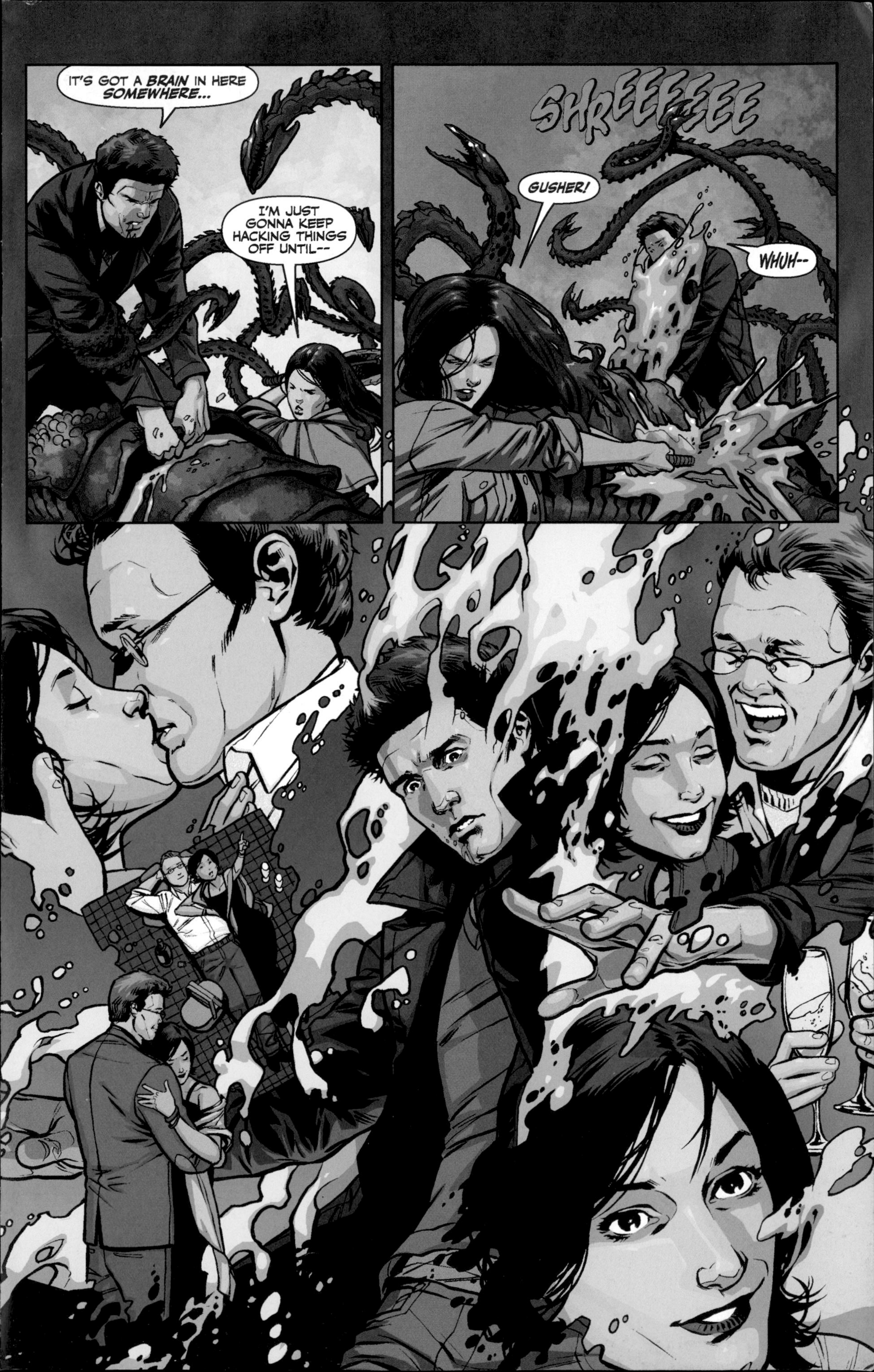
IT'S GOT A BRAIN IN HERE SOMEWHERE...
I'M JUST GONNA KEEP HACKING THINGS OFF UNTIL--
SHREEEEEEE
GUSHER!
WHUH--

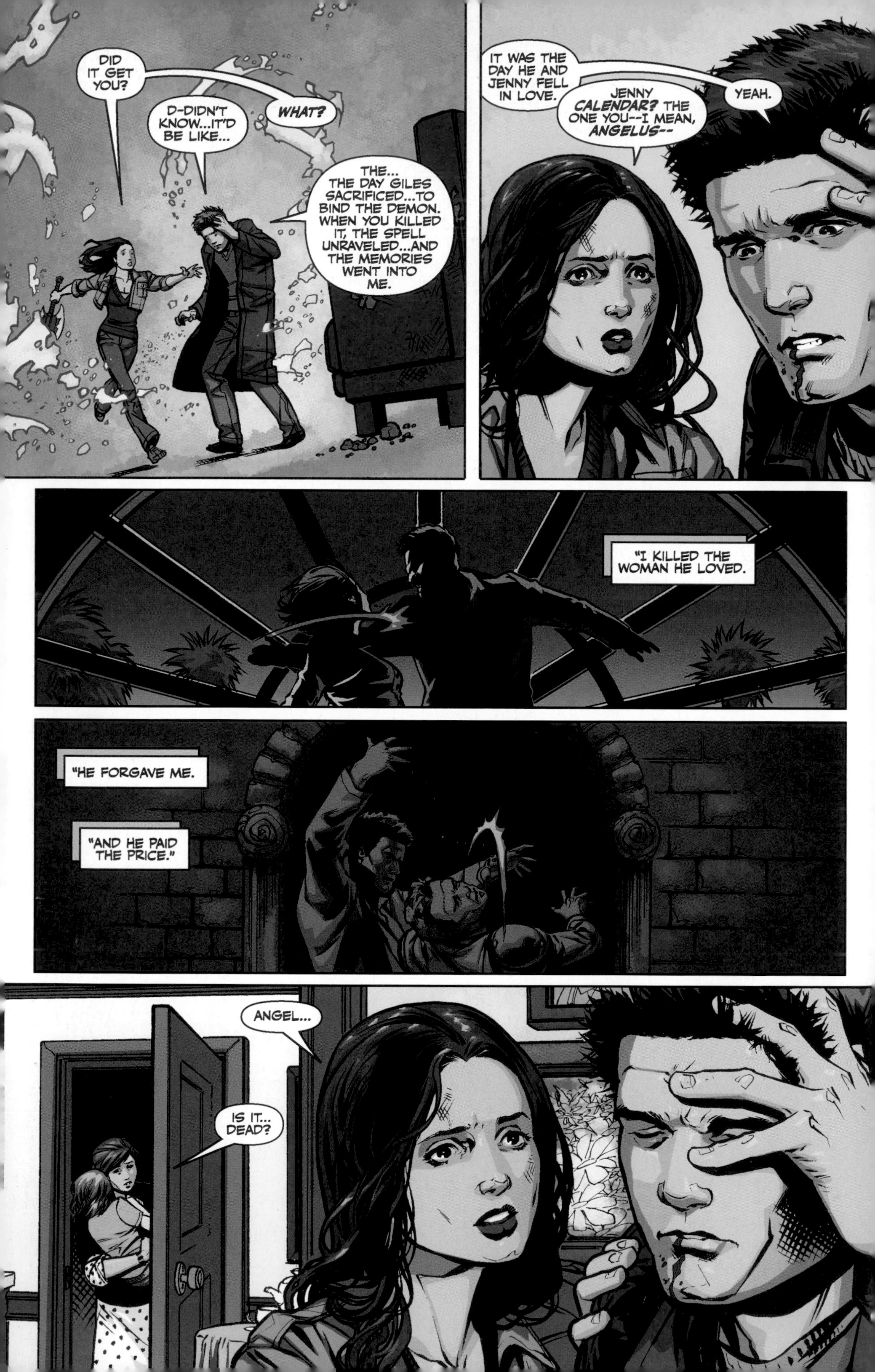
DID IT GET YOU?
D-DIDN'T KNOW...IT'D BE LIKE...
WHAT?
THE... THE DAY GILES SACRIFICED...TO BIND THE DEMON. WHEN YOU KILLED IT, THE SPELL UNRAVELED...AND THE MEMORIES WENT INTO ME.
IT WAS THE DAY HE AND JENNY FELL IN LOVE.
JENNY CALENDAR? THE ONE YOU--I MEAN, ANGELUS--
YEAH.
"I KILLED THE WOMAN HE LOVED.
"HE FORGAVE ME.
"AND HE PAID THE PRICE."
ANGEL...
IS IT... DEAD?

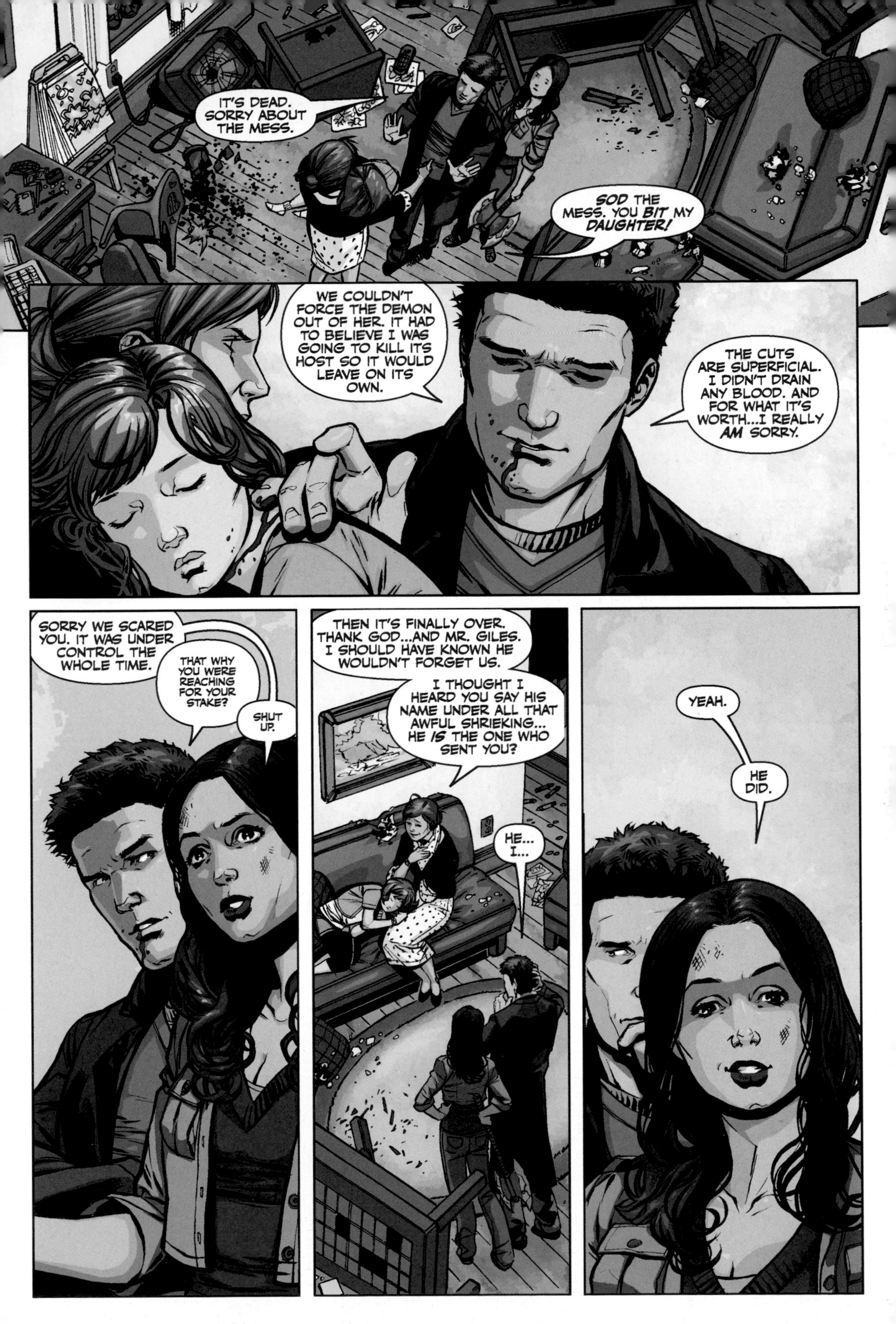
IT'S DEAD. SORRY ABOUT THE MESS.
SOD THE MESS. YOU BIT MY DAUGHTER!
WE COULDN'T FORCE THE DEMON OUT OF HER. IT HAD TO BELIEVE I WAS GOING TO KILL ITS HOST SO IT WOULD LEAVE ON ITS OWN.
THE CUTS ARE SUPERFICIAL. I DIDN'T DRAIN ANY BLOOD. AND FOR WHAT IT'S WORTH...I REALLY AM SORRY.
SORRY WE SCARED YOU. IT WAS UNDER CONTROL THE WHOLE TIME.
THAT WHY YOU WERE REACHING FOR YOUR STAKE?
SHUT UP.
THEN IT'S FINALLY OVER. THANK GOD...AND MR. GILES. I SHOULD HAVE KNOWN HE WOULDN'T FORGET US.
I THOUGHT I HEARD YOU SAY HIS NAME UNDER ALL THAT AWFUL SHRIEKING... HE IS THE ONE WHO SENT YOU?
HE... I...
YEAH.
HE DID.

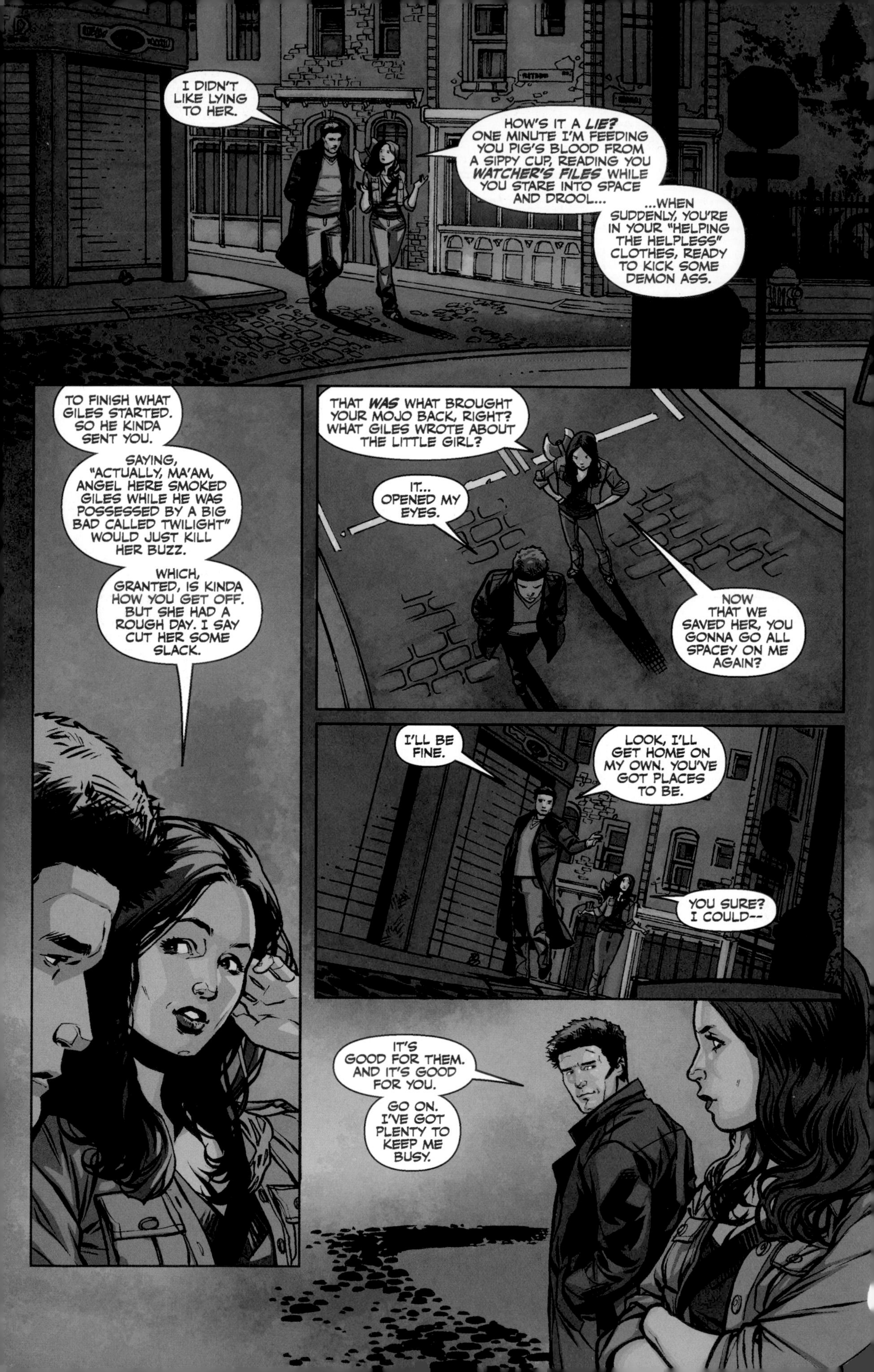
I DIDN'T LIKE LYING TO HER.
HOW'S IT A *LIE?* ONE MINUTE I'M FEEDING YOU PIG'S BLOOD FROM A SIPPY CUP, READING YOU *WATCHER'S FILES* WHILE YOU STARE INTO SPACE AND DROOL...
...WHEN SUDDENLY, YOU'RE IN YOUR "HELPING THE HELPLESS" CLOTHES, READY TO KICK SOME DEMON ASS.
TO FINISH WHAT GILES STARTED. SO HE KINDA SENT YOU.
SAYING, "ACTUALLY, MA'AM, ANGEL HERE SMOKED GILES WHILE HE WAS POSSESSED BY A BIG BAD CALLED TWILIGHT" WOULD JUST KILL HER BUZZ.
WHICH, GRANTED, IS KINDA HOW YOU GET OFF. BUT SHE HAD A ROUGH DAY. I SAY CUT HER SOME SLACK.
THAT *WAS* WHAT BROUGHT YOUR MOJO BACK, RIGHT? WHAT GILES WROTE ABOUT THE LITTLE GIRL?
IT... OPENED MY EYES.
NOW THAT WE SAVED HER, YOU GONNA GO ALL SPACEY ON ME AGAIN?
I'LL BE FINE.
LOOK, I'LL GET HOME ON MY OWN. YOU'VE GOT PLACES TO BE.
YOU SURE? I COULD--
IT'S GOOD FOR THEM. AND IT'S GOOD FOR YOU.
GO ON. I'VE GOT PLENTY TO KEEP ME BUSY.

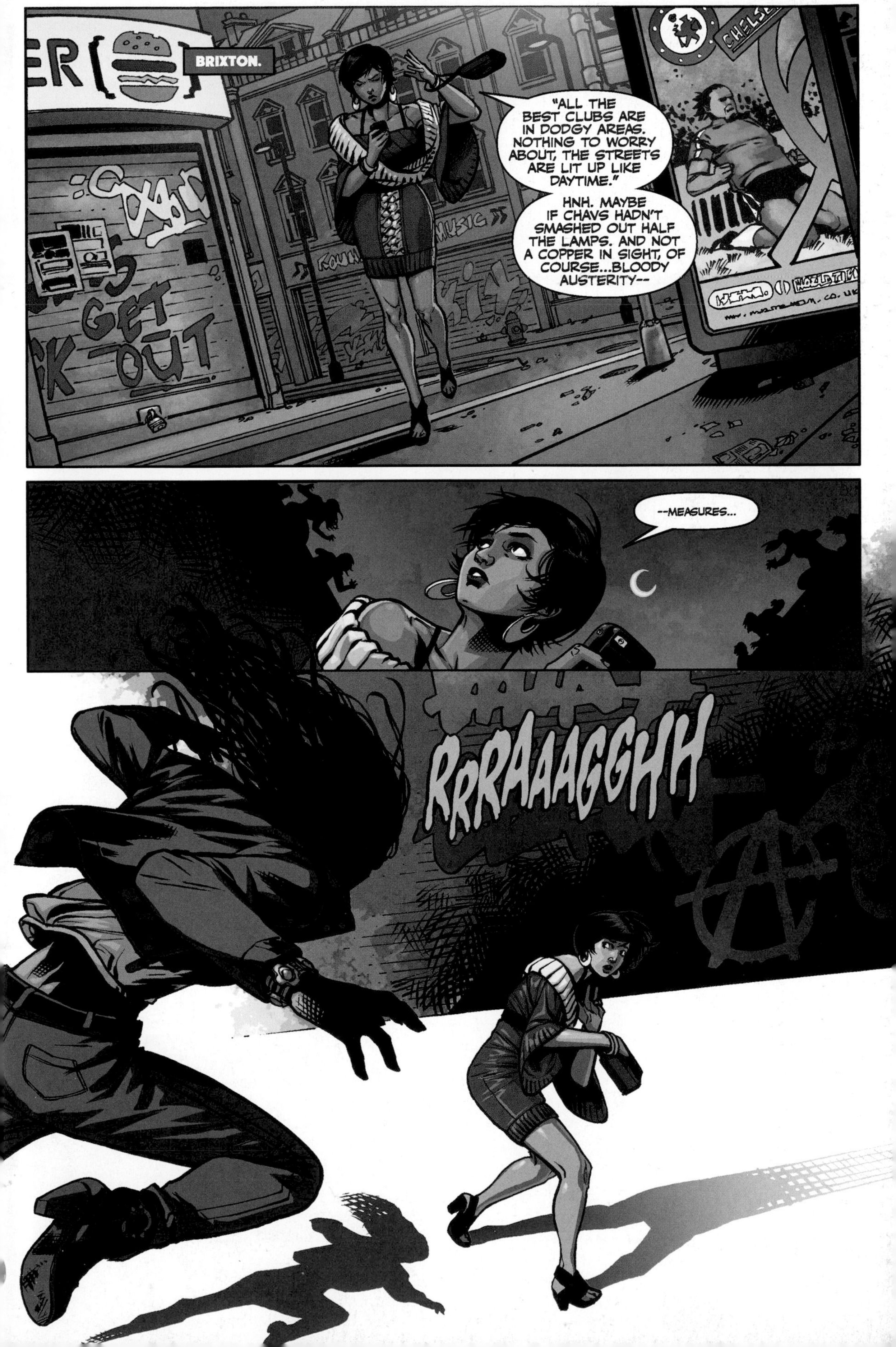
BRIXTON.
"ALL THE BEST CLUBS ARE IN DODGY AREAS. NOTHING TO WORRY ABOUT, THE STREETS ARE LIT UP LIKE DAYTIME."
HNH. MAYBE IF CHAVS HADN'T SMASHED OUT HALF THE LAMPS. AND NOT A COPPER IN SIGHT, OF COURSE...BLOODY AUSTERITY--
GET OUT
--MEASURES...
RRRAAAGGHH

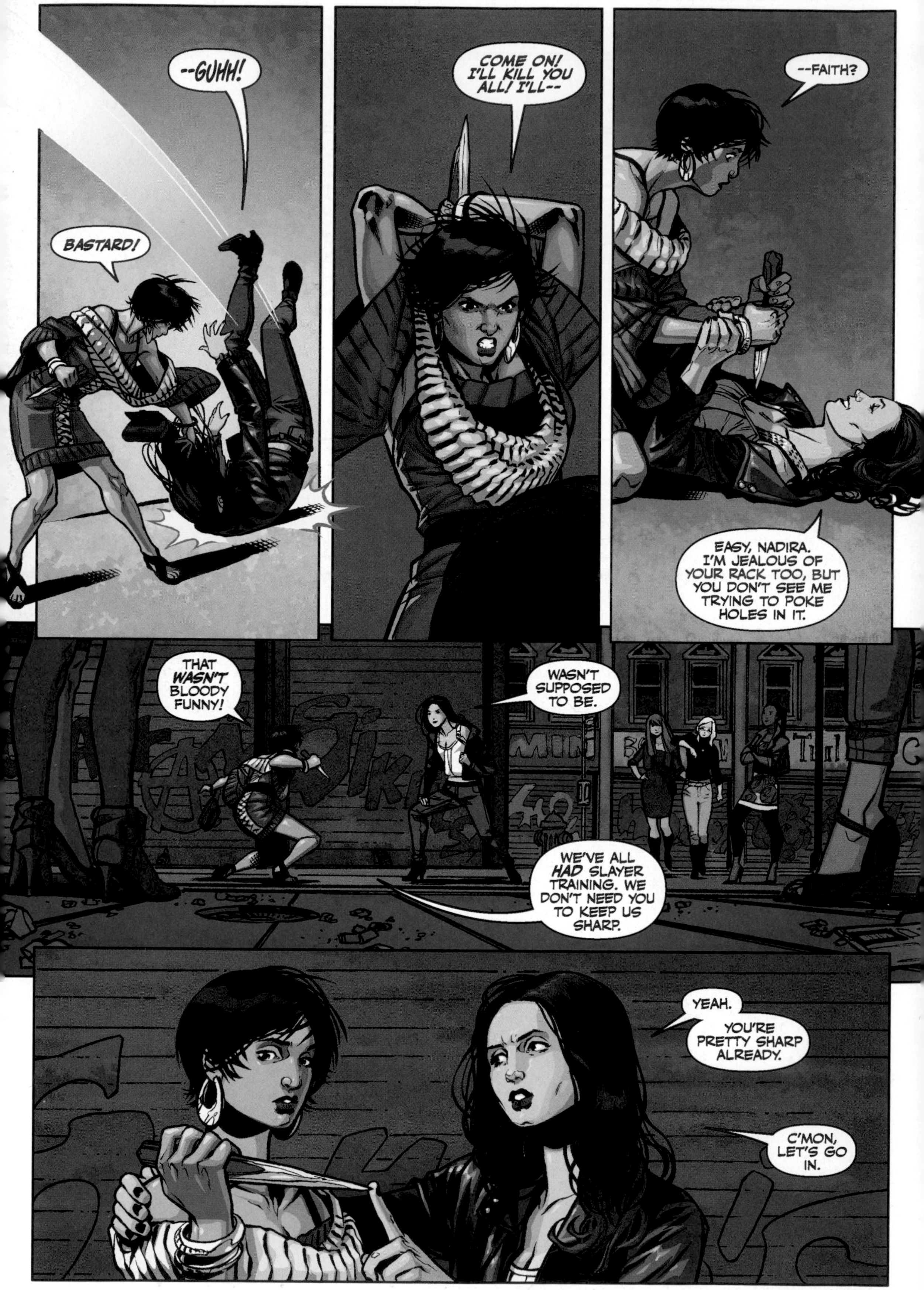
--GUHH!
BASTARD!
COME ON! I'LL KILL YOU ALL! I'LL--
--FAITH?
EASY, NADIRA. I'M JEALOUS OF YOUR RACK TOO, BUT YOU DON'T SEE ME TRYING TO POKE HOLES IN IT.
THAT WASN'T BLOODY FUNNY!
WASN'T SUPPOSED TO BE.
WE'VE ALL HAD SLAYER TRAINING. WE DON'T NEED YOU TO KEEP US SHARP.
YEAH.
YOU'RE PRETTY SHARP ALREADY.
C'MON, LET'S GO IN.

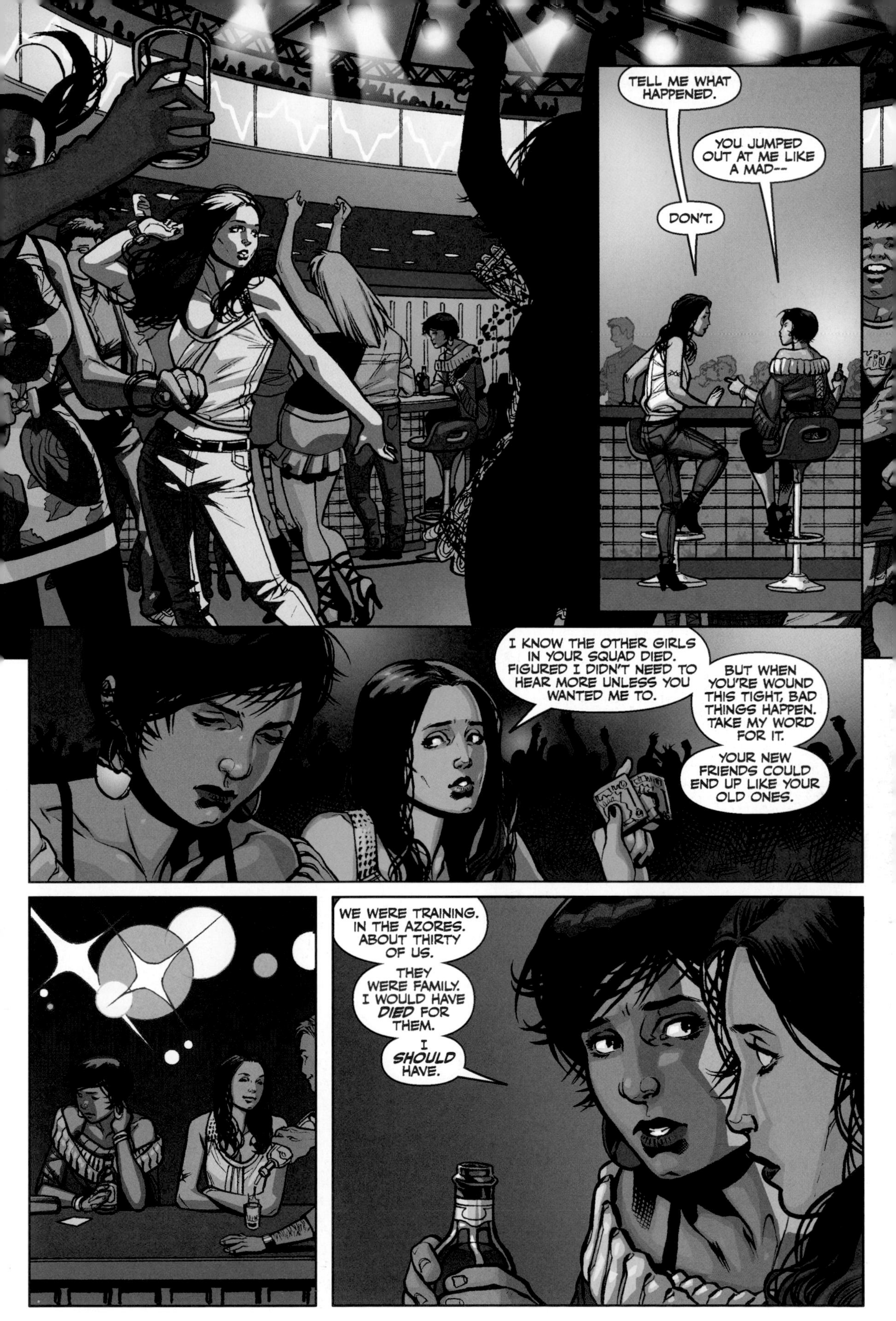
TELL ME WHAT HAPPENED.
YOU JUMPED OUT AT ME LIKE A MAD--
DON'T.
I KNOW THE OTHER GIRLS IN YOUR SQUAD DIED. FIGURED I DIDN'T NEED TO HEAR MORE UNLESS YOU WANTED ME TO.
BUT WHEN YOU'RE WOUND THIS TIGHT, BAD THINGS HAPPEN. TAKE MY WORD FOR IT.
YOUR NEW FRIENDS COULD END UP LIKE YOUR OLD ONES.
WE WERE TRAINING. IN THE AZORES. ABOUT THIRTY OF US.
THEY WERE FAMILY. I WOULD HAVE *DIED* FOR THEM.
I *SHOULD* HAVE.

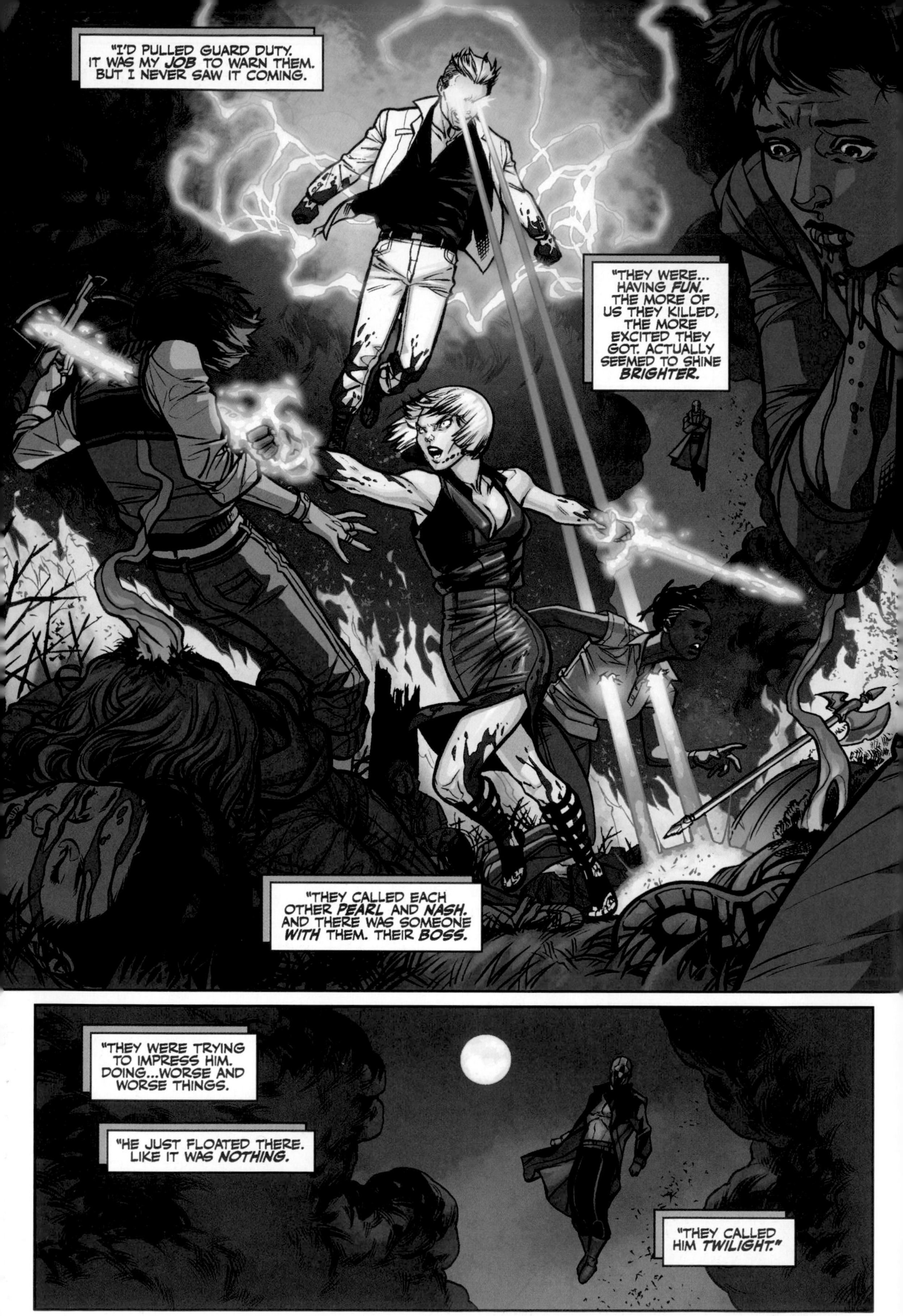
"I'D PULLED GUARD DUTY. IT WAS MY *JOB* TO WARN THEM. BUT I NEVER SAW IT COMING.
"THEY WERE... HAVING *FUN*. THE MORE OF US THEY KILLED, THE MORE EXCITED THEY GOT. ACTUALLY SEEMED TO SHINE *BRIGHTER*.
"THEY CALLED EACH OTHER *PEARL* AND *NASH*. AND THERE WAS SOMEONE *WITH* THEM. THEIR *BOSS*.
"THEY WERE TRYING TO IMPRESS HIM. DOING...WORSE AND WORSE THINGS.
"HE JUST FLOATED THERE. LIKE IT WAS *NOTHING*.
"THEY CALLED HIM *TWILIGHT*."

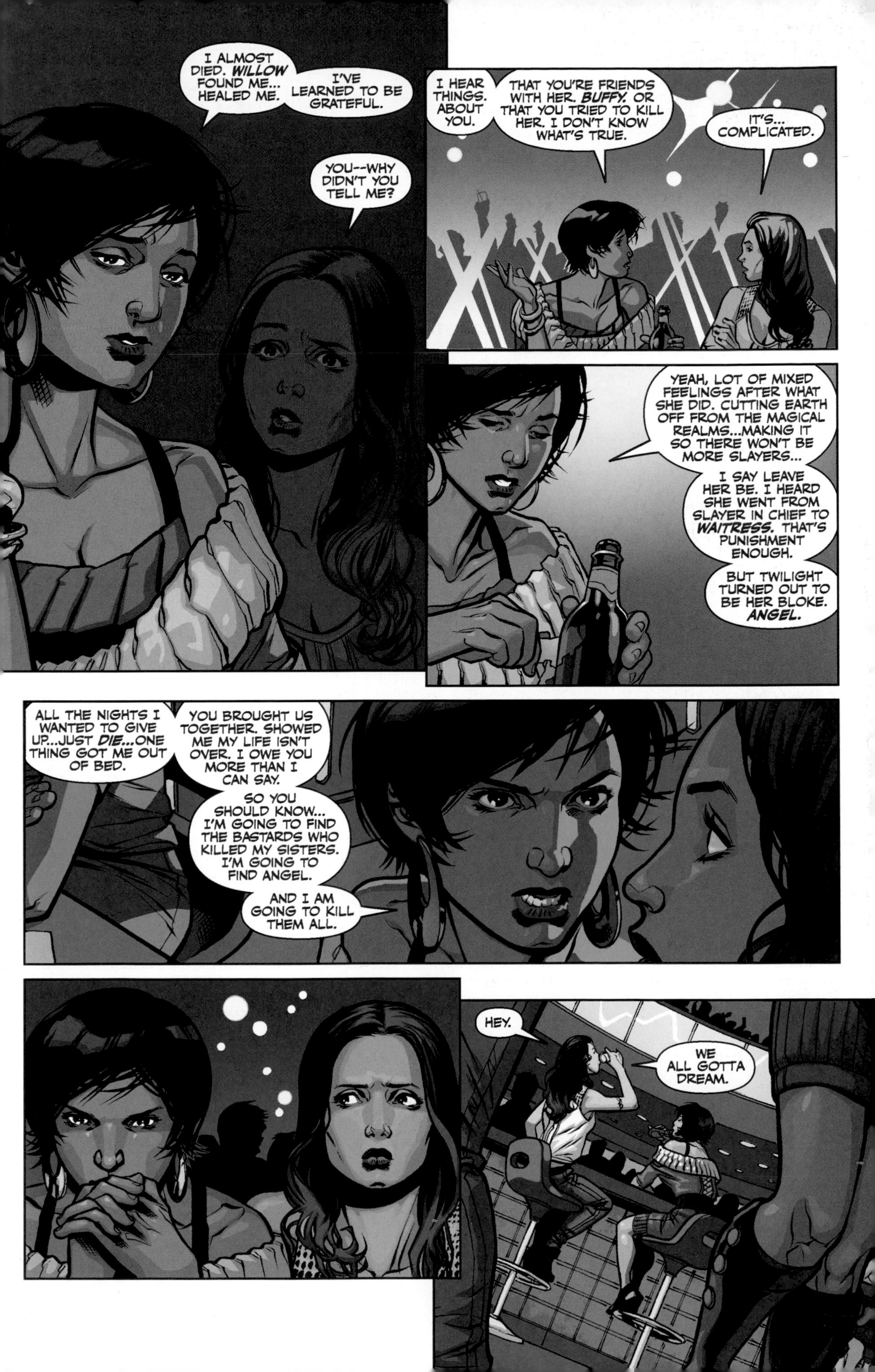
I ALMOST DIED. *WILLOW* FOUND ME... HEALED ME.
I'VE LEARNED TO BE GRATEFUL.
YOU--WHY DIDN'T YOU TELL ME?
I HEAR THINGS. ABOUT YOU.
THAT YOU'RE FRIENDS WITH HER. *BUFFY.* OR THAT YOU TRIED TO KILL HER. I DON'T KNOW WHAT'S TRUE.
IT'S... COMPLICATED.
YEAH, LOT OF MIXED FEELINGS AFTER WHAT SHE DID. CUTTING EARTH OFF FROM THE MAGICAL REALMS...MAKING IT SO THERE WON'T BE MORE SLAYERS...
I SAY LEAVE HER BE. I HEARD SHE WENT FROM SLAYER IN CHIEF TO *WAITRESS.* THAT'S PUNISHMENT ENOUGH.
BUT TWILIGHT TURNED OUT TO BE HER BLOKE. *ANGEL.*
ALL THE NIGHTS I WANTED TO GIVE UP...JUST *DIE...*ONE THING GOT ME OUT OF BED.
YOU BROUGHT US TOGETHER. SHOWED ME MY LIFE ISN'T OVER. I OWE YOU MORE THAN I CAN SAY.
SO YOU SHOULD KNOW... I'M GOING TO FIND THE BASTARDS WHO KILLED MY SISTERS. I'M GOING TO FIND ANGEL.
AND I AM GOING TO KILL THEM ALL.
HEY.
WE ALL GOTTA DREAM.

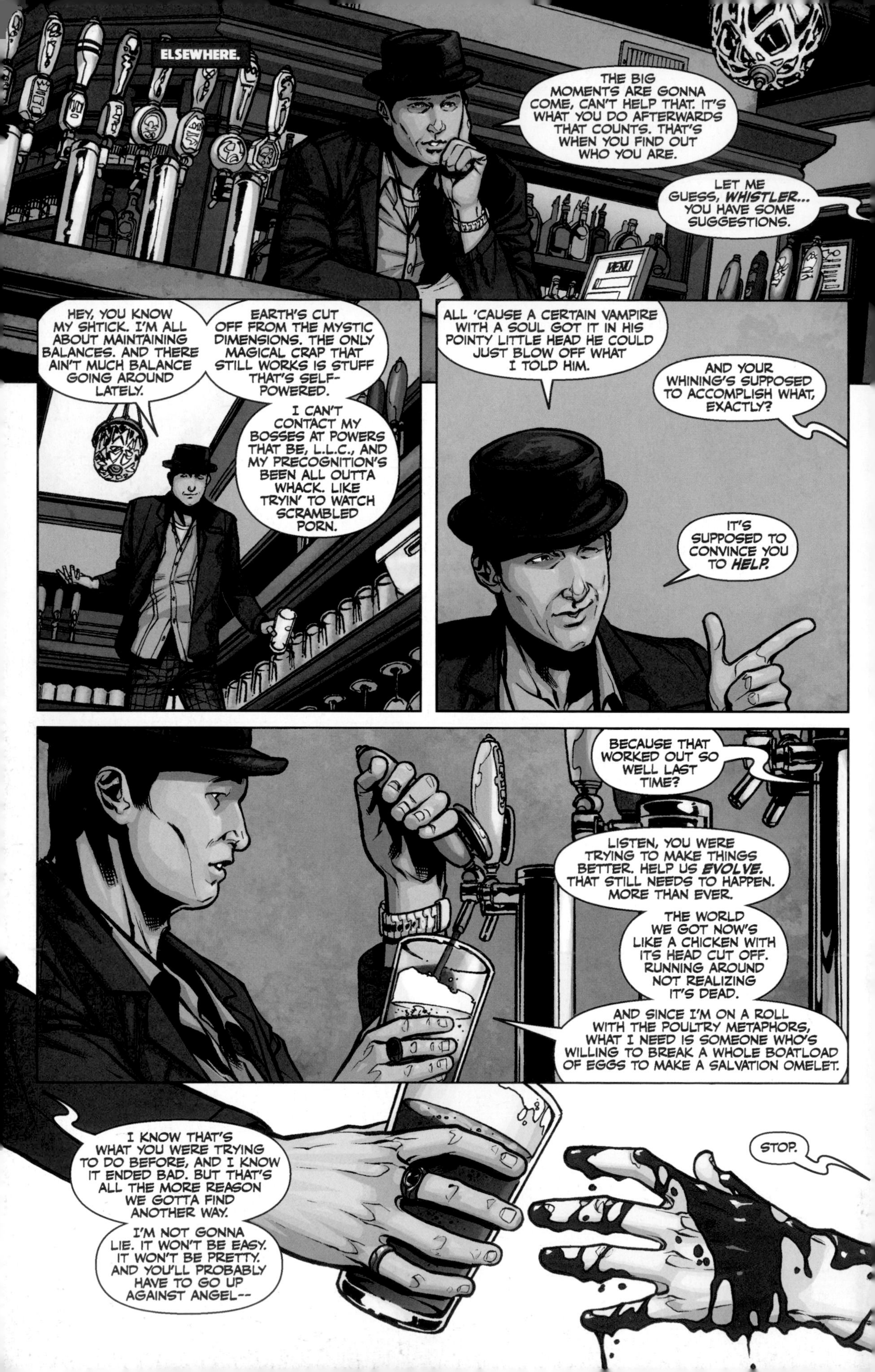
ELSEWHERE.
THE BIG MOMENTS ARE GONNA COME, CAN'T HELP THAT. IT'S WHAT YOU DO AFTERWARDS THAT COUNTS. THAT'S WHEN YOU FIND OUT WHO YOU ARE.
LET ME GUESS, WHISTLER... YOU HAVE SOME SUGGESTIONS.
HEY, YOU KNOW MY SHTICK. I'M ALL ABOUT MAINTAINING BALANCES. AND THERE AIN'T MUCH BALANCE GOING AROUND LATELY.
EARTH'S CUT OFF FROM THE MYSTIC DIMENSIONS. THE ONLY MAGICAL CRAP THAT STILL WORKS IS STUFF THAT'S SELF-POWERED.
I CAN'T CONTACT MY BOSSES AT POWERS THAT BE, L.L.C., AND MY PRECOGNITION'S BEEN ALL OUTTA WHACK. LIKE TRYIN' TO WATCH SCRAMBLED PORN.
ALL 'CAUSE A CERTAIN VAMPIRE WITH A SOUL GOT IT IN HIS POINTY LITTLE HEAD HE COULD JUST BLOW OFF WHAT I TOLD HIM.
AND YOUR WHINING'S SUPPOSED TO ACCOMPLISH WHAT, EXACTLY?
IT'S SUPPOSED TO CONVINCE YOU TO HELP.
BECAUSE THAT WORKED OUT SO WELL LAST TIME?
LISTEN, YOU WERE TRYING TO MAKE THINGS BETTER. HELP US EVOLVE. THAT STILL NEEDS TO HAPPEN. MORE THAN EVER.
THE WORLD WE GOT NOW'S LIKE A CHICKEN WITH ITS HEAD CUT OFF. RUNNING AROUND NOT REALIZING IT'S DEAD.
AND SINCE I'M ON A ROLL WITH THE POULTRY METAPHORS, WHAT I NEED IS SOMEONE WHO'S WILLING TO BREAK A WHOLE BOATLOAD OF EGGS TO MAKE A SALVATION OMELET.
I KNOW THAT'S WHAT YOU WERE TRYING TO DO BEFORE, AND I KNOW IT ENDED BAD. BUT THAT'S ALL THE MORE REASON WE GOTTA FIND ANOTHER WAY.
I'M NOT GONNA LIE. IT WON'T BE EASY. IT WON'T BE PRETTY. AND YOU'LL PROBABLY HAVE TO GO UP AGAINST ANGEL--
STOP.

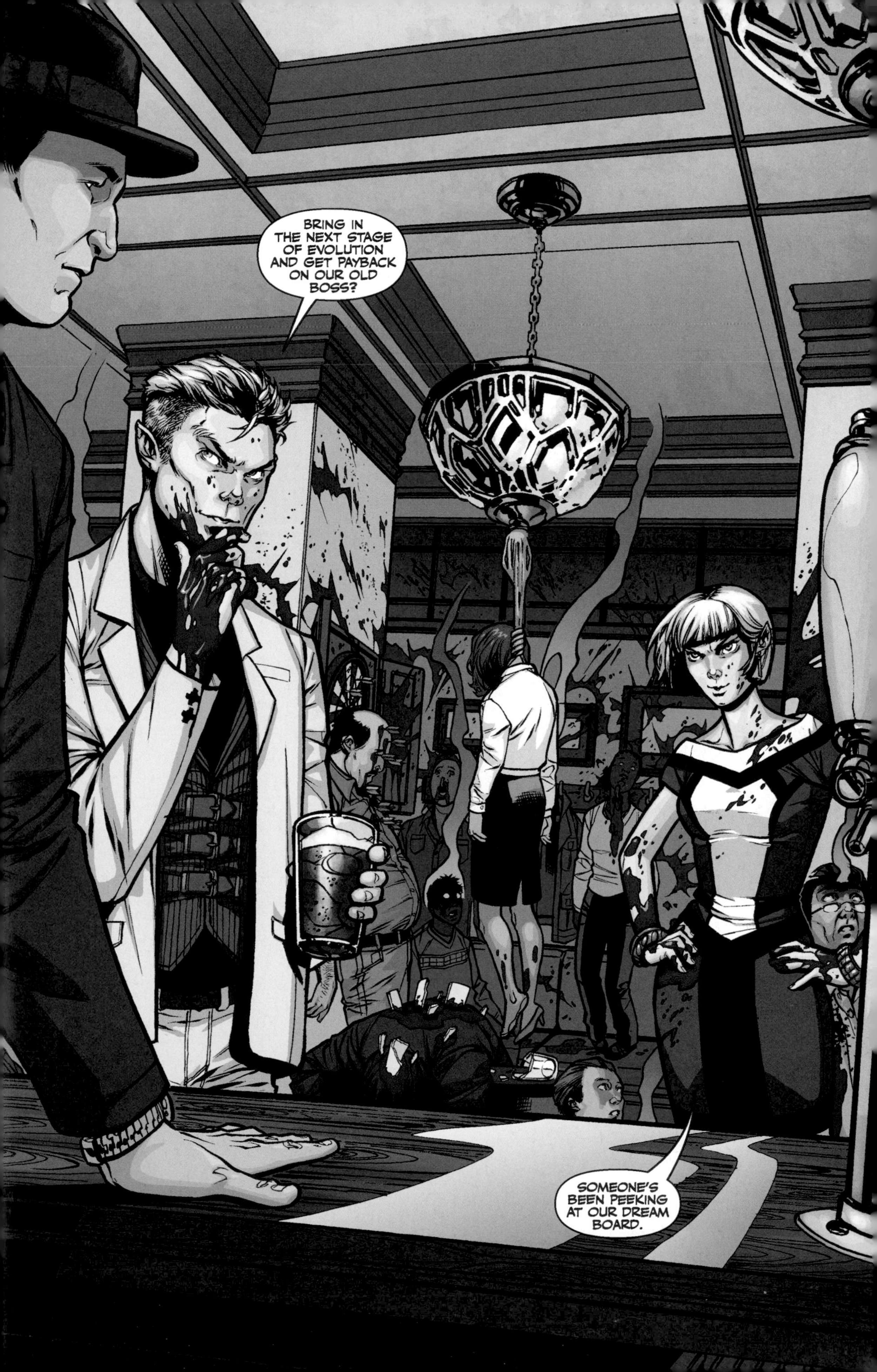
BRING IN THE NEXT STAGE OF EVOLUTION AND GET PAYBACK ON OUR OLD BOSS?
SOMEONE'S BEEN PEEKING AT OUR DREAM BOARD.

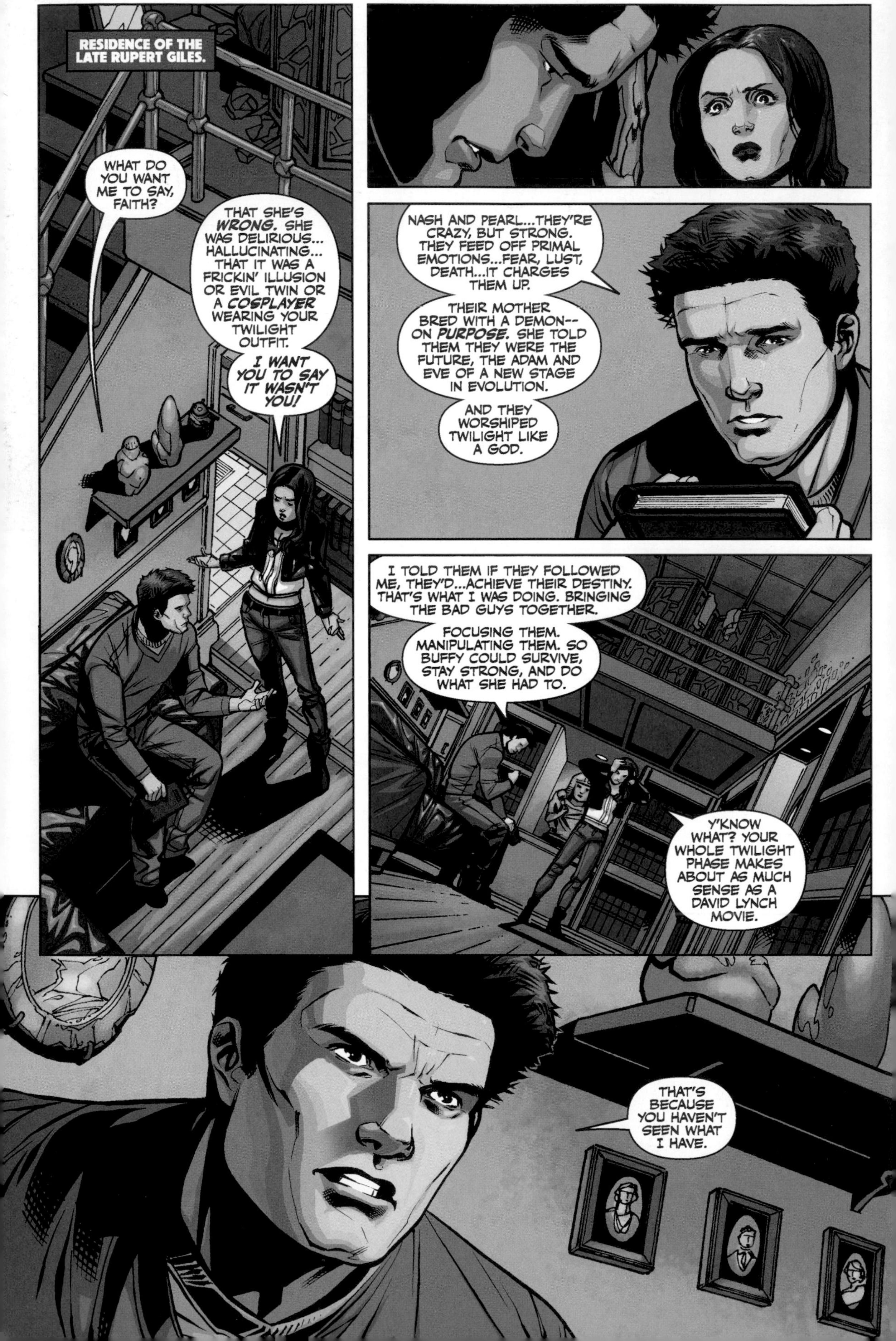
RESIDENCE OF THE LATE RUPERT GILES.
WHAT DO YOU WANT ME TO SAY, FAITH?
THAT SHE'S WRONG. SHE WAS DELIRIOUS... HALLUCINATING... THAT IT WAS A FRICKIN' ILLUSION OR EVIL TWIN OR A COSPLAYER WEARING YOUR TWILIGHT OUTFIT.
I WANT YOU TO SAY IT WASN'T YOU!
NASH AND PEARL...THEY'RE CRAZY, BUT STRONG. THEY FEED OFF PRIMAL EMOTIONS...FEAR, LUST, DEATH...IT CHARGES THEM UP.
THEIR MOTHER BRED WITH A DEMON-- ON PURPOSE. SHE TOLD THEM THEY WERE THE FUTURE, THE ADAM AND EVE OF A NEW STAGE IN EVOLUTION.
AND THEY WORSHIPED TWILIGHT LIKE A GOD.
I TOLD THEM IF THEY FOLLOWED ME, THEY'D...ACHIEVE THEIR DESTINY. THAT'S WHAT I WAS DOING. BRINGING THE BAD GUYS TOGETHER.
FOCUSING THEM. MANIPULATING THEM. SO BUFFY COULD SURVIVE, STAY STRONG, AND DO WHAT SHE HAD TO.
Y'KNOW WHAT? YOUR WHOLE TWILIGHT PHASE MAKES ABOUT AS MUCH SENSE AS A DAVID LYNCH MOVIE.
THAT'S BECAUSE YOU HAVEN'T SEEN WHAT I HAVE.

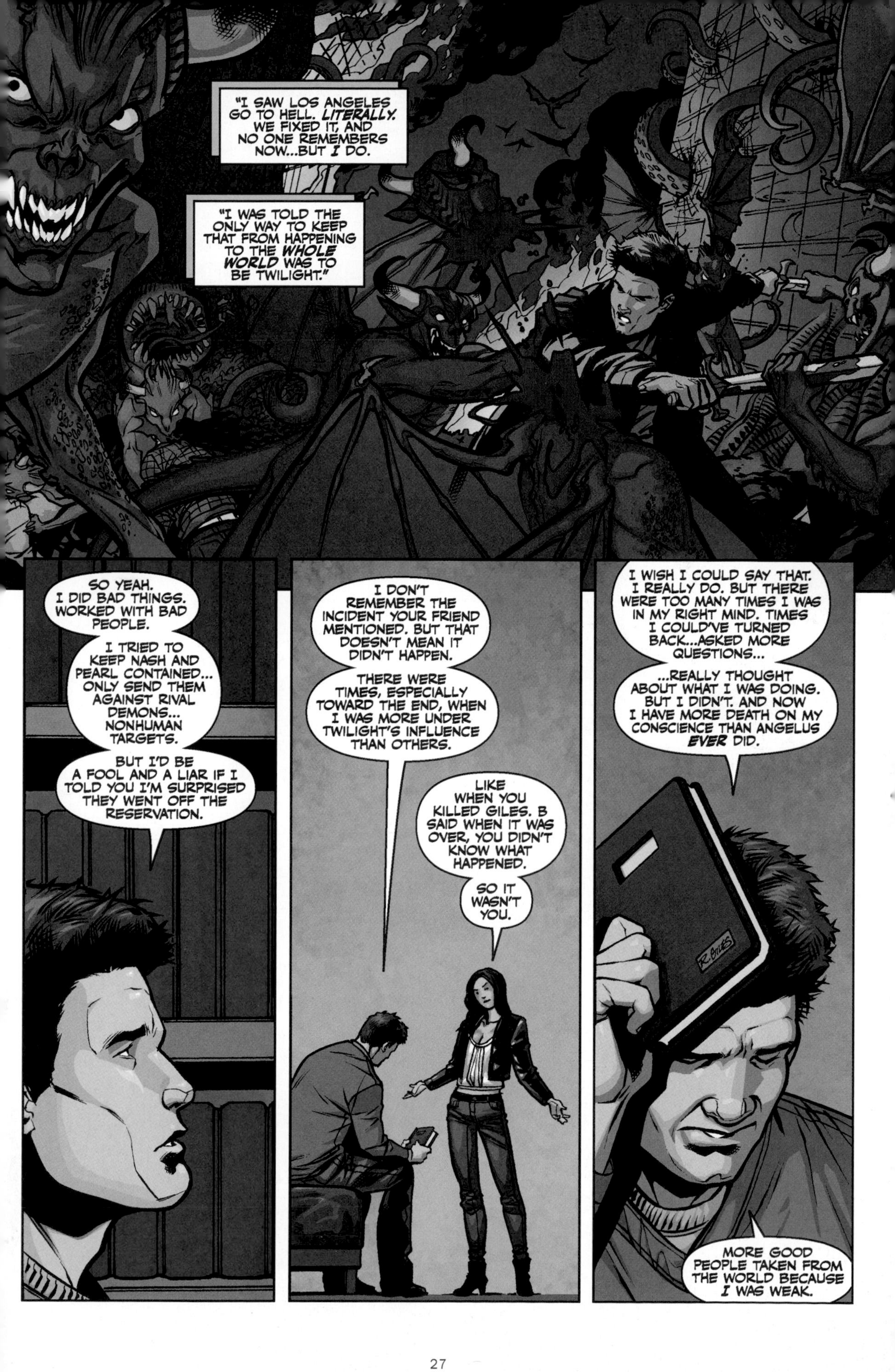
"I SAW LOS ANGELES GO TO HELL. LITERALLY. WE FIXED IT, AND NO ONE REMEMBERS NOW...BUT I DO.
"I WAS TOLD THE ONLY WAY TO KEEP THAT FROM HAPPENING TO THE WHOLE WORLD WAS TO BE TWILIGHT."
SO YEAH. I DID BAD THINGS. WORKED WITH BAD PEOPLE.
I TRIED TO KEEP NASH AND PEARL CONTAINED... ONLY SEND THEM AGAINST RIVAL DEMONS... NONHUMAN TARGETS.
BUT I'D BE A FOOL AND A LIAR IF I TOLD YOU I'M SURPRISED THEY WENT OFF THE RESERVATION.
I DON'T REMEMBER THE INCIDENT YOUR FRIEND MENTIONED. BUT THAT DOESN'T MEAN IT DIDN'T HAPPEN.
THERE WERE TIMES, ESPECIALLY TOWARD THE END, WHEN I WAS MORE UNDER TWILIGHT'S INFLUENCE THAN OTHERS.
LIKE WHEN YOU KILLED GILES. B SAID WHEN IT WAS OVER, YOU DIDN'T KNOW WHAT HAPPENED.
SO IT WASN'T YOU.
I WISH I COULD SAY THAT. I REALLY DO. BUT THERE WERE TOO MANY TIMES I WAS IN MY RIGHT MIND. TIMES I COULD'VE TURNED BACK...ASKED MORE QUESTIONS...
...REALLY THOUGHT ABOUT WHAT I WAS DOING. BUT I DIDN'T. AND NOW I HAVE MORE DEATH ON MY CONSCIENCE THAN ANGELUS EVER DID.
R. GILES
MORE GOOD PEOPLE TAKEN FROM THE WORLD BECAUSE I WAS WEAK.

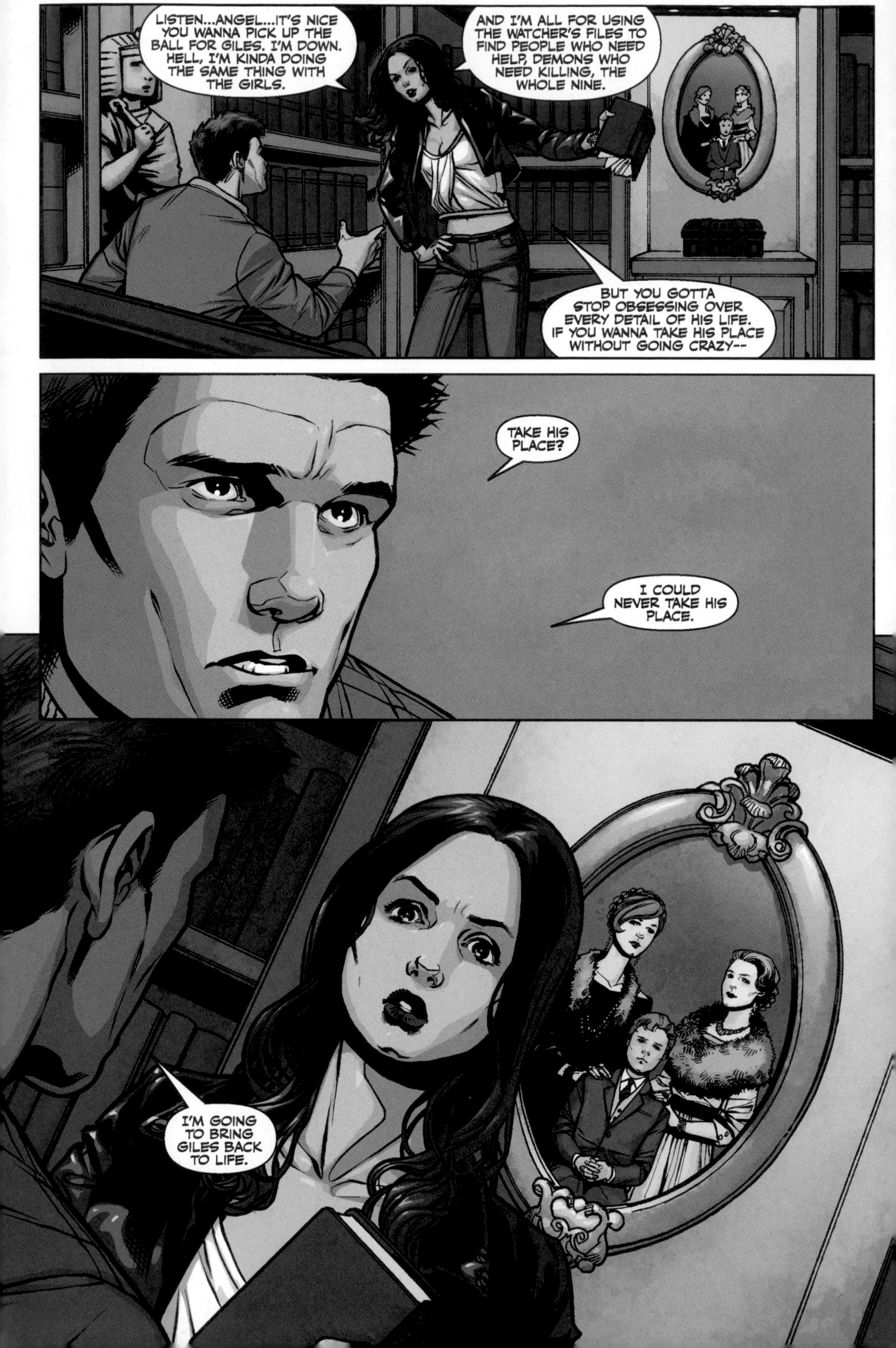
LISTEN...ANGEL...IT'S NICE YOU WANNA PICK UP THE BALL FOR GILES. I'M DOWN. HELL, I'M KINDA DOING THE SAME THING WITH THE GIRLS.
AND I'M ALL FOR USING THE WATCHER'S FILES TO FIND PEOPLE WHO NEED HELP, DEMONS WHO NEED KILLING, THE WHOLE NINE.
BUT YOU GOTTA STOP OBSESSING OVER EVERY DETAIL OF HIS LIFE. IF YOU WANNA TAKE HIS PLACE WITHOUT GOING CRAZY--
TAKE HIS PLACE?
I COULD NEVER TAKE HIS PLACE.
I'M GOING TO BRING GILES BACK TO LIFE.

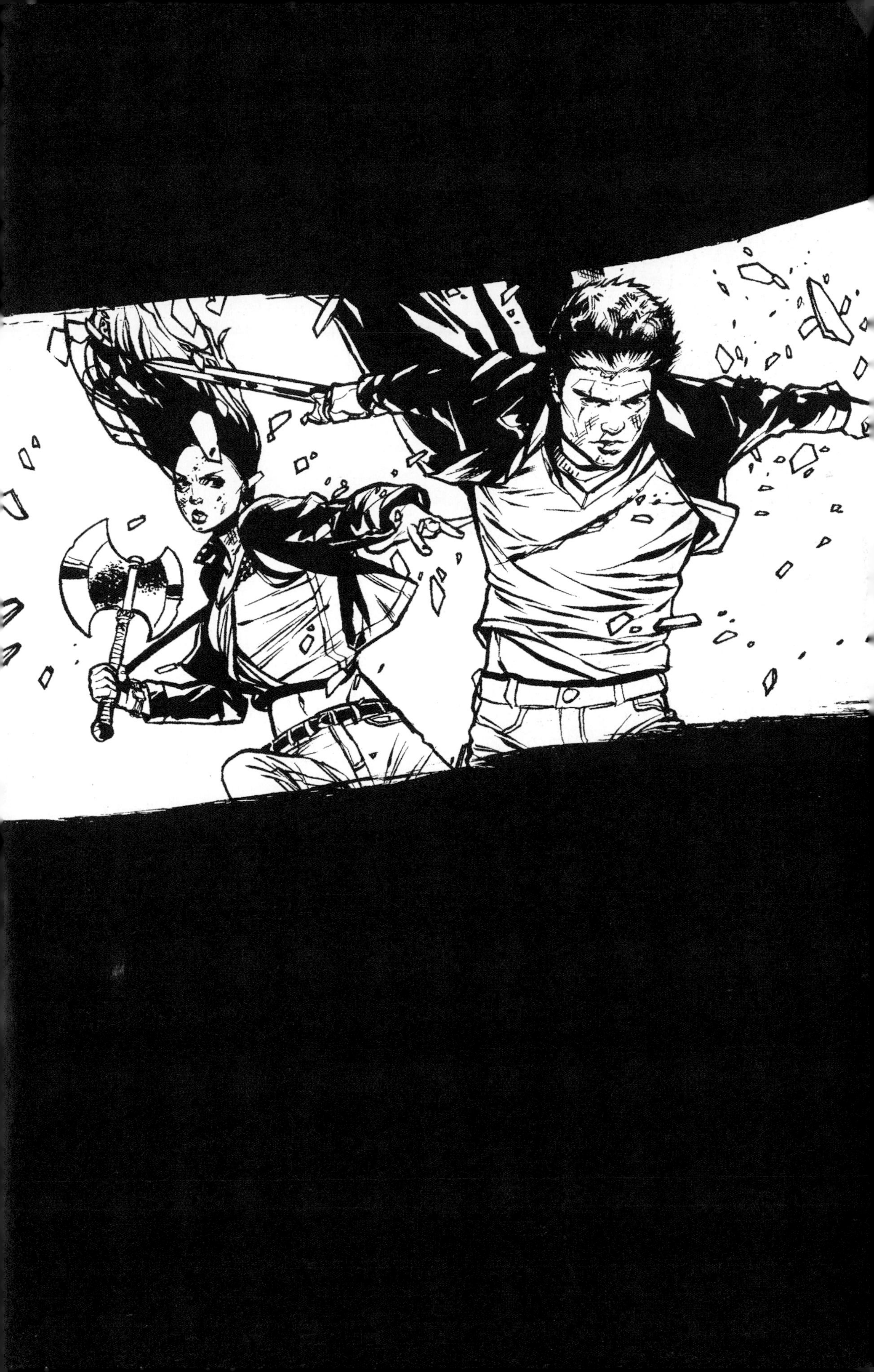

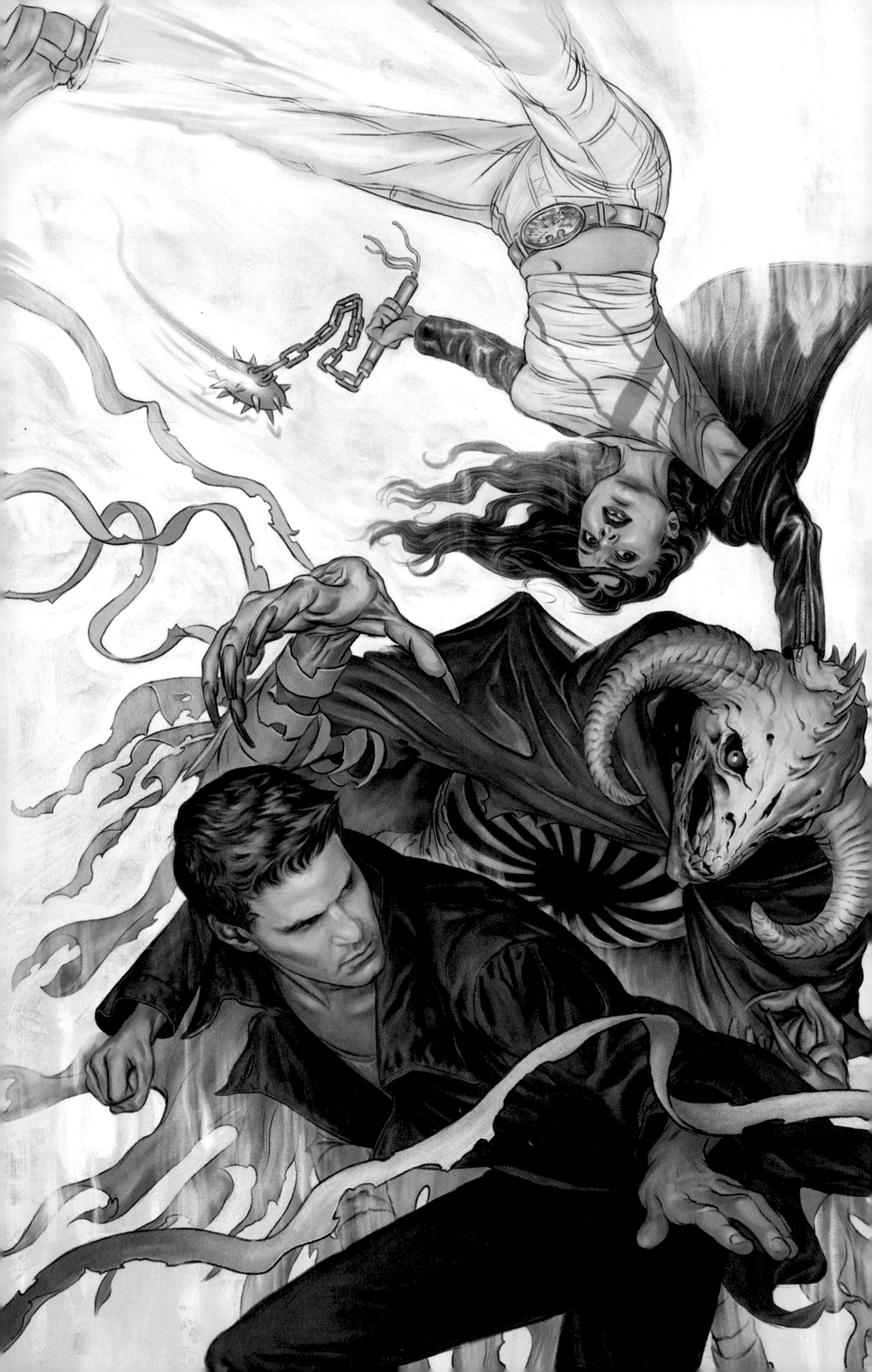

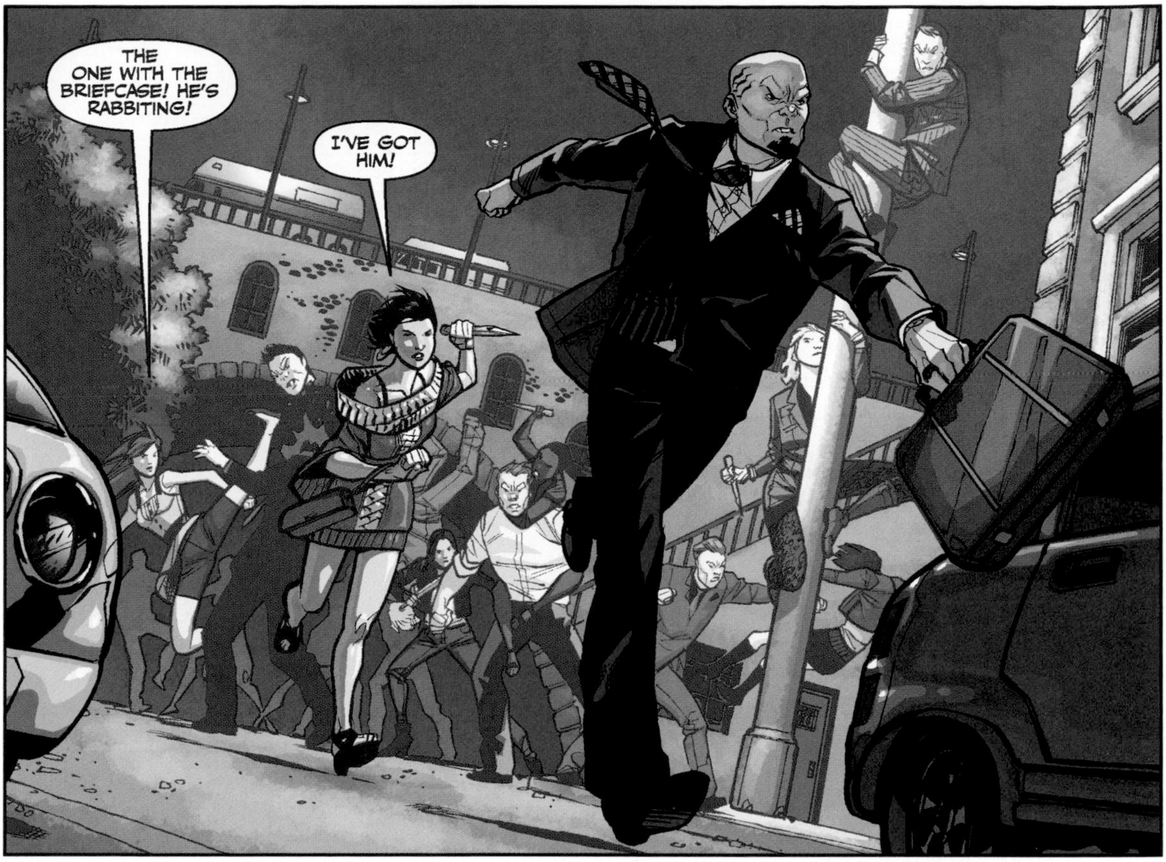
THE ONE WITH THE BRIEFCASE! HE'S RABBITING!
I'VE GOT HIM!

LIVE THROUGH THIS PART TWO

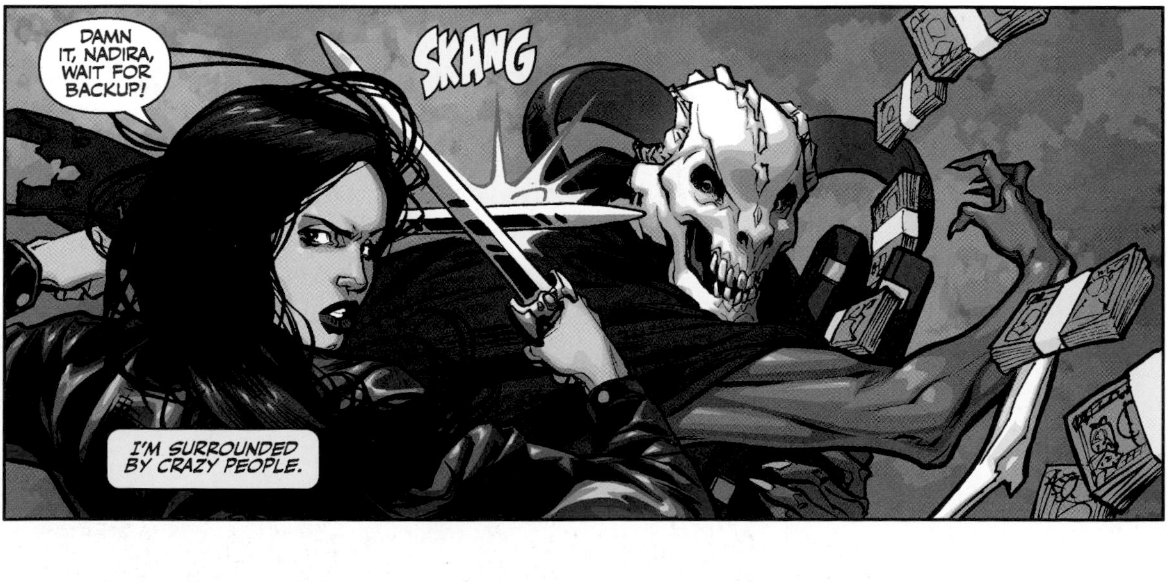
DAMN IT, NADIRA, WAIT FOR BACKUP!
SKANG
I'M SURROUNDED BY CRAZY PEOPLE.

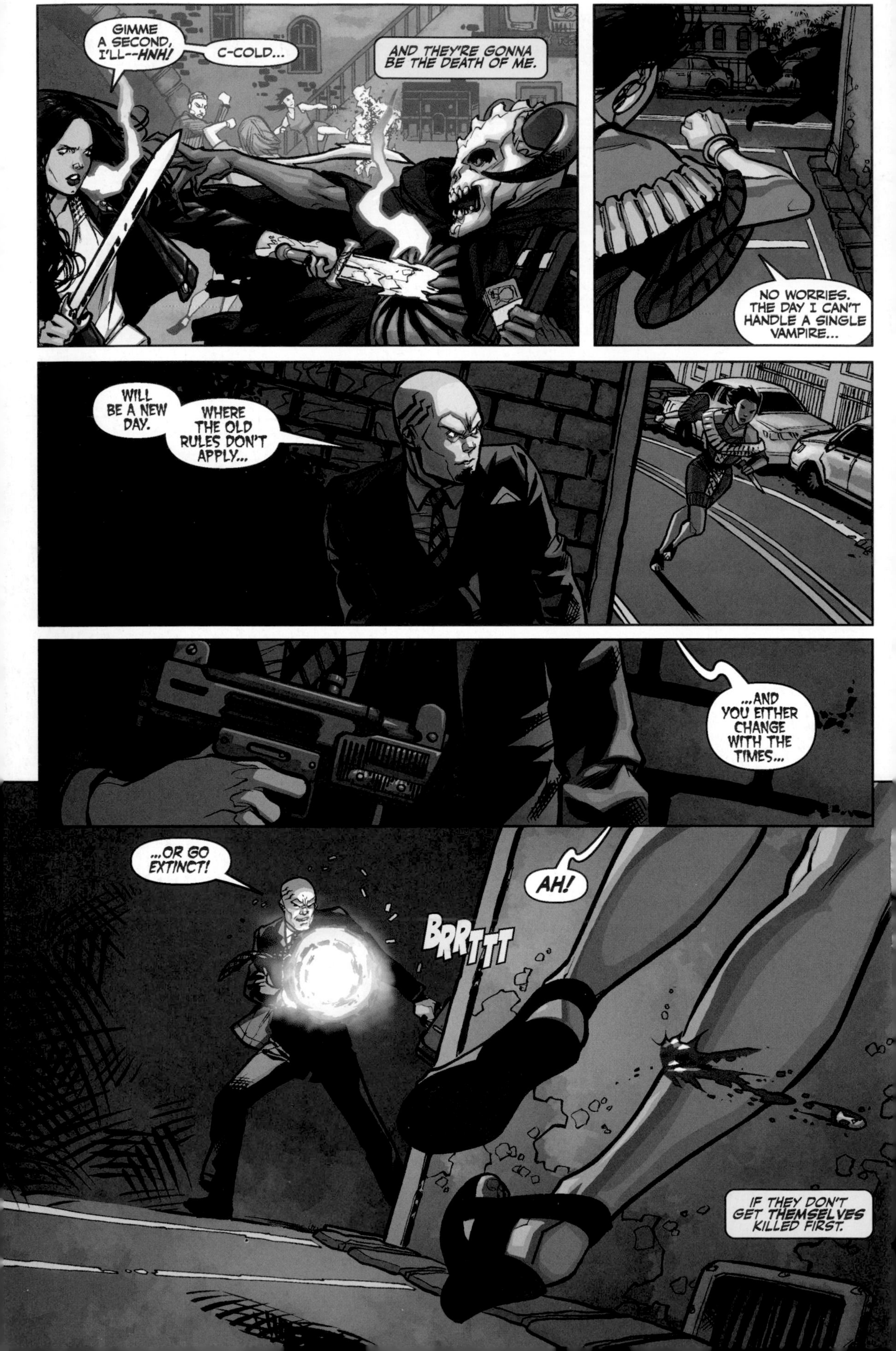
GIMME A SECOND, I'LL--HNH!
C-COLD...
AND THEY'RE GONNA BE THE DEATH OF ME.
NO WORRIES. THE DAY I CAN'T HANDLE A SINGLE VAMPIRE...
WILL BE A NEW DAY.
WHERE THE OLD RULES DON'T APPLY...
...AND YOU EITHER CHANGE WITH THE TIMES...
...OR GO EXTINCT!
AH!
BRRTTT
IF THEY DON'T GET THEMSELVES KILLED FIRST.

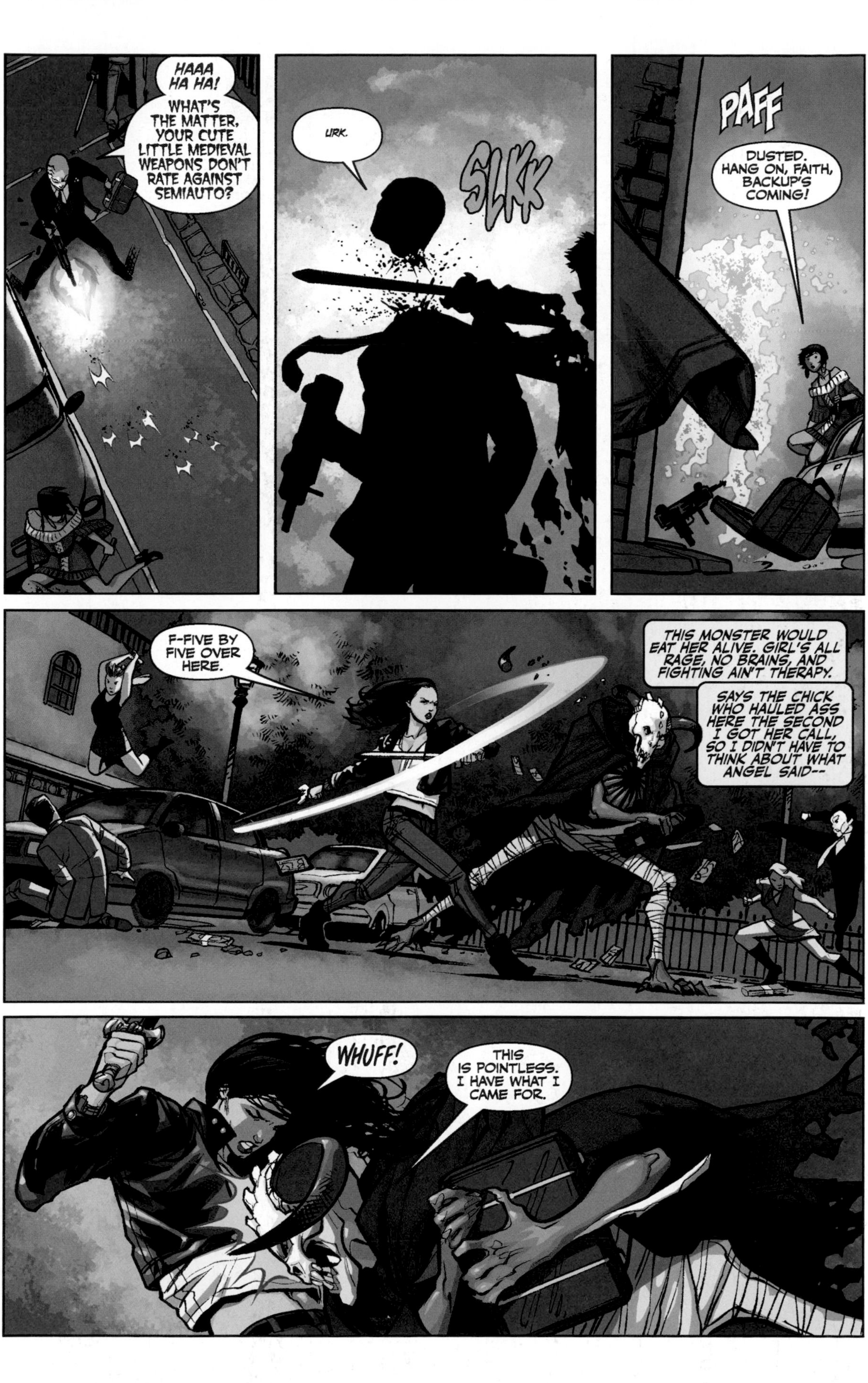
HAAAA HA HA!
WHAT'S THE MATTER, YOUR CUTE LITTLE MEDIEVAL WEAPONS DON'T RATE AGAINST SEMIAUTO?
URK.
SLKK
PAFF
DUSTED. HANG ON, FAITH, BACKUP'S COMING!
F-FIVE BY FIVE OVER HERE.
THIS MONSTER WOULD EAT HER ALIVE. GIRL'S ALL RAGE, NO BRAINS, AND FIGHTING AIN'T THERAPY.
SAYS THE CHICK WHO HAULED ASS HERE THE SECOND I GOT HER CALL, SO I DIDN'T HAVE TO THINK ABOUT WHAT ANGEL SAID--
WHUFF!
THIS IS POINTLESS. I HAVE WHAT I CAME FOR.

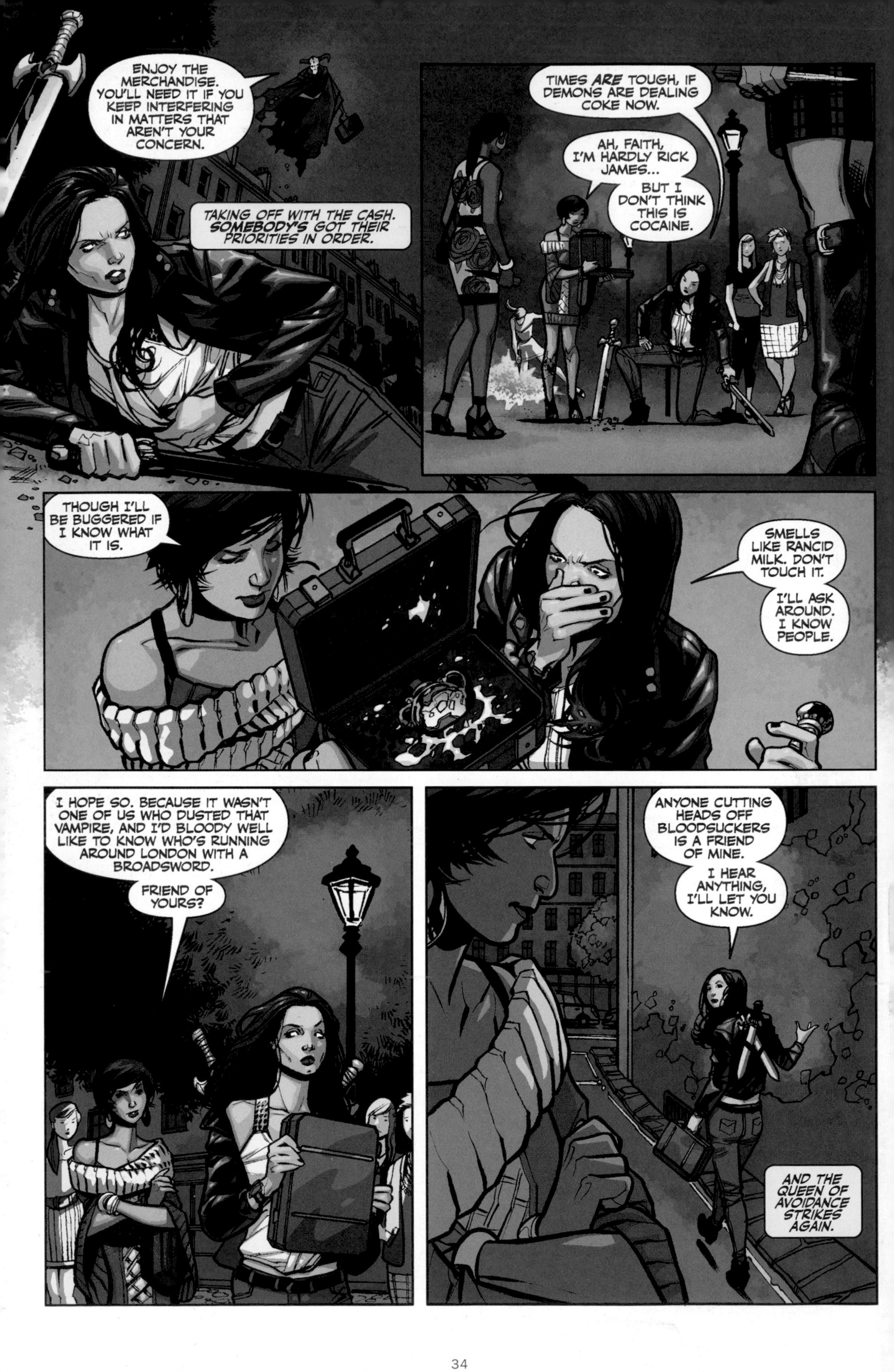
ENJOY THE MERCHANDISE. YOU'LL NEED IT IF YOU KEEP INTERFERING IN MATTERS THAT AREN'T YOUR CONCERN.
TAKING OFF WITH THE CASH. SOMEBODY'S GOT THEIR PRIORITIES IN ORDER.
TIMES ARE TOUGH, IF DEMONS ARE DEALING COKE NOW.
AH, FAITH, I'M HARDLY RICK JAMES...
BUT I DON'T THINK THIS IS COCAINE.
THOUGH I'LL BE BUGGERED IF I KNOW WHAT IT IS.
SMELLS LIKE RANCID MILK. DON'T TOUCH IT.
I'LL ASK AROUND. I KNOW PEOPLE.
I HOPE SO. BECAUSE IT WASN'T ONE OF US WHO DUSTED THAT VAMPIRE, AND I'D BLOODY WELL LIKE TO KNOW WHO'S RUNNING AROUND LONDON WITH A BROADSWORD.
FRIEND OF YOURS?
ANYONE CUTTING HEADS OFF BLOODSUCKERS IS A FRIEND OF MINE.
I HEAR ANYTHING, I'LL LET YOU KNOW.
AND THE QUEEN OF AVOIDANCE STRIKES AGAIN.

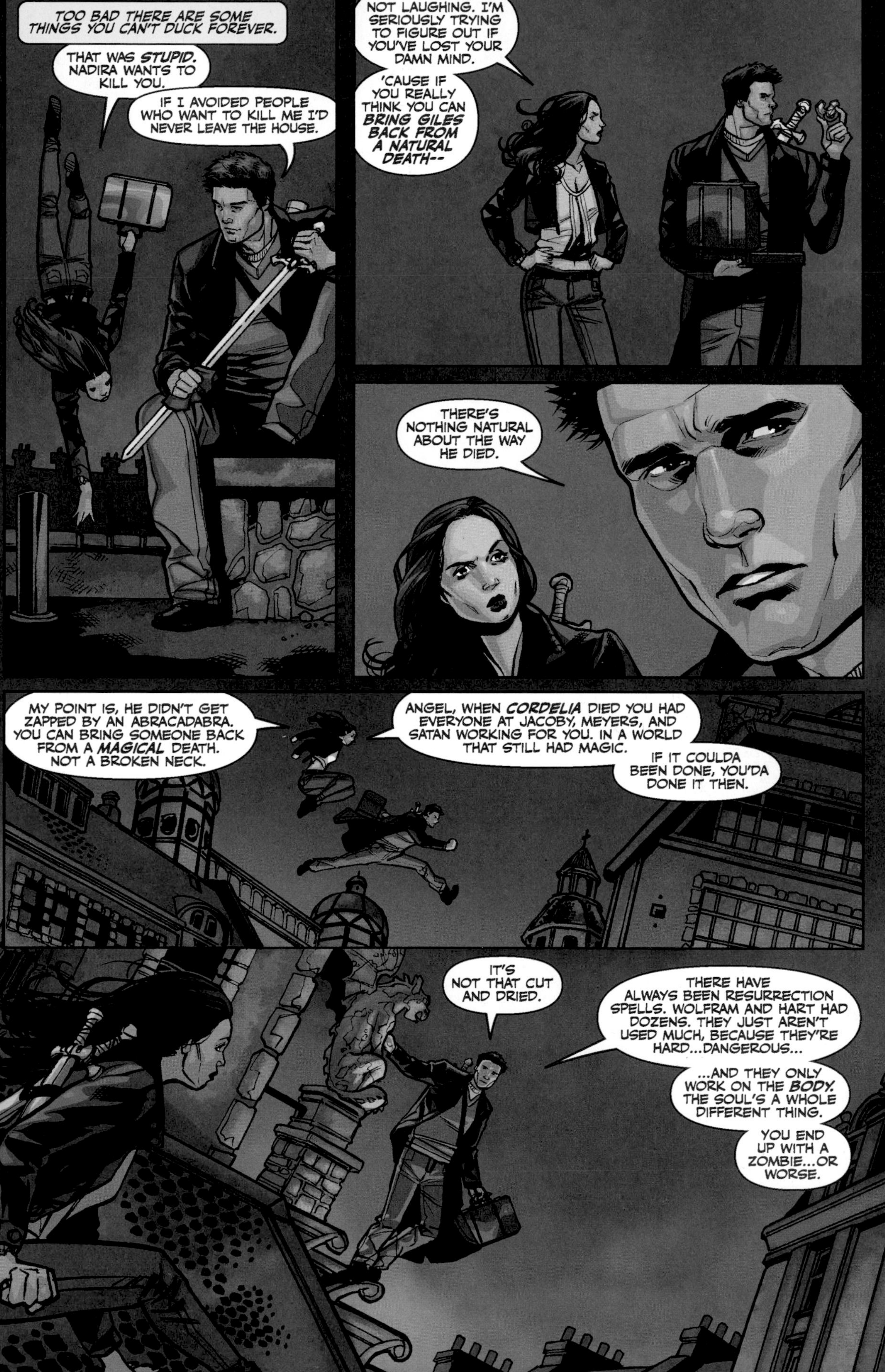
TOO BAD THERE ARE SOME THINGS YOU CAN'T DUCK FOREVER.
THAT WAS STUPID. NADIRA WANTS TO KILL YOU.
IF I AVOIDED PEOPLE WHO WANT TO KILL ME I'D NEVER LEAVE THE HOUSE.
NOT LAUGHING. I'M SERIOUSLY TRYING TO FIGURE OUT IF YOU'VE LOST YOUR DAMN MIND.
'CAUSE IF YOU REALLY THINK YOU CAN BRING GILES BACK FROM A NATURAL DEATH--
THERE'S NOTHING NATURAL ABOUT THE WAY HE DIED.
MY POINT IS, HE DIDN'T GET ZAPPED BY AN ABRACADABRA. YOU CAN BRING SOMEONE BACK FROM A MAGICAL DEATH. NOT A BROKEN NECK.
ANGEL, WHEN CORDELIA DIED YOU HAD EVERYONE AT JACOBY, MEYERS, AND SATAN WORKING FOR YOU. IN A WORLD THAT STILL HAD MAGIC.
IF IT COULDA BEEN DONE, YOU'DA DONE IT THEN.
IT'S NOT THAT CUT AND DRIED.
THERE HAVE ALWAYS BEEN RESURRECTION SPELLS. WOLFRAM AND HART HAD DOZENS. THEY JUST AREN'T USED MUCH, BECAUSE THEY'RE HARD...DANGEROUS...
...AND THEY ONLY WORK ON THE BODY. THE SOUL'S A WHOLE DIFFERENT THING.
YOU END UP WITH A ZOMBIE...OR WORSE.

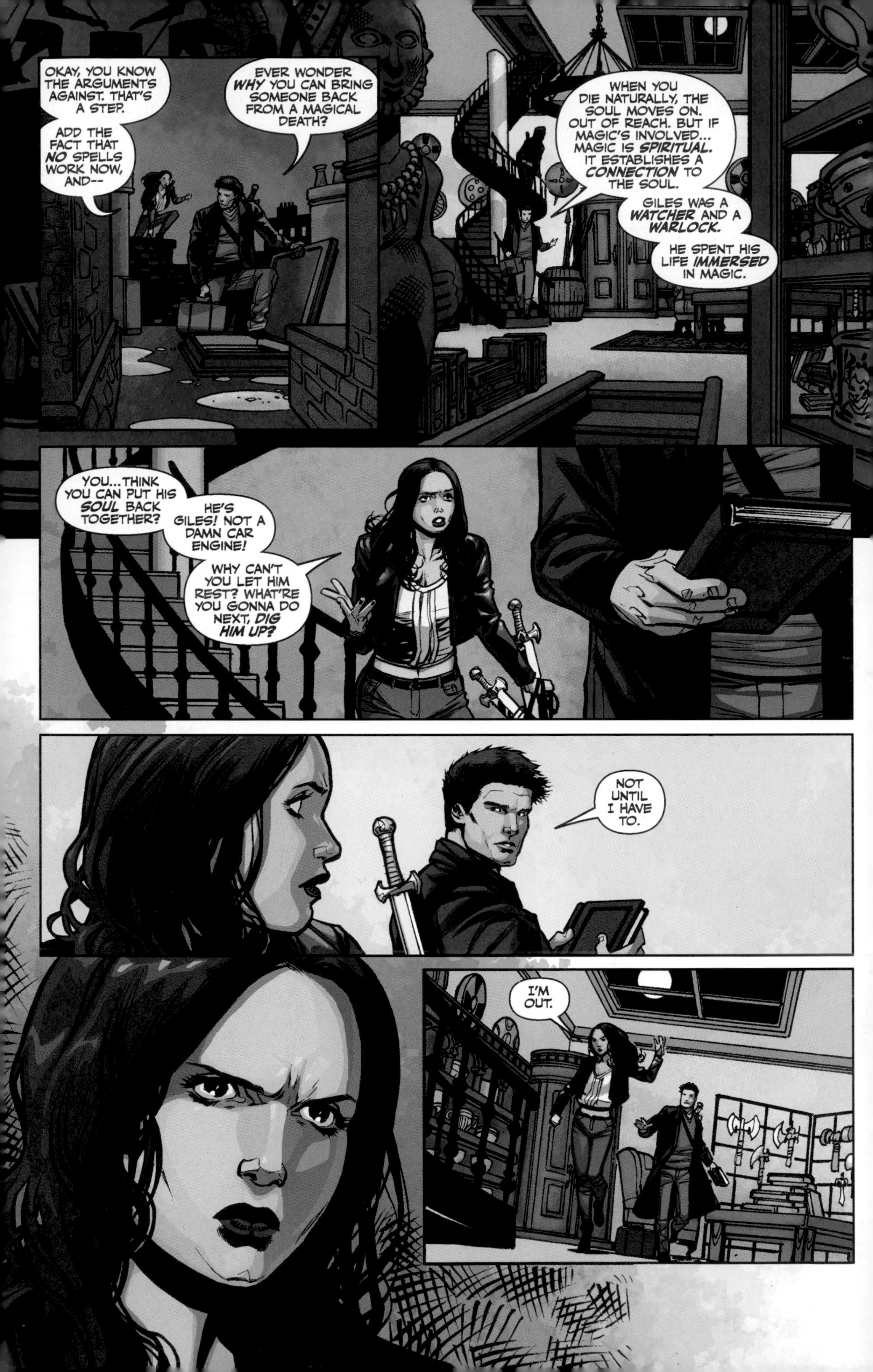
OKAY, YOU KNOW THE ARGUMENTS AGAINST. THAT'S A STEP.
ADD THE FACT THAT *NO* SPELLS WORK NOW, AND--
EVER WONDER *WHY* YOU CAN BRING SOMEONE BACK FROM A MAGICAL DEATH?
WHEN YOU DIE NATURALLY, THE SOUL MOVES ON. OUT OF REACH. BUT IF MAGIC'S INVOLVED... MAGIC IS *SPIRITUAL.* IT ESTABLISHES A *CONNECTION* TO THE SOUL.
GILES WAS A *WATCHER* AND A *WARLOCK.*
HE SPENT HIS LIFE *IMMERSED* IN MAGIC.
YOU...THINK YOU CAN PUT HIS *SOUL* BACK TOGETHER?
HE'S GILES! NOT A DAMN CAR ENGINE!
WHY CAN'T YOU LET HIM REST? WHAT'RE YOU GONNA DO NEXT, *DIG HIM UP?*
NOT UNTIL I HAVE TO.
I'M OUT.

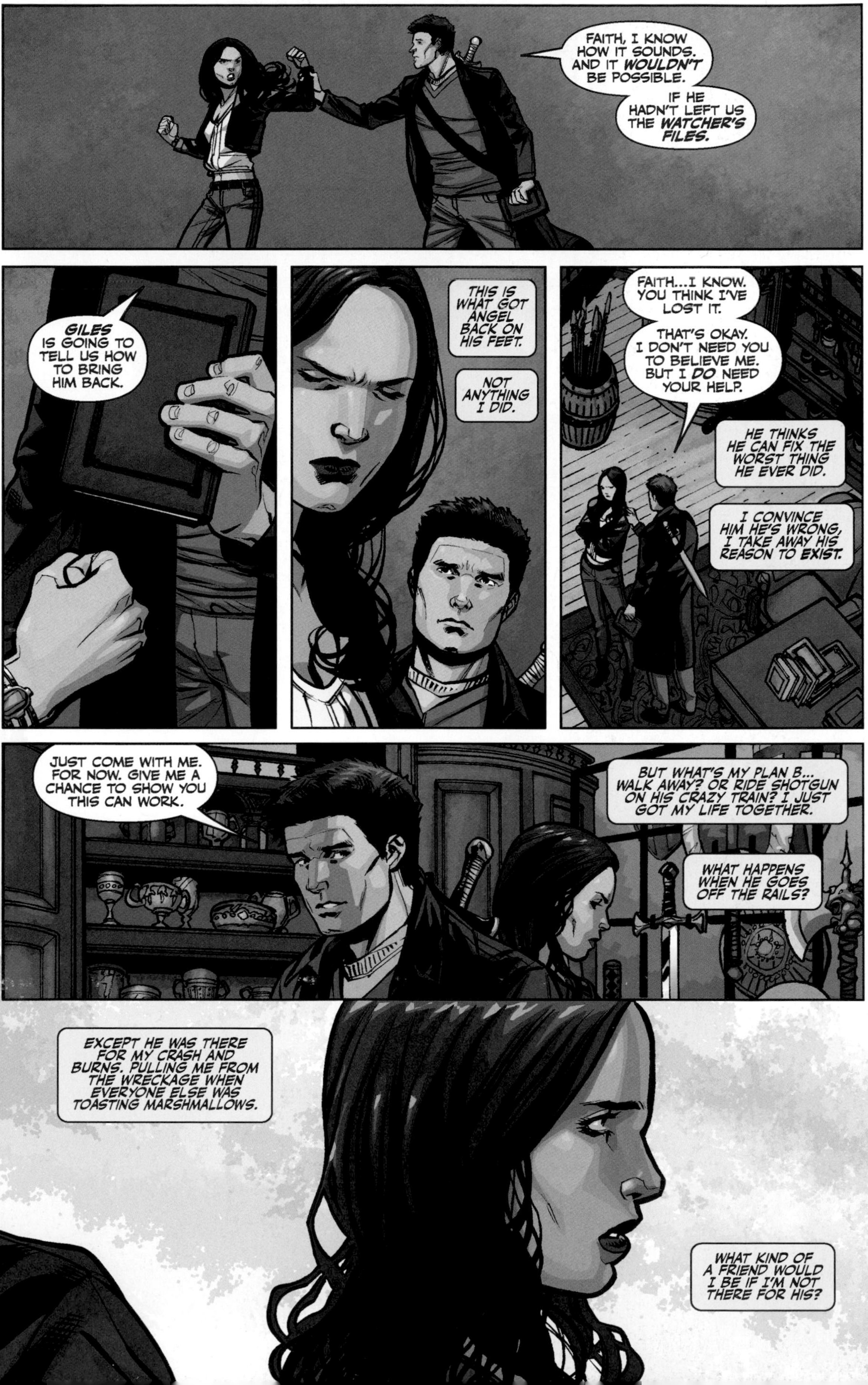
FAITH, I KNOW HOW IT SOUNDS. AND IT WOULDN'T BE POSSIBLE.
IF HE HADN'T LEFT US THE WATCHER'S FILES.
GILES IS GOING TO TELL US HOW TO BRING HIM BACK.
THIS IS WHAT GOT ANGEL BACK ON HIS FEET.
NOT ANYTHING I DID.
FAITH...I KNOW. YOU THINK I'VE LOST IT.
THAT'S OKAY. I DON'T NEED YOU TO BELIEVE ME. BUT I DO NEED YOUR HELP.
HE THINKS HE CAN FIX THE WORST THING HE EVER DID.
I CONVINCE HIM HE'S WRONG, I TAKE AWAY HIS REASON TO EXIST.
JUST COME WITH ME. FOR NOW. GIVE ME A CHANCE TO SHOW YOU THIS CAN WORK.
BUT WHAT'S MY PLAN B... WALK AWAY? OR RIDE SHOTGUN ON HIS CRAZY TRAIN? I JUST GOT MY LIFE TOGETHER.
WHAT HAPPENS WHEN HE GOES OFF THE RAILS?
EXCEPT HE WAS THERE FOR MY CRASH AND BURNS. PULLING ME FROM THE WRECKAGE WHEN EVERYONE ELSE WAS TOASTING MARSHMALLOWS.
WHAT KIND OF A FRIEND WOULD I BE IF I'M NOT THERE FOR HIS?

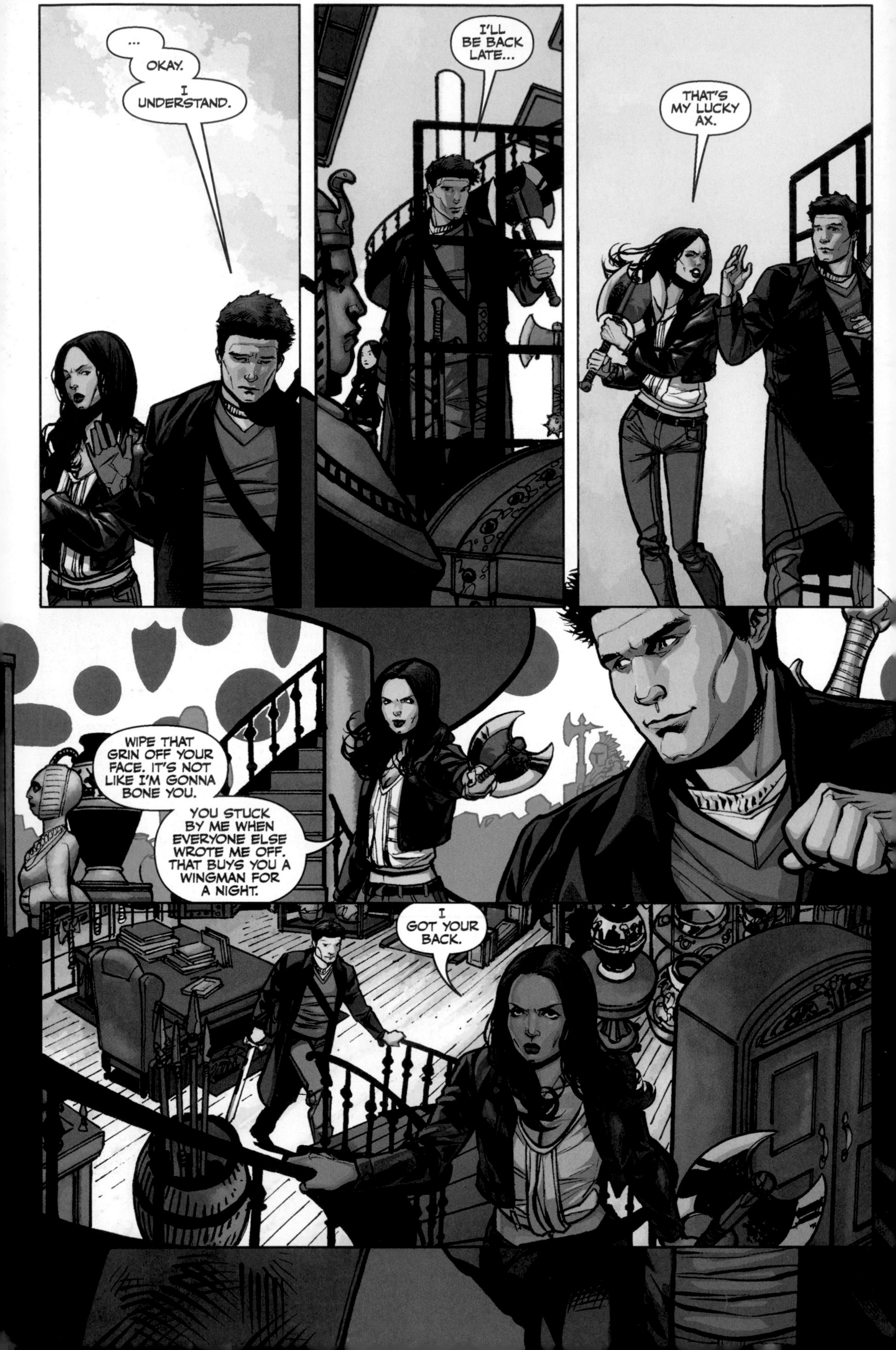
...
OKAY.
I UNDERSTAND.
I'LL BE BACK LATE...
THAT'S MY LUCKY AX.
WIPE THAT GRIN OFF YOUR FACE. IT'S NOT LIKE I'M GONNA BONE YOU.
YOU STUCK BY ME WHEN EVERYONE ELSE WROTE ME OFF. THAT BUYS YOU A WINGMAN FOR A NIGHT.
I GOT YOUR BACK.

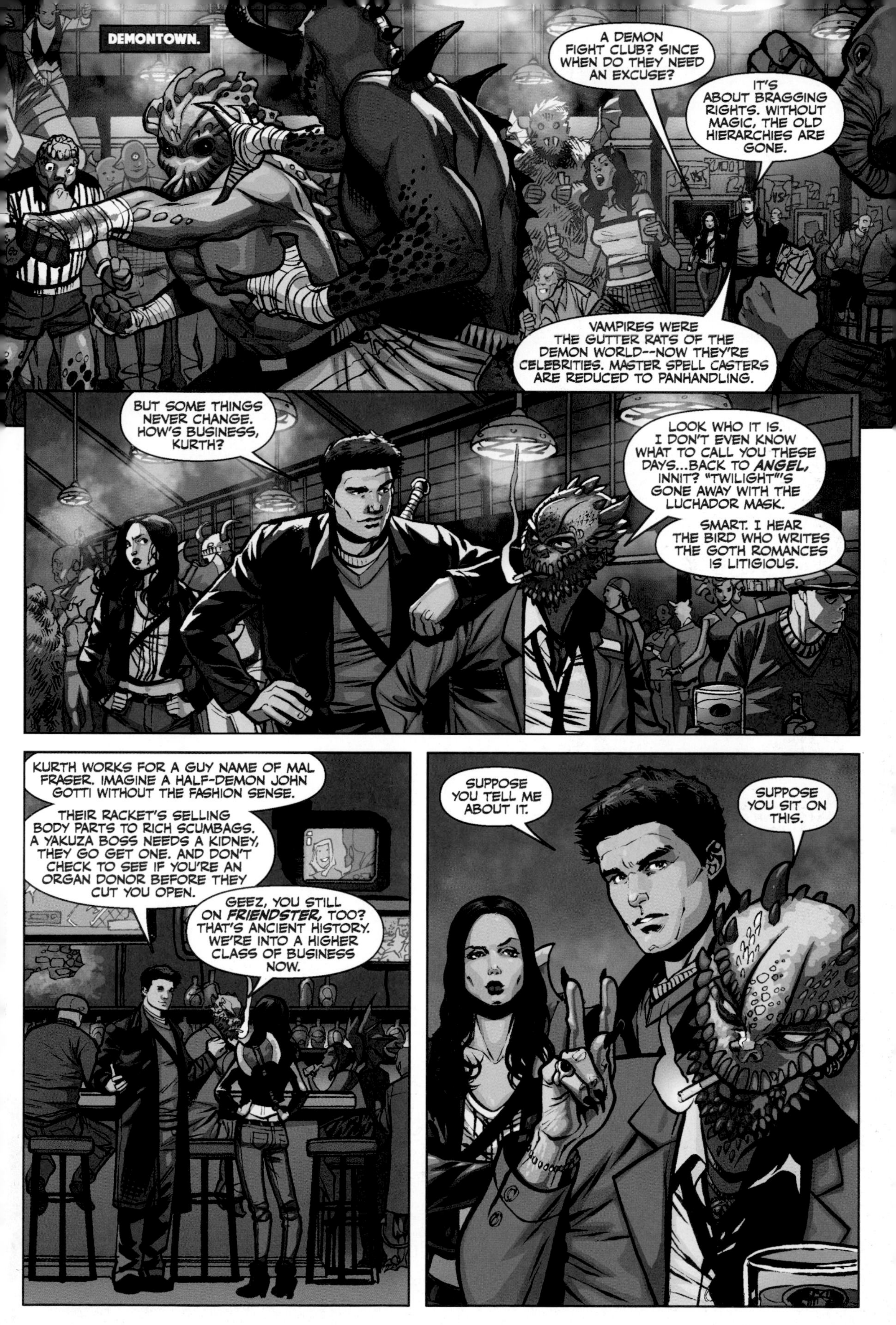
DEMONTOWN.
A DEMON FIGHT CLUB? SINCE WHEN DO THEY NEED AN EXCUSE?
IT'S ABOUT BRAGGING RIGHTS. WITHOUT MAGIC, THE OLD HIERARCHIES ARE GONE.
VAMPIRES WERE THE GUTTER RATS OF THE DEMON WORLD--NOW THEY'RE CELEBRITIES. MASTER SPELL CASTERS ARE REDUCED TO PANHANDLING.
BUT SOME THINGS NEVER CHANGE. HOW'S BUSINESS, KURTH?
LOOK WHO IT IS. I DON'T EVEN KNOW WHAT TO CALL YOU THESE DAYS...BACK TO *ANGEL,* INNIT? "TWILIGHT"'S GONE AWAY WITH THE LUCHADOR MASK.
SMART. I HEAR THE BIRD WHO WRITES THE GOTH ROMANCES IS LITIGIOUS.
KURTH WORKS FOR A GUY NAME OF MAL FRASER. IMAGINE A HALF-DEMON JOHN GOTTI WITHOUT THE FASHION SENSE.
THEIR RACKET'S SELLING BODY PARTS TO RICH SCUMBAGS. A YAKUZA BOSS NEEDS A KIDNEY, THEY GO GET ONE. AND DON'T CHECK TO SEE IF YOU'RE AN ORGAN DONOR BEFORE THEY CUT YOU OPEN.
GEEZ, YOU STILL ON *FRIENDSTER,* TOO? THAT'S ANCIENT HISTORY. WE'RE INTO A HIGHER CLASS OF BUSINESS NOW.
SUPPOSE YOU TELL ME ABOUT IT.
SUPPOSE YOU SIT ON THIS.

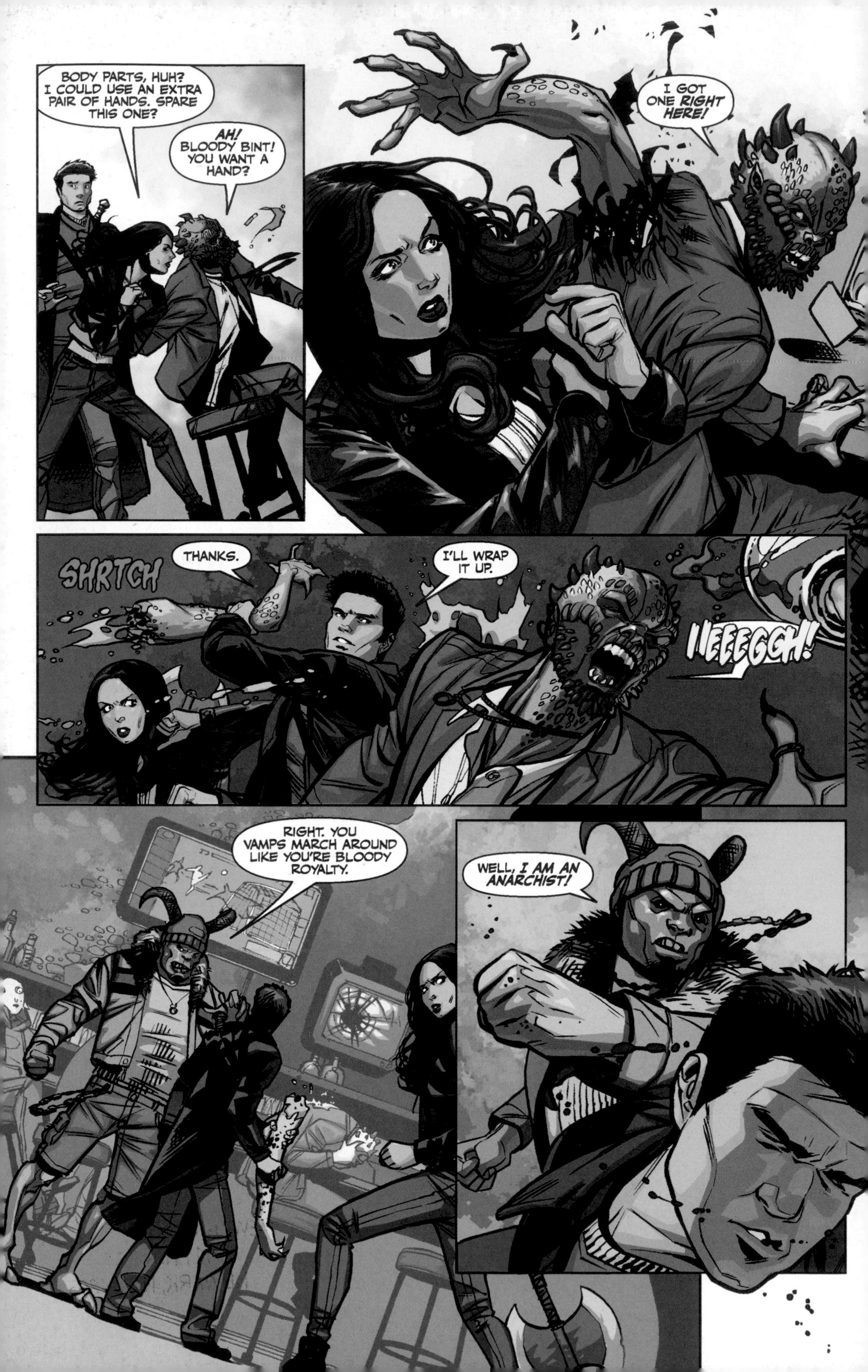
BODY PARTS, HUH? I COULD USE AN EXTRA PAIR OF HANDS. SPARE THIS ONE?
AH! BLOODY BINT! YOU WANT A HAND?
I GOT ONE RIGHT HERE!
SHRTCH
THANKS.
I'LL WRAP IT UP.
IEEEEGGH!
RIGHT. YOU VAMPS MARCH AROUND LIKE YOU'RE BLOODY ROYALTY.
WELL, I AM AN ANARCHIST!

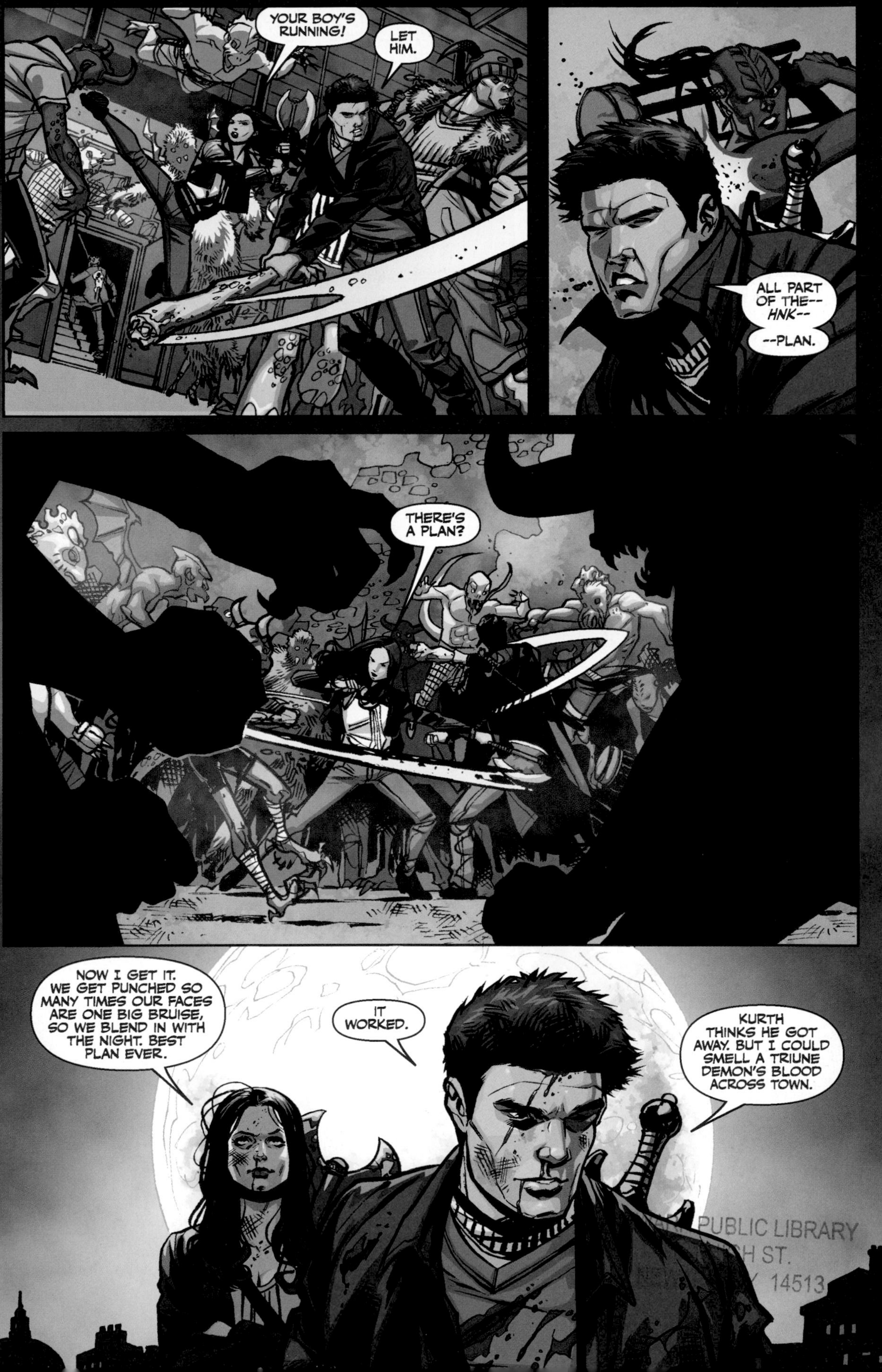
YOUR BOY'S RUNNING!
LET HIM.
ALL PART OF THE-- HNK--
--PLAN.
THERE'S A PLAN?
NOW I GET IT. WE GET PUNCHED SO MANY TIMES OUR FACES ARE ONE BIG BRUISE, SO WE BLEND IN WITH THE NIGHT. BEST PLAN EVER.
IT WORKED.
KURTH THINKS HE GOT AWAY. BUT I COULD SMELL A TRIUNE DEMON'S BLOOD ACROSS TOWN.

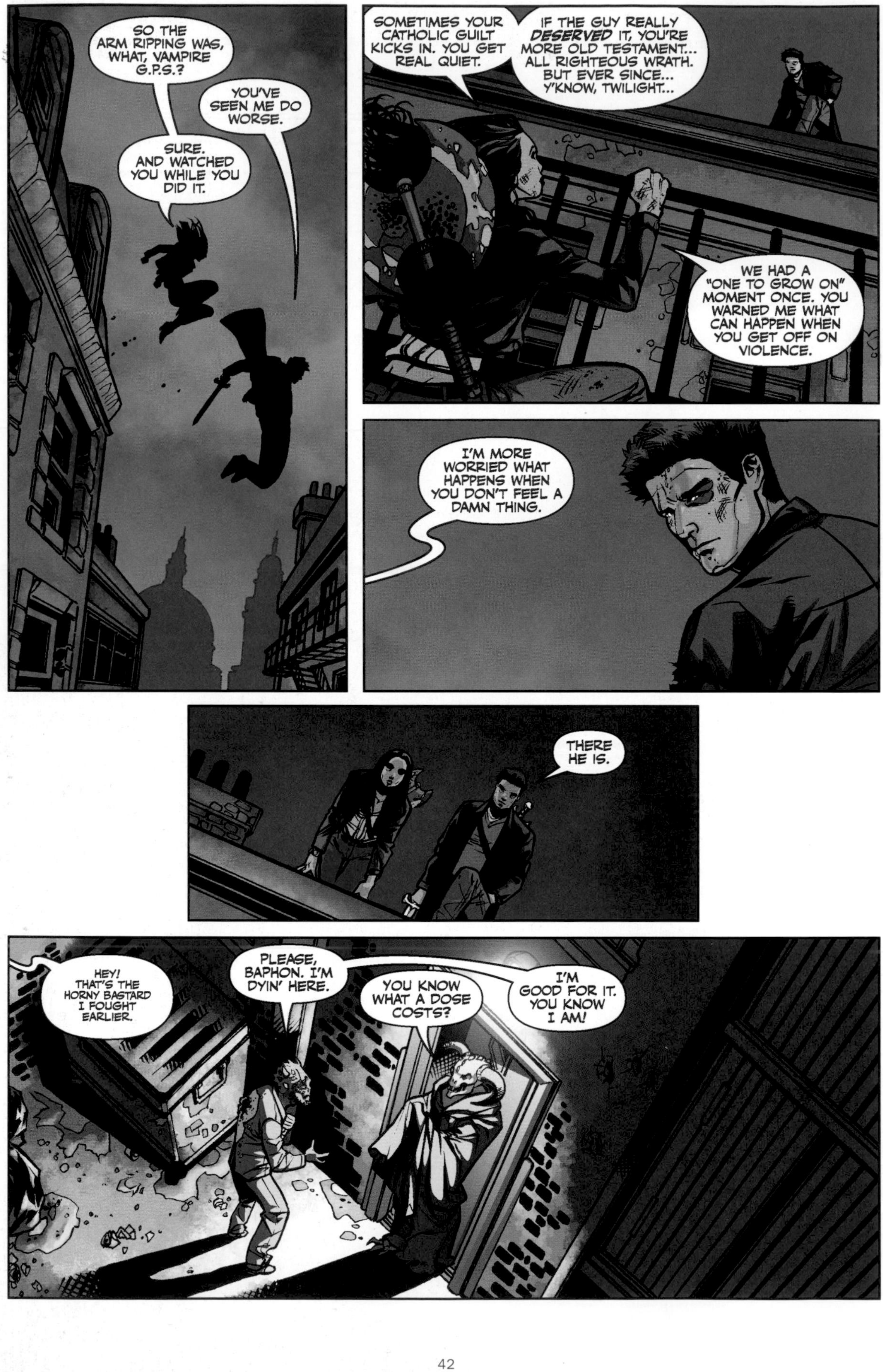
SO THE ARM RIPPING WAS, WHAT, VAMPIRE G.P.S.?
YOU'VE SEEN ME DO WORSE.
SURE. AND WATCHED YOU WHILE YOU DID IT.
SOMETIMES YOUR CATHOLIC GUILT KICKS IN. YOU GET REAL QUIET.
IF THE GUY REALLY DESERVED IT, YOU'RE MORE OLD TESTAMENT... ALL RIGHTEOUS WRATH. BUT EVER SINCE... Y'KNOW, TWILIGHT...
WE HAD A "ONE TO GROW ON" MOMENT ONCE. YOU WARNED ME WHAT CAN HAPPEN WHEN YOU GET OFF ON VIOLENCE.
I'M MORE WORRIED WHAT HAPPENS WHEN YOU DON'T FEEL A DAMN THING.
THERE HE IS.
HEY! THAT'S THE HORNY BASTARD I FOUGHT EARLIER.
PLEASE, BAPHON. I'M DYIN' HERE.
YOU KNOW WHAT A DOSE COSTS?
I'M GOOD FOR IT. YOU KNOW I AM!

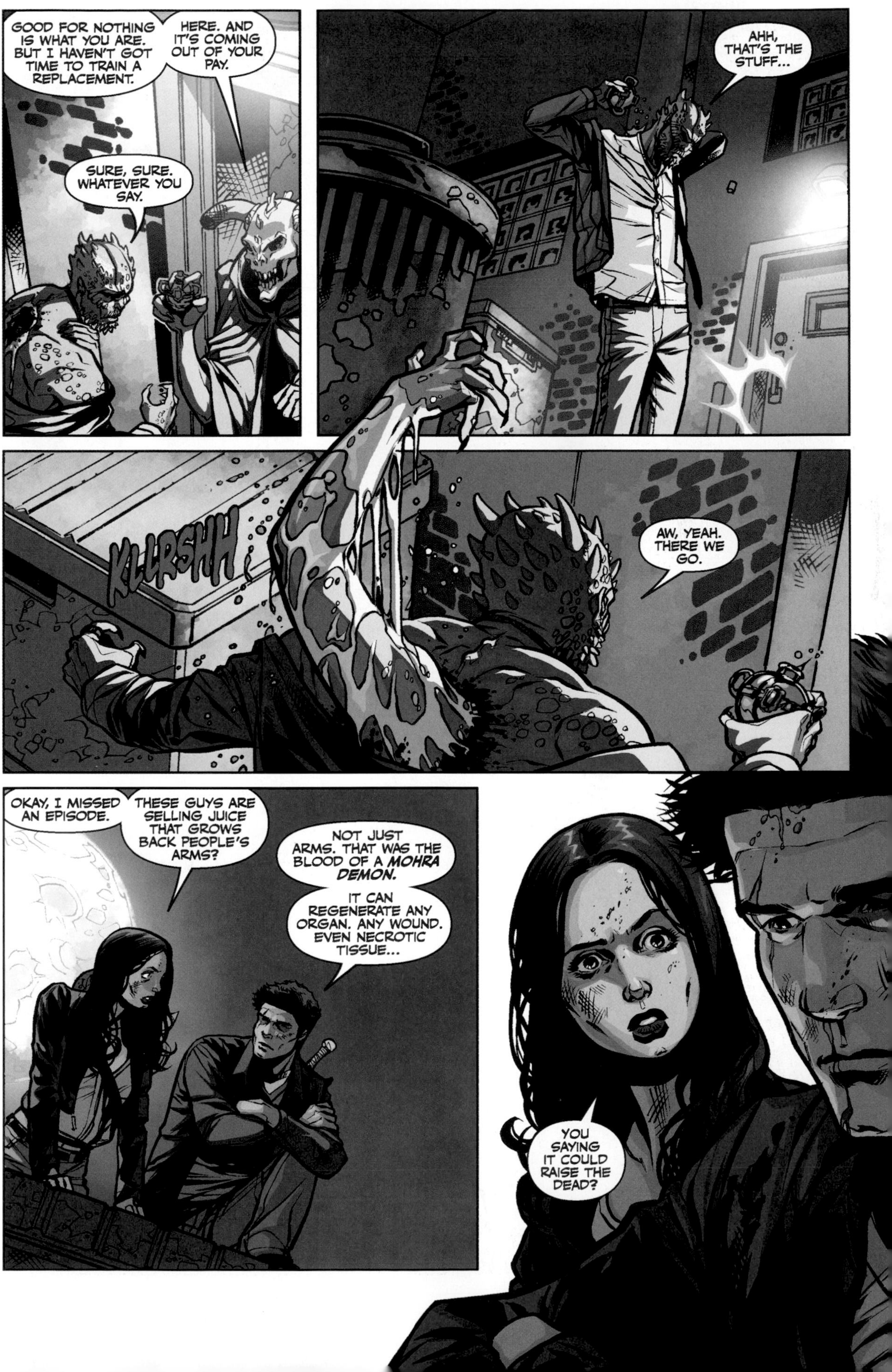
GOOD FOR NOTHING IS WHAT YOU ARE. BUT I HAVEN'T GOT TIME TO TRAIN A REPLACEMENT.
HERE. AND IT'S COMING OUT OF YOUR PAY.
SURE, SURE. WHATEVER YOU SAY.
AHH, THAT'S THE STUFF...
KLLRSHH
AW, YEAH. THERE WE GO.
OKAY, I MISSED AN EPISODE.
THESE GUYS ARE SELLING JUICE THAT GROWS BACK PEOPLE'S ARMS?
NOT JUST ARMS. THAT WAS THE BLOOD OF A *MOHRA DEMON.*
IT CAN REGENERATE ANY ORGAN. ANY WOUND. EVEN NECROTIC TISSUE...
YOU SAYING IT COULD RAISE THE DEAD?

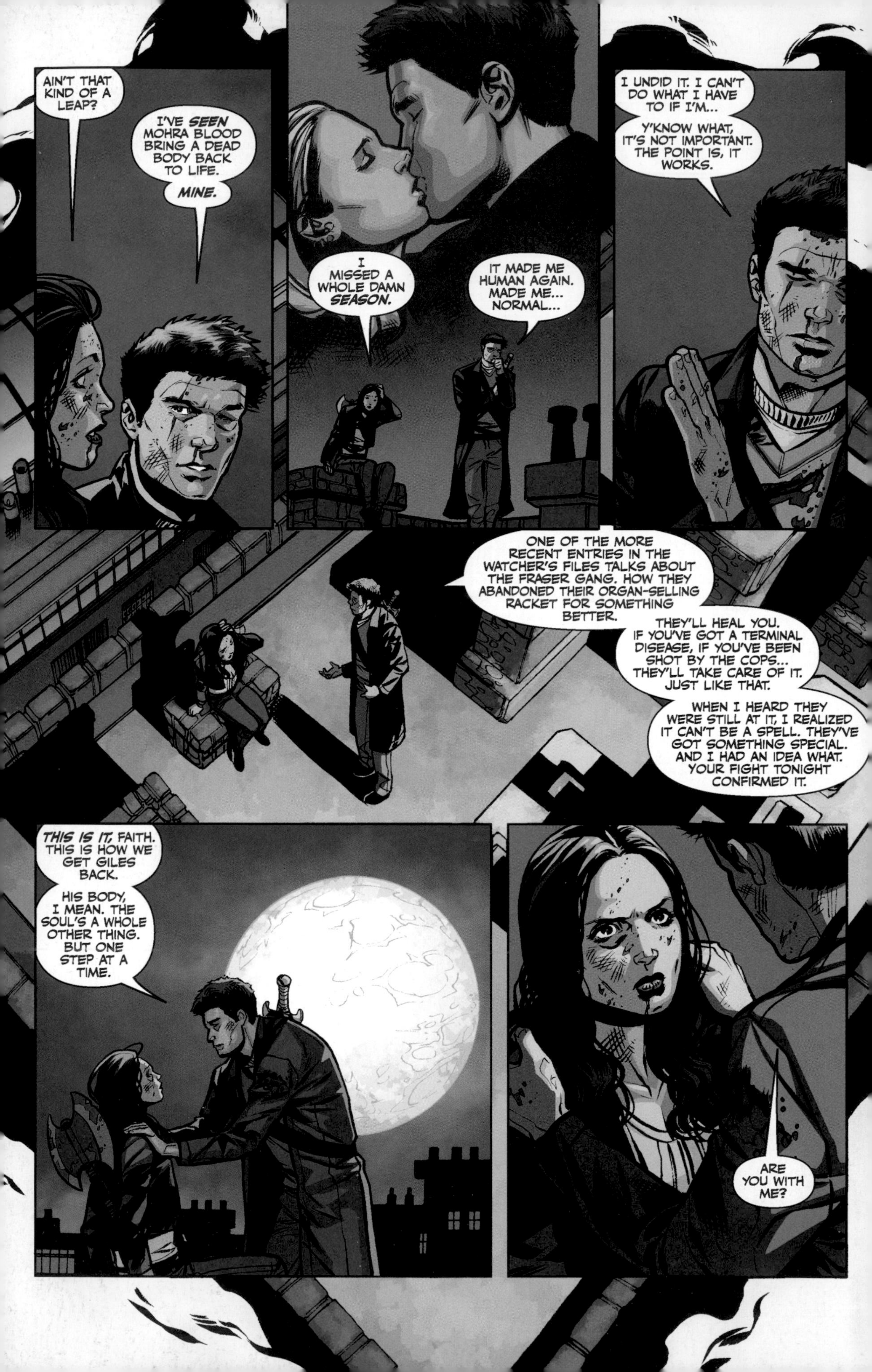
AIN'T THAT KIND OF A LEAP?
I'VE *SEEN* MOHRA BLOOD BRING A DEAD BODY BACK TO LIFE.
MINE.
I MISSED A WHOLE DAMN *SEASON.*
IT MADE ME HUMAN AGAIN. MADE ME... NORMAL...
I UNDID IT. I CAN'T DO WHAT I HAVE TO IF I'M...
Y'KNOW WHAT, IT'S NOT IMPORTANT. THE POINT IS, IT WORKS.
ONE OF THE MORE RECENT ENTRIES IN THE WATCHER'S FILES TALKS ABOUT THE FRASER GANG. HOW THEY ABANDONED THEIR ORGAN-SELLING RACKET FOR SOMETHING BETTER.
THEY'LL HEAL YOU. IF YOU'VE GOT A TERMINAL DISEASE, IF YOU'VE BEEN SHOT BY THE COPS... THEY'LL TAKE CARE OF IT. JUST LIKE THAT.
WHEN I HEARD THEY WERE STILL AT IT, I REALIZED IT CAN'T BE A SPELL. THEY'VE GOT SOMETHING SPECIAL. AND I HAD AN IDEA WHAT. YOUR FIGHT TONIGHT CONFIRMED IT.
THIS IS IT, FAITH. THIS IS HOW WE GET GILES BACK.
HIS BODY, I MEAN. THE SOUL'S A WHOLE OTHER THING. BUT ONE STEP AT A TIME.
ARE YOU WITH ME?

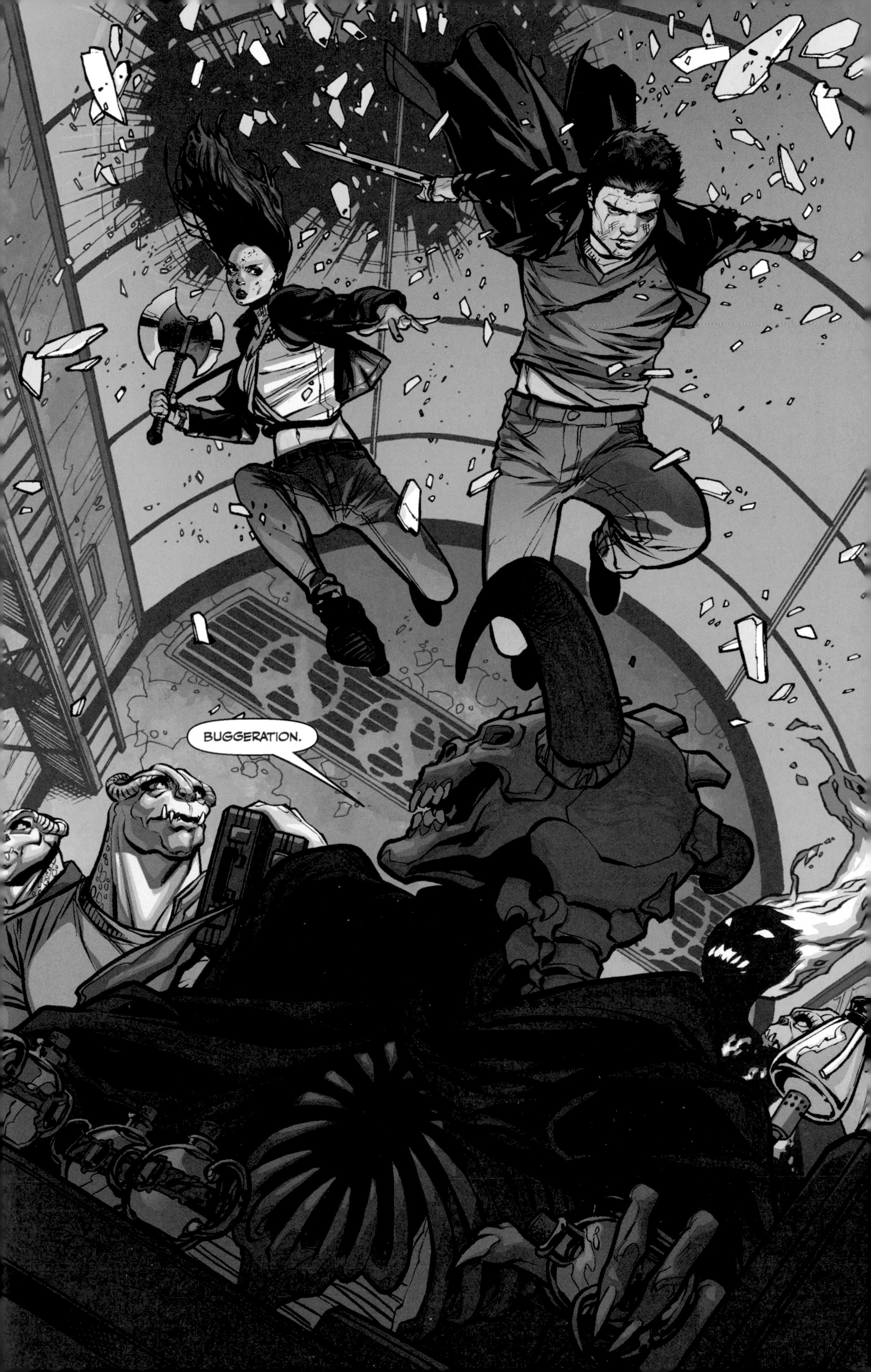
BUGGERATION.

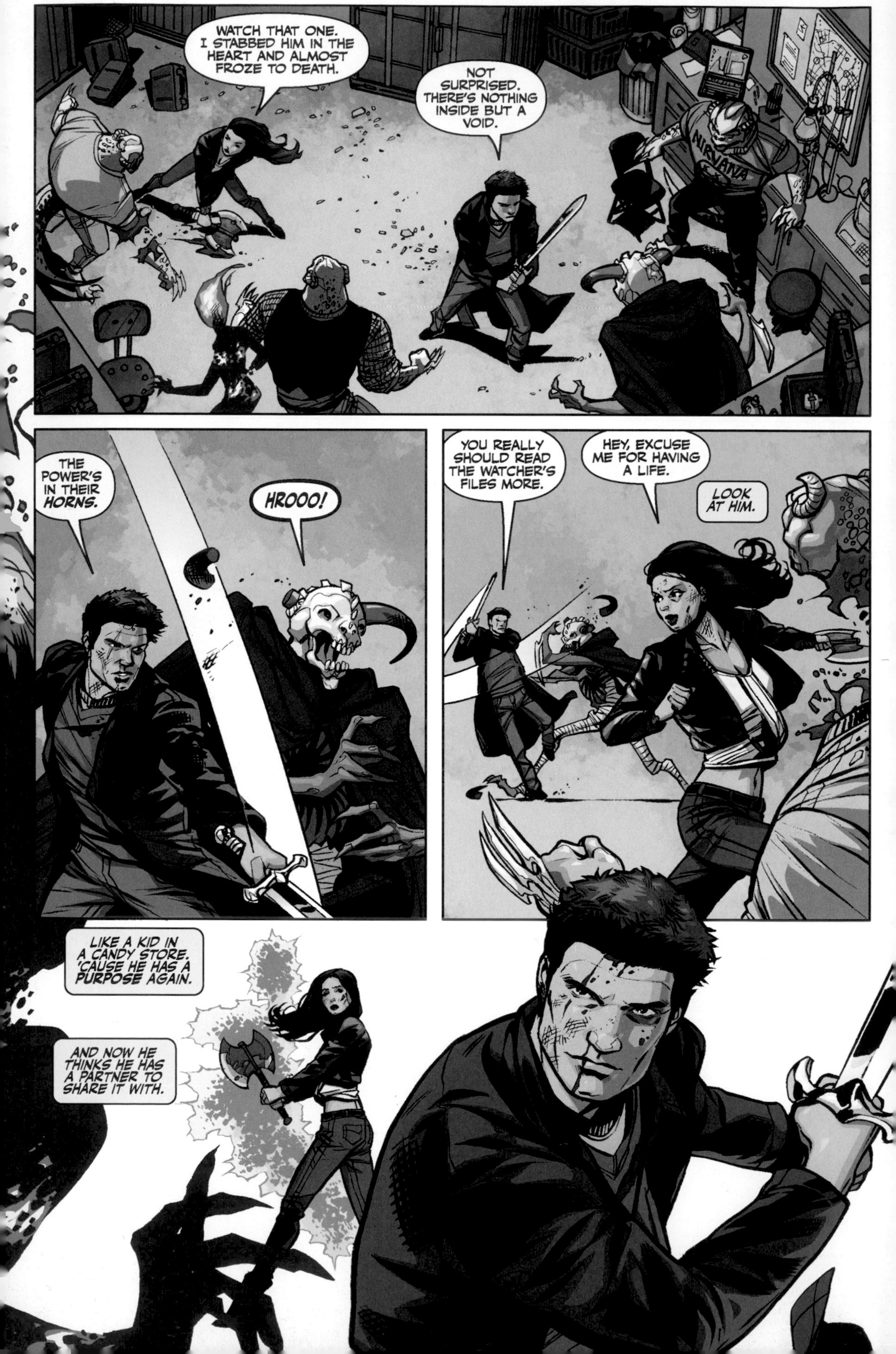
WATCH THAT ONE. I STABBED HIM IN THE HEART AND ALMOST FROZE TO DEATH.
NOT SURPRISED. THERE'S NOTHING INSIDE BUT A VOID.
NIRVANA
THE POWER'S IN THEIR *HORNS*.
HROOO!
YOU REALLY SHOULD READ THE WATCHER'S FILES MORE.
HEY, EXCUSE ME FOR HAVING A LIFE.
LOOK AT HIM.
LIKE A KID IN A CANDY STORE. 'CAUSE HE HAS A PURPOSE AGAIN.
AND NOW HE THINKS HE HAS A PARTNER TO SHARE IT WITH.

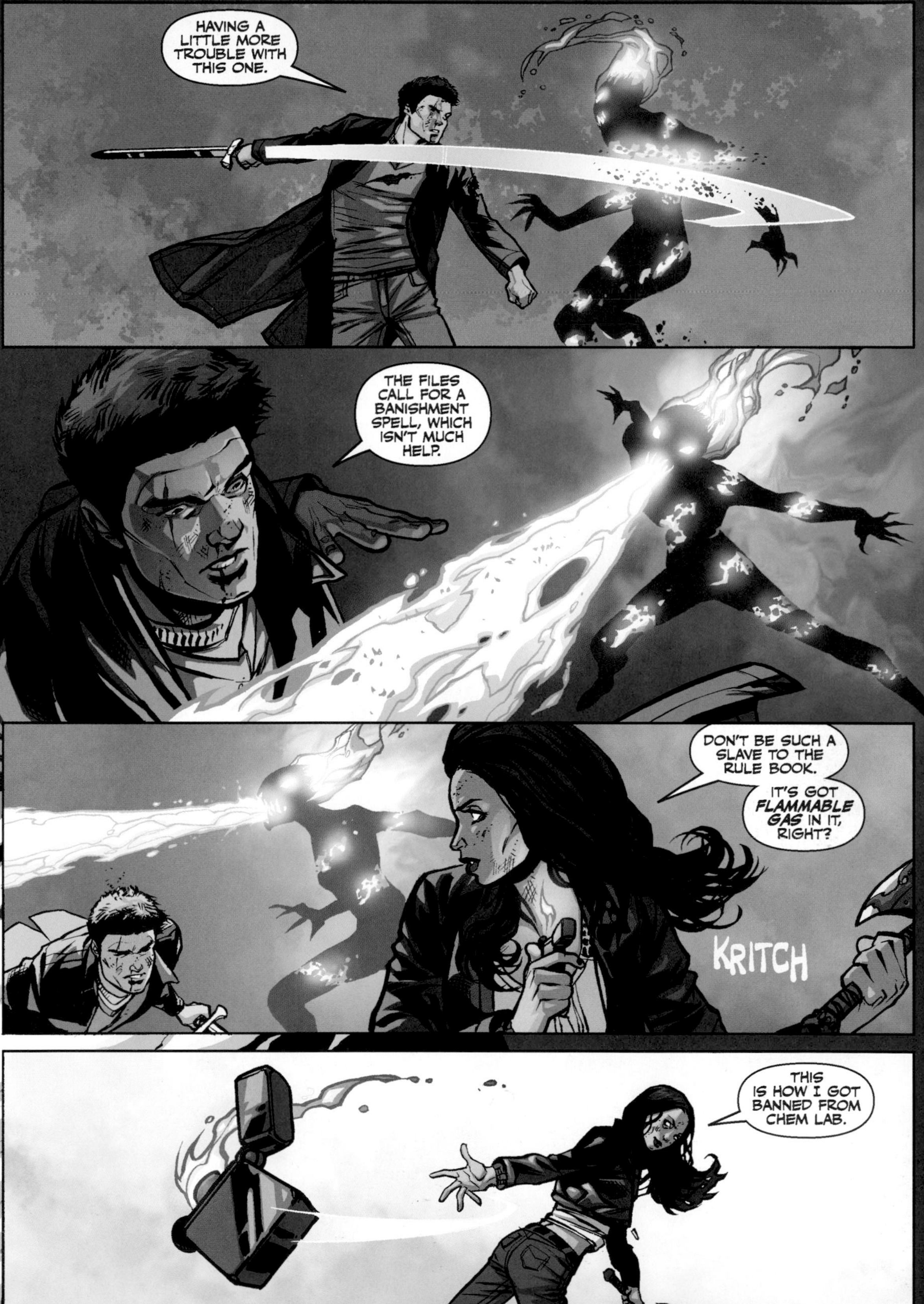
HAVING A LITTLE MORE TROUBLE WITH THIS ONE.
THE FILES CALL FOR A BANISHMENT SPELL, WHICH ISN'T MUCH HELP.
DON'T BE SUCH A SLAVE TO THE RULE BOOK.
IT'S GOT FLAMMABLE GAS IN IT, RIGHT?
KRITCH
THIS IS HOW I GOT BANNED FROM CHEM LAB.

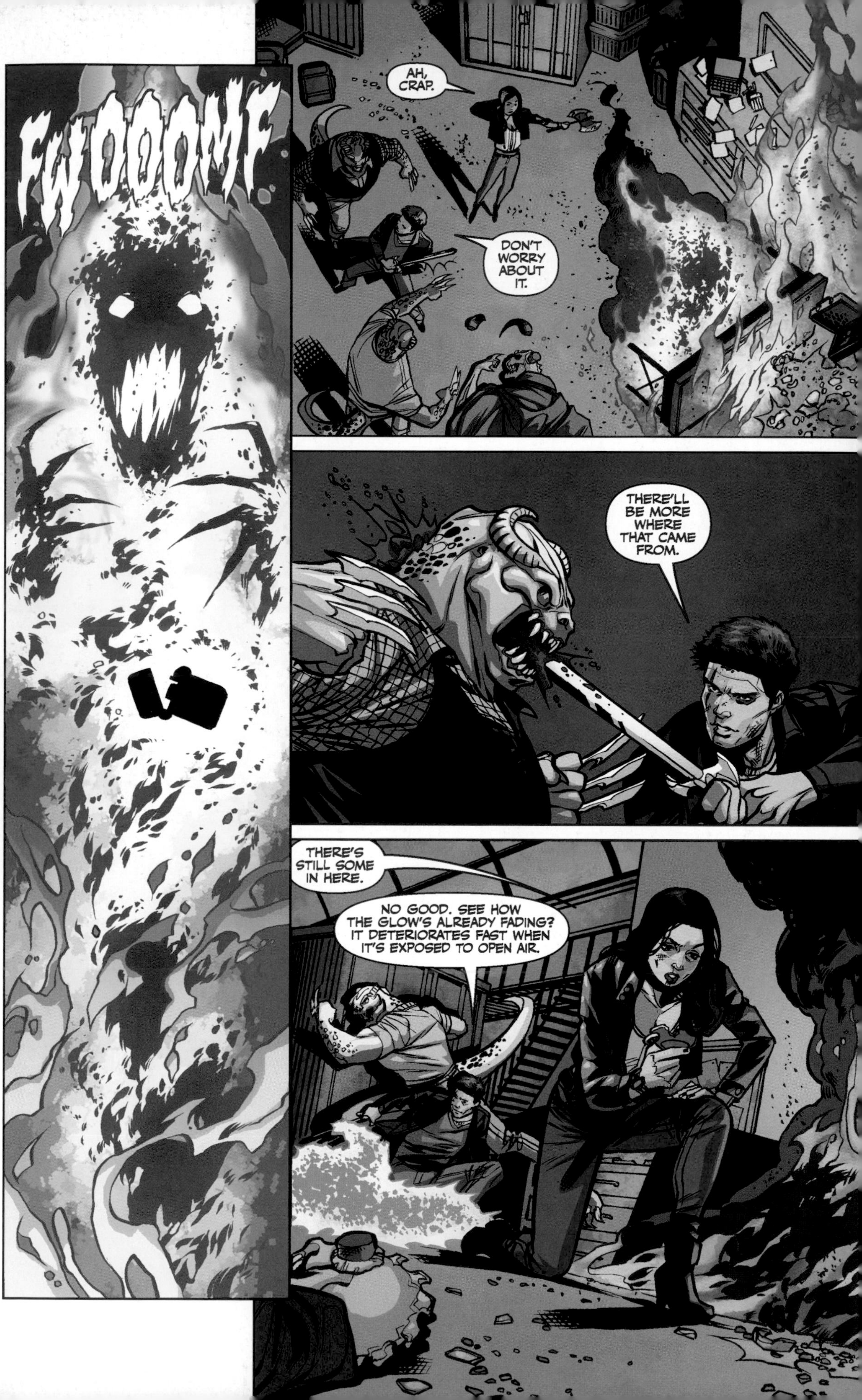
FWOOMF
AH, CRAP.
DON'T WORRY ABOUT IT.
THERE'LL BE MORE WHERE THAT CAME FROM.
THERE'S STILL SOME IN HERE.
NO GOOD. SEE HOW THE GLOW'S ALREADY FADING? IT DETERIORATES FAST WHEN IT'S EXPOSED TO OPEN AIR.

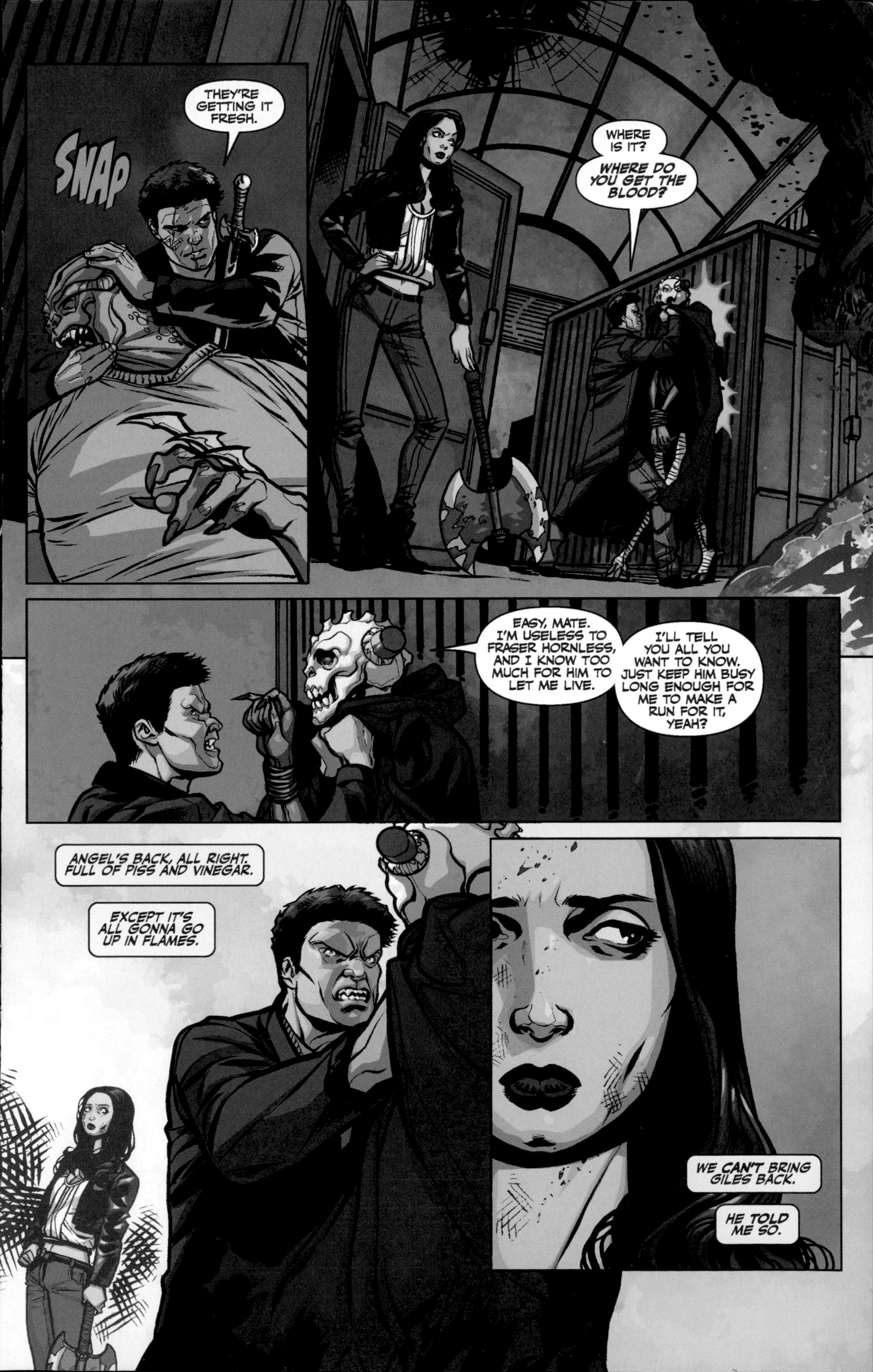
THEY'RE GETTING IT FRESH.
SNAP
WHERE IS IT? WHERE DO YOU GET THE BLOOD?
EASY, MATE. I'M USELESS TO FRASER HORNLESS, AND I KNOW TOO MUCH FOR HIM TO LET ME LIVE.
I'LL TELL YOU ALL YOU WANT TO KNOW. JUST KEEP HIM BUSY LONG ENOUGH FOR ME TO MAKE A RUN FOR IT, YEAH?
ANGEL'S BACK, ALL RIGHT. FULL OF PISS AND VINEGAR.
EXCEPT IT'S ALL GONNA GO UP IN FLAMES.
WE CAN'T BRING GILES BACK.
HE TOLD ME SO.

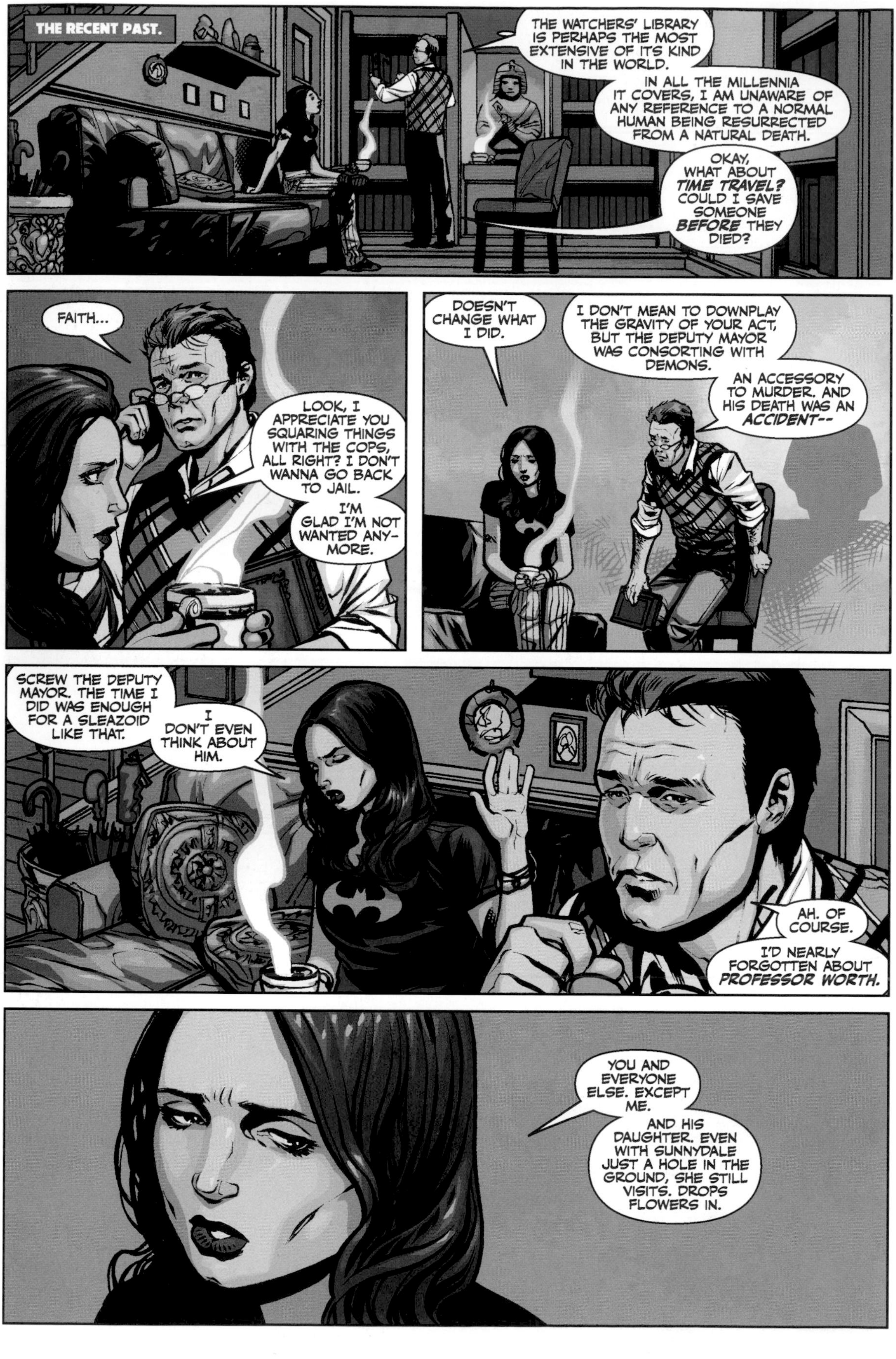
THE RECENT PAST.
THE WATCHERS' LIBRARY IS PERHAPS THE MOST EXTENSIVE OF ITS KIND IN THE WORLD.
IN ALL THE MILLENNIA IT COVERS, I AM UNAWARE OF ANY REFERENCE TO A NORMAL HUMAN BEING RESURRECTED FROM A NATURAL DEATH.
OKAY, WHAT ABOUT *TIME TRAVEL?* COULD I SAVE SOMEONE *BEFORE* THEY DIED?
FAITH...
LOOK, I APPRECIATE YOU SQUARING THINGS WITH THE COPS, ALL RIGHT? I DON'T WANNA GO BACK TO JAIL.
I'M GLAD I'M NOT WANTED ANY-MORE.
DOESN'T CHANGE WHAT I DID.
I DON'T MEAN TO DOWNPLAY THE GRAVITY OF YOUR ACT, BUT THE DEPUTY MAYOR WAS CONSORTING WITH DEMONS.
AN ACCESSORY TO MURDER. AND HIS DEATH WAS AN *ACCIDENT--*
SCREW THE DEPUTY MAYOR. THE TIME I DID WAS ENOUGH FOR A SLEAZOID LIKE THAT.
I DON'T EVEN THINK ABOUT HIM.
AH. OF COURSE.
I'D NEARLY FORGOTTEN ABOUT *PROFESSOR WORTH.*
YOU AND EVERYONE ELSE. EXCEPT ME.
AND HIS DAUGHTER. EVEN WITH SUNNYDALE JUST A HOLE IN THE GROUND, SHE STILL VISITS. DROPS FLOWERS IN.

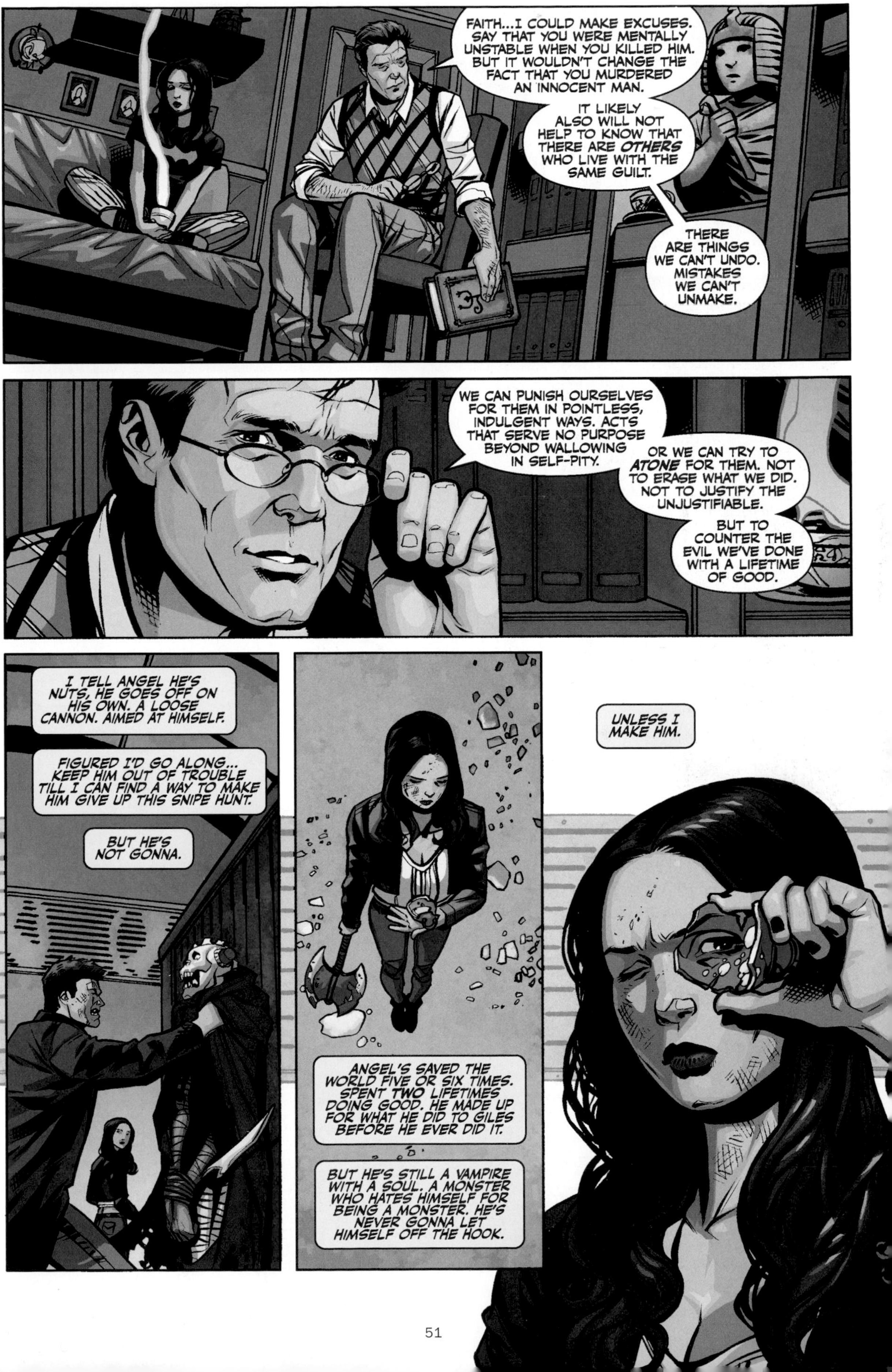
FAITH...I COULD MAKE EXCUSES. SAY THAT YOU WERE MENTALLY UNSTABLE WHEN YOU KILLED HIM. BUT IT WOULDN'T CHANGE THE FACT THAT YOU MURDERED AN INNOCENT MAN.
IT LIKELY ALSO WILL NOT HELP TO KNOW THAT THERE ARE OTHERS WHO LIVE WITH THE SAME GUILT.
THERE ARE THINGS WE CAN'T UNDO. MISTAKES WE CAN'T UNMAKE.
WE CAN PUNISH OURSELVES FOR THEM IN POINTLESS, INDULGENT WAYS. ACTS THAT SERVE NO PURPOSE BEYOND WALLOWING IN SELF-PITY.
OR WE CAN TRY TO ATONE FOR THEM. NOT TO ERASE WHAT WE DID. NOT TO JUSTIFY THE UNJUSTIFIABLE.
BUT TO COUNTER THE EVIL WE'VE DONE WITH A LIFETIME OF GOOD.
I TELL ANGEL HE'S NUTS, HE GOES OFF ON HIS OWN. A LOOSE CANNON. AIMED AT HIMSELF.
FIGURED I'D GO ALONG... KEEP HIM OUT OF TROUBLE TILL I CAN FIND A WAY TO MAKE HIM GIVE UP THIS SNIPE HUNT.
BUT HE'S NOT GONNA.
ANGEL'S SAVED THE WORLD FIVE OR SIX TIMES. SPENT TWO LIFETIMES DOING GOOD. HE MADE UP FOR WHAT HE DID TO GILES BEFORE HE EVER DID IT.
BUT HE'S STILL A VAMPIRE WITH A SOUL. A MONSTER WHO HATES HIMSELF FOR BEING A MONSTER. HE'S NEVER GONNA LET HIMSELF OFF THE HOOK.
UNLESS I MAKE HIM.

HELLO, KURTH.

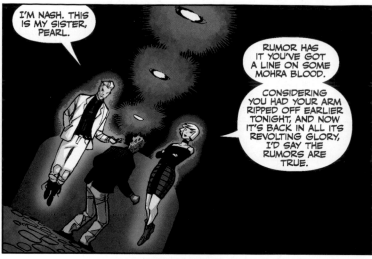

I'M NASH. THIS IS MY SISTER, PEARL.

RUMOR HAS IT YOU'VE GOT A LINE ON SOME MOHRA BLOOD.

CONSIDERING YOU HAD YOUR ARM RIPPED OFF EARLIER TONIGHT, AND NOW IT'S BACK IN ALL ITS REVOLTING GLORY, I'D SAY THE RUMORS ARE TRUE.

SORRY, FRESH OUT. MIGHT GET A NEW DELIVERY IN A WEEK OR SO. COME SEE ME THEN.

I'M AFRAID WE CAN'T WAIT.

GNNAAA!

AND NOW NEITHER CAN YOU.

YOU KNOW THE KIDS WHO LIKED TO PULL WINGS OFF FLIES?

WE LIKED TO PULL THINGS OFF THEM.

TAKE US TO YOUR SOURCE. OR WE DEMONSTRATE.

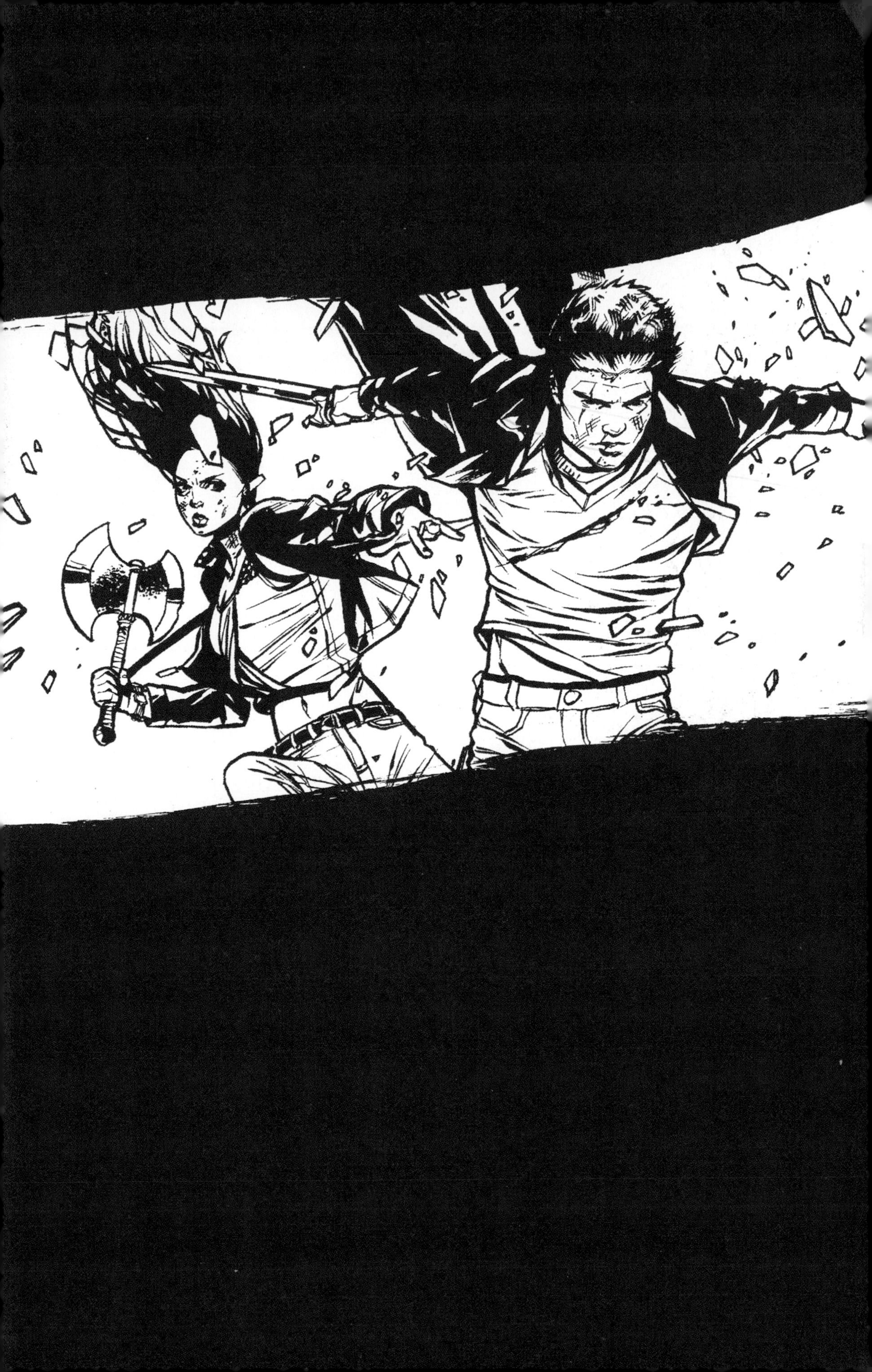

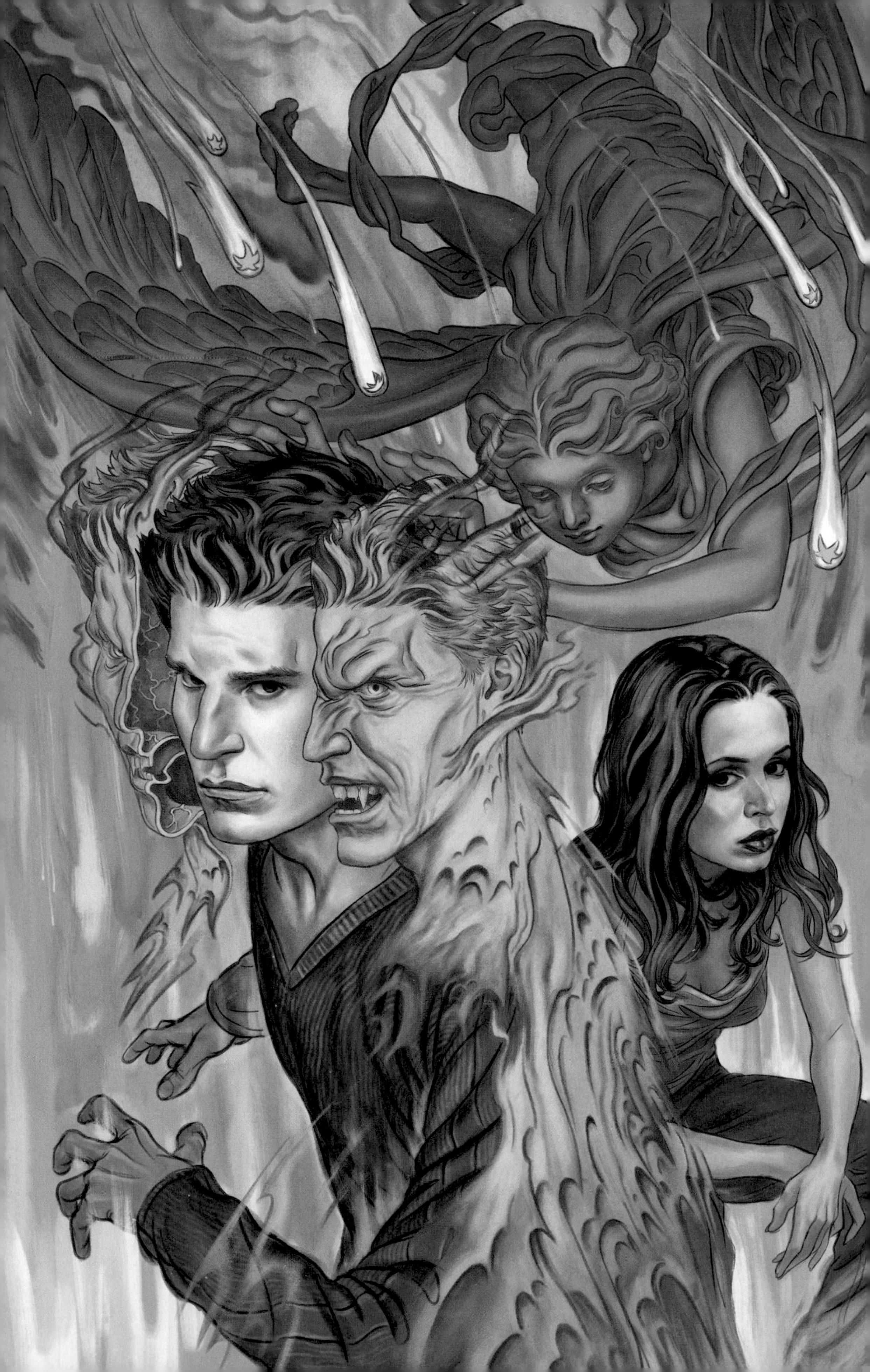

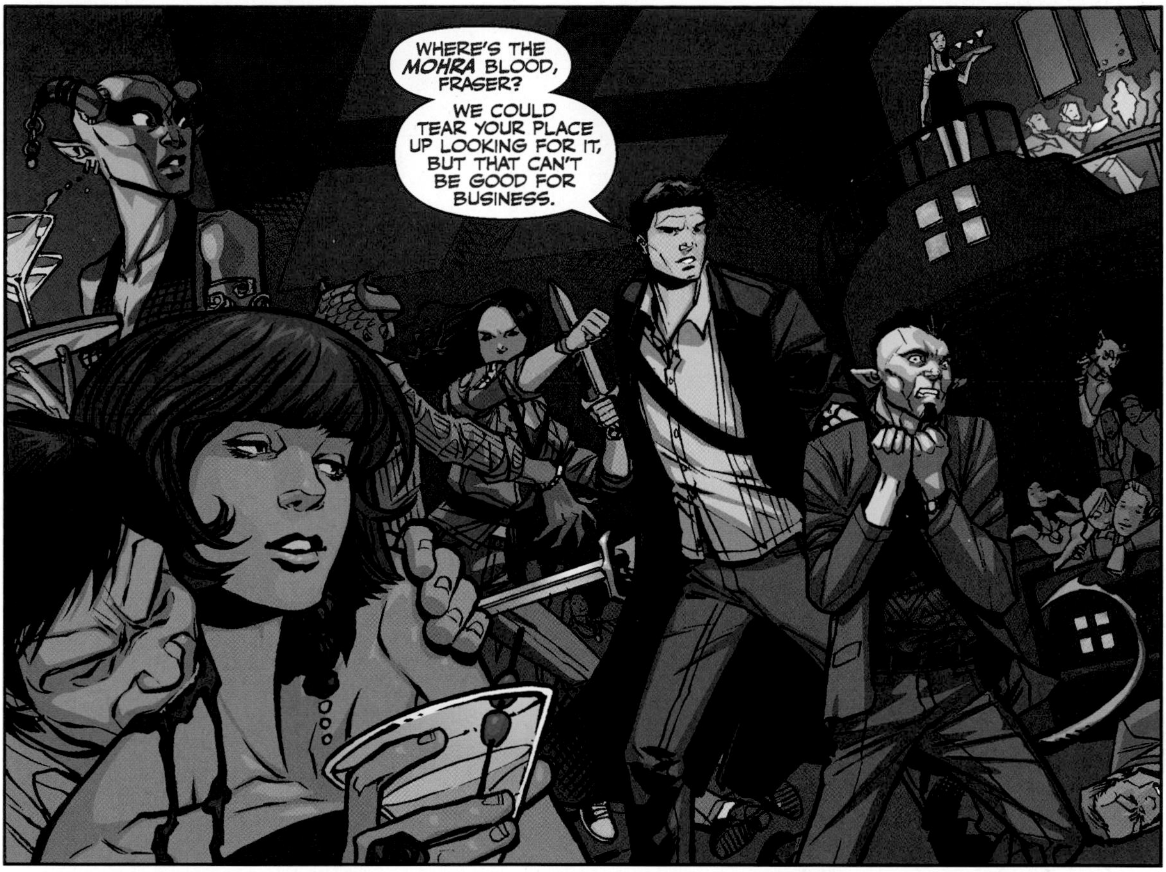
WHERE'S THE *MOHRA* BLOOD, FRASER?
WE COULD TEAR YOUR PLACE UP LOOKING FOR IT, BUT THAT CAN'T BE GOOD FOR BUSINESS.

LIVE THROUGH THIS PART THREE

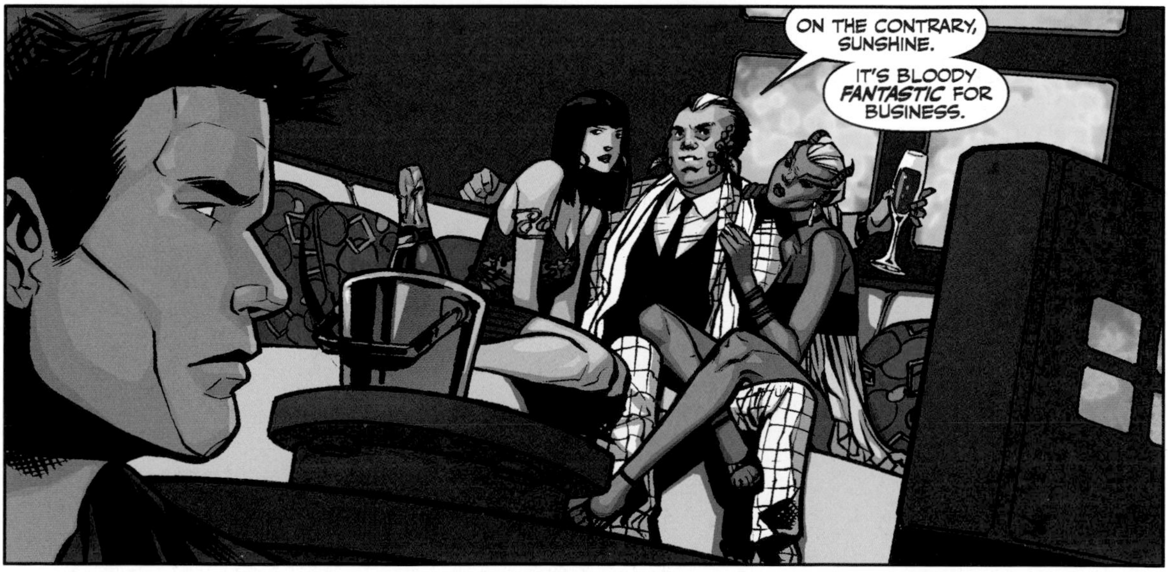
ON THE CONTRARY, SUNSHINE.
IT'S BLOODY *FANTASTIC* FOR BUSINESS.

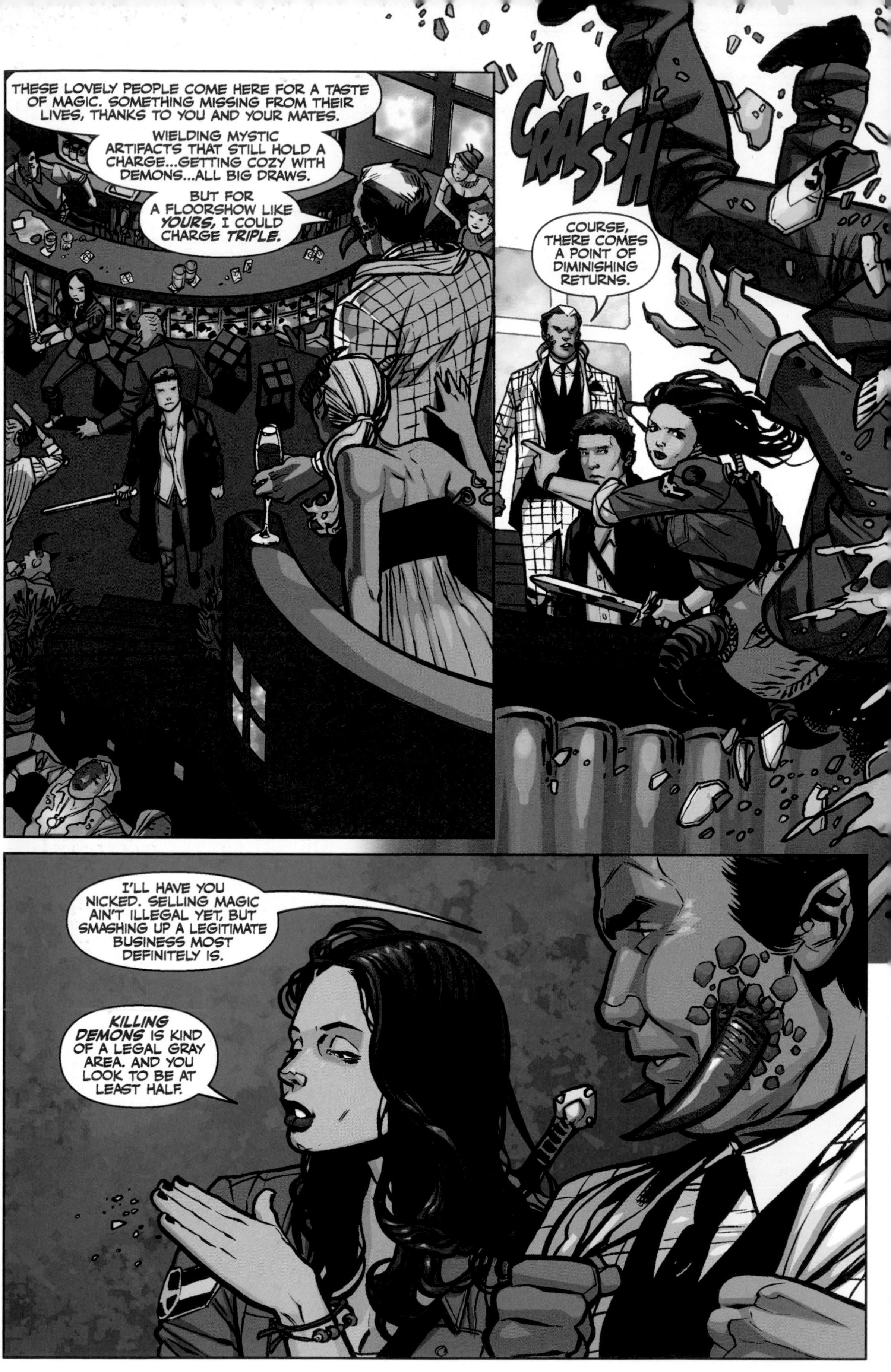
THESE LOVELY PEOPLE COME HERE FOR A TASTE OF MAGIC. SOMETHING MISSING FROM THEIR LIVES, THANKS TO YOU AND YOUR MATES.
WIELDING MYSTIC ARTIFACTS THAT STILL HOLD A CHARGE...GETTING COZY WITH DEMONS...ALL BIG DRAWS.
BUT FOR A FLOORSHOW LIKE *YOURS*, I COULD CHARGE *TRIPLE*.
CRASSH
COURSE, THERE COMES A POINT OF DIMINISHING RETURNS.
I'LL HAVE YOU NICKED. SELLING MAGIC AIN'T ILLEGAL YET, BUT SMASHING UP A LEGITIMATE BUSINESS MOST DEFINITELY IS.
KILLING DEMONS IS KIND OF A LEGAL GRAY AREA. AND YOU LOOK TO BE AT LEAST HALF.

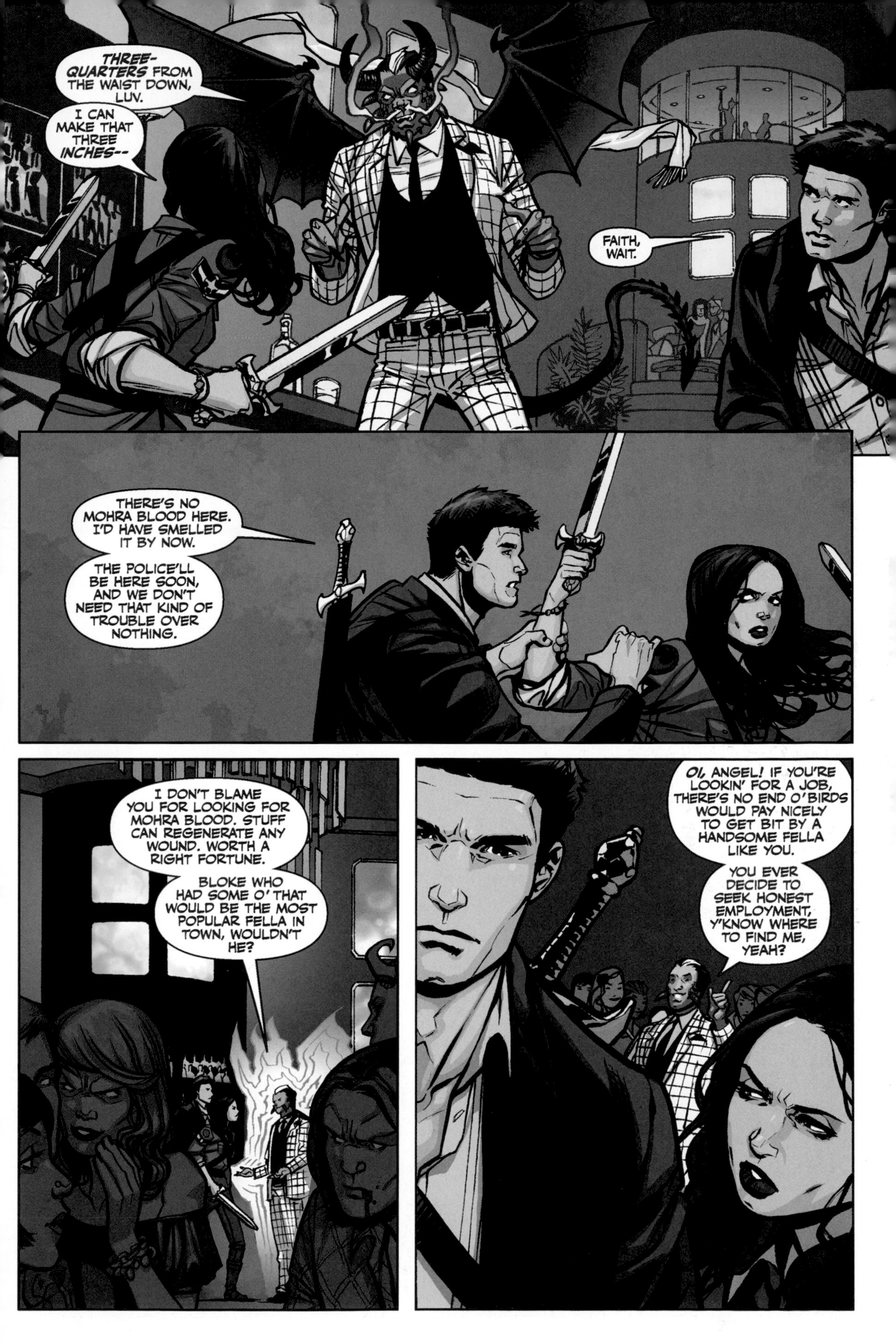

THREE-QUARTERS FROM THE WAIST DOWN, LUV.
I CAN MAKE THAT THREE INCHES--
FAITH, WAIT.
THERE'S NO MOHRA BLOOD HERE. I'D HAVE SMELLED IT BY NOW.
THE POLICE'LL BE HERE SOON, AND WE DON'T NEED THAT KIND OF TROUBLE OVER NOTHING.
I DON'T BLAME YOU FOR LOOKING FOR MOHRA BLOOD. STUFF CAN REGENERATE ANY WOUND. WORTH A RIGHT FORTUNE.
BLOKE WHO HAD SOME O' THAT WOULD BE THE MOST POPULAR FELLA IN TOWN, WOULDN'T HE?
OI, ANGEL! IF YOU'RE LOOKIN' FOR A JOB, THERE'S NO END O'BIRDS WOULD PAY NICELY TO GET BIT BY A HANDSOME FELLA LIKE YOU.
YOU EVER DECIDE TO SEEK HONEST EMPLOYMENT, Y'KNOW WHERE TO FIND ME, YEAH?

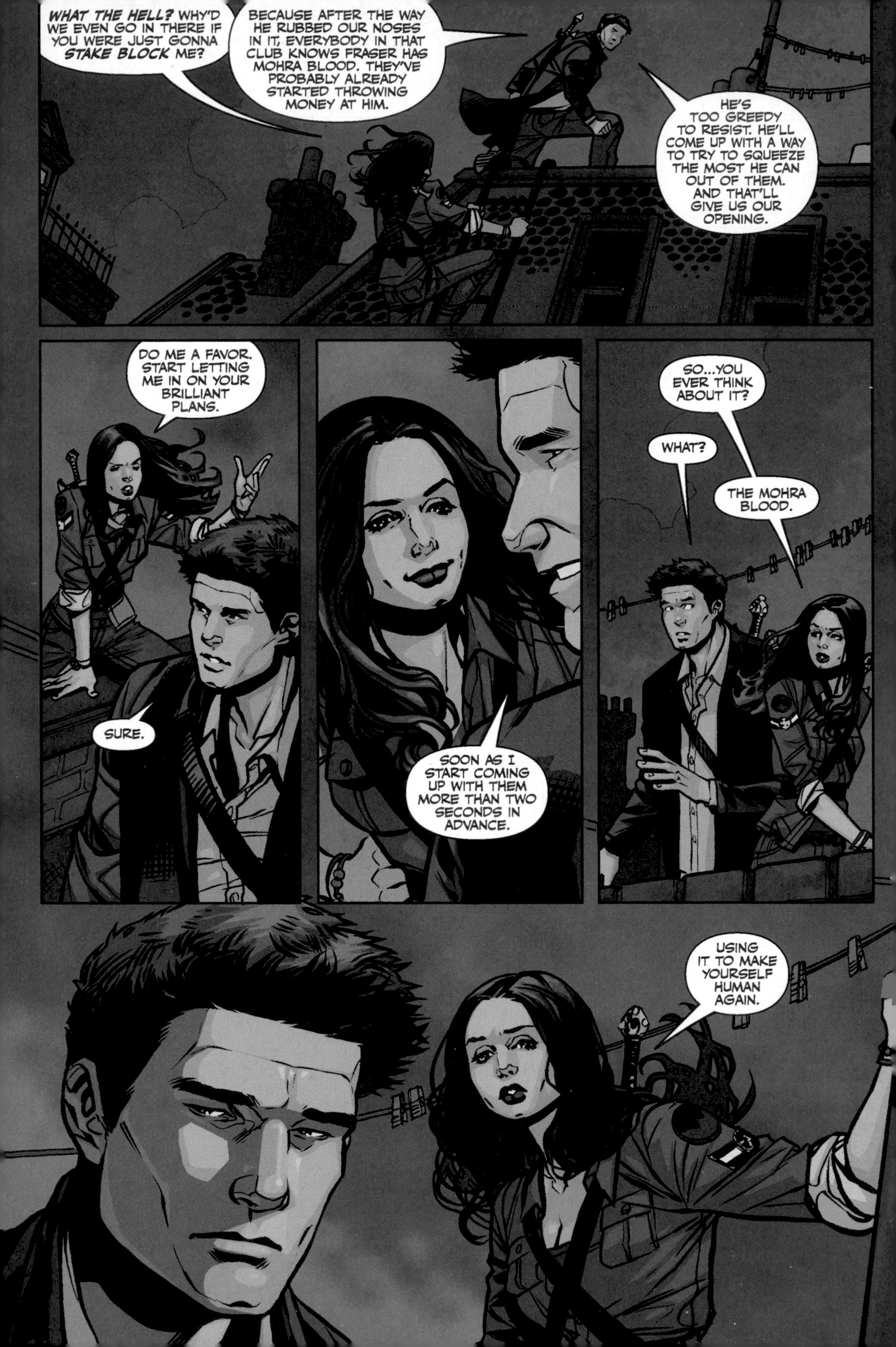
WHAT THE HELL? WHY'D WE EVEN GO IN THERE IF YOU WERE JUST GONNA *STAKE BLOCK* ME?
BECAUSE AFTER THE WAY HE RUBBED OUR NOSES IN IT, EVERYBODY IN THAT CLUB KNOWS FRASER HAS MOHRA BLOOD. THEY'VE PROBABLY ALREADY STARTED THROWING MONEY AT HIM.
HE'S TOO GREEDY TO RESIST. HE'LL COME UP WITH A WAY TO TRY TO SQUEEZE THE MOST HE CAN OUT OF THEM. AND THAT'LL GIVE US OUR OPENING.
DO ME A FAVOR. START LETTING ME IN ON YOUR BRILLIANT PLANS.
SURE.
SOON AS I START COMING UP WITH THEM MORE THAN TWO SECONDS IN ADVANCE.
SO...YOU EVER THINK ABOUT IT?
WHAT?
THE MOHRA BLOOD.
USING IT TO MAKE YOURSELF HUMAN AGAIN.

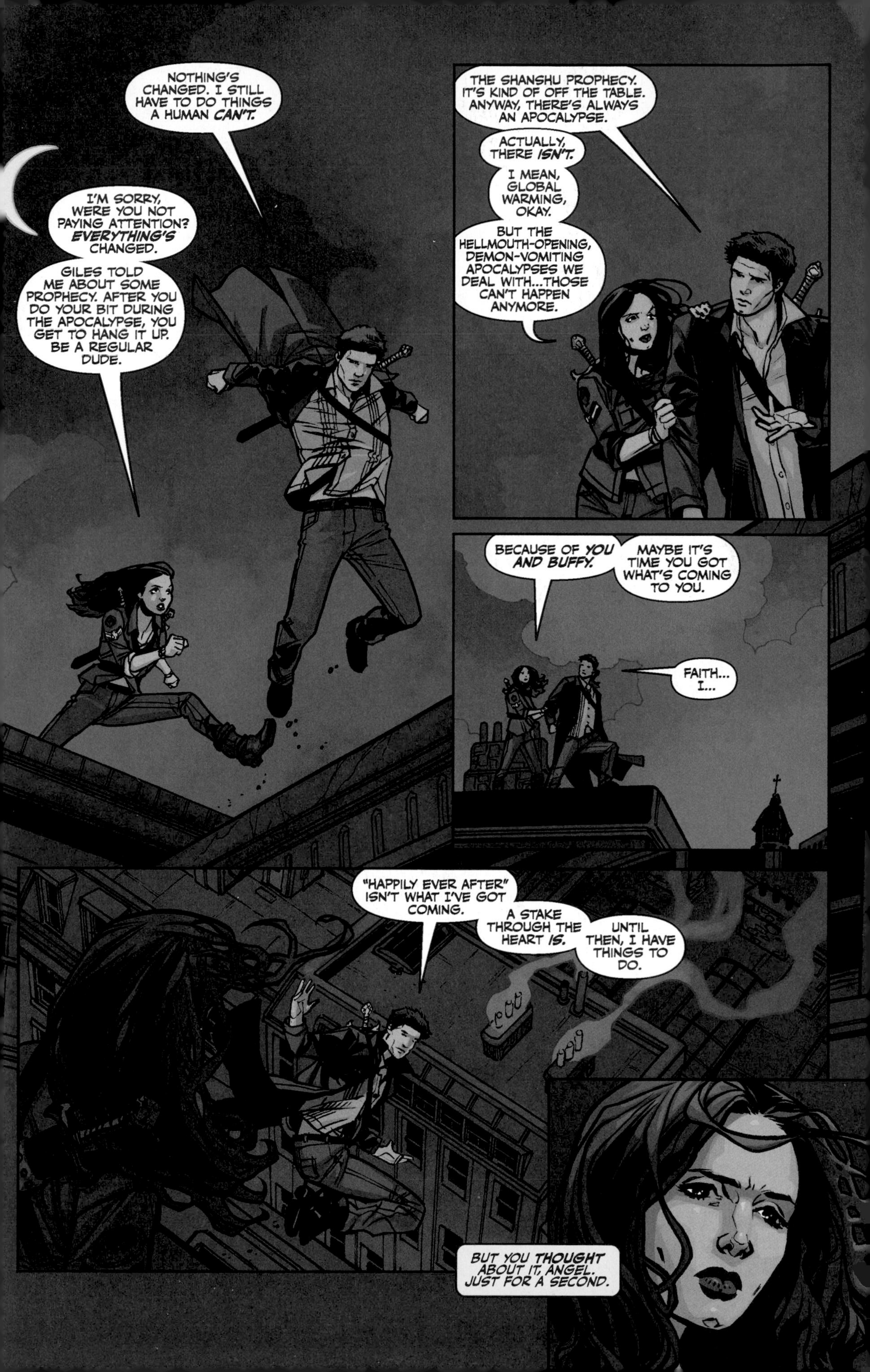
NOTHING'S CHANGED. I STILL HAVE TO DO THINGS A HUMAN *CAN'T.*
I'M SORRY, WERE YOU NOT PAYING ATTENTION? *EVERYTHING'S* CHANGED.
GILES TOLD ME ABOUT SOME PROPHECY. AFTER YOU DO YOUR BIT DURING THE APOCALYPSE, YOU GET TO HANG IT UP. BE A REGULAR DUDE.
THE SHANSHU PROPHECY. IT'S KIND OF OFF THE TABLE. ANYWAY, THERE'S ALWAYS AN APOCALYPSE.
ACTUALLY, THERE *ISN'T.*
I MEAN, GLOBAL WARMING, OKAY.
BUT THE HELLMOUTH-OPENING, DEMON-VOMITING APOCALYPSES WE DEAL WITH...THOSE CAN'T HAPPEN ANYMORE.
BECAUSE OF *YOU AND BUFFY.*
MAYBE IT'S TIME YOU GOT WHAT'S COMING TO YOU.
FAITH... I...
"HAPPILY EVER AFTER" ISN'T WHAT I'VE GOT COMING.
A STAKE THROUGH THE HEART *IS.*
UNTIL THEN, I HAVE THINGS TO DO.
*BUT YOU **THOUGHT** ABOUT IT, ANGEL. JUST FOR A SECOND.*

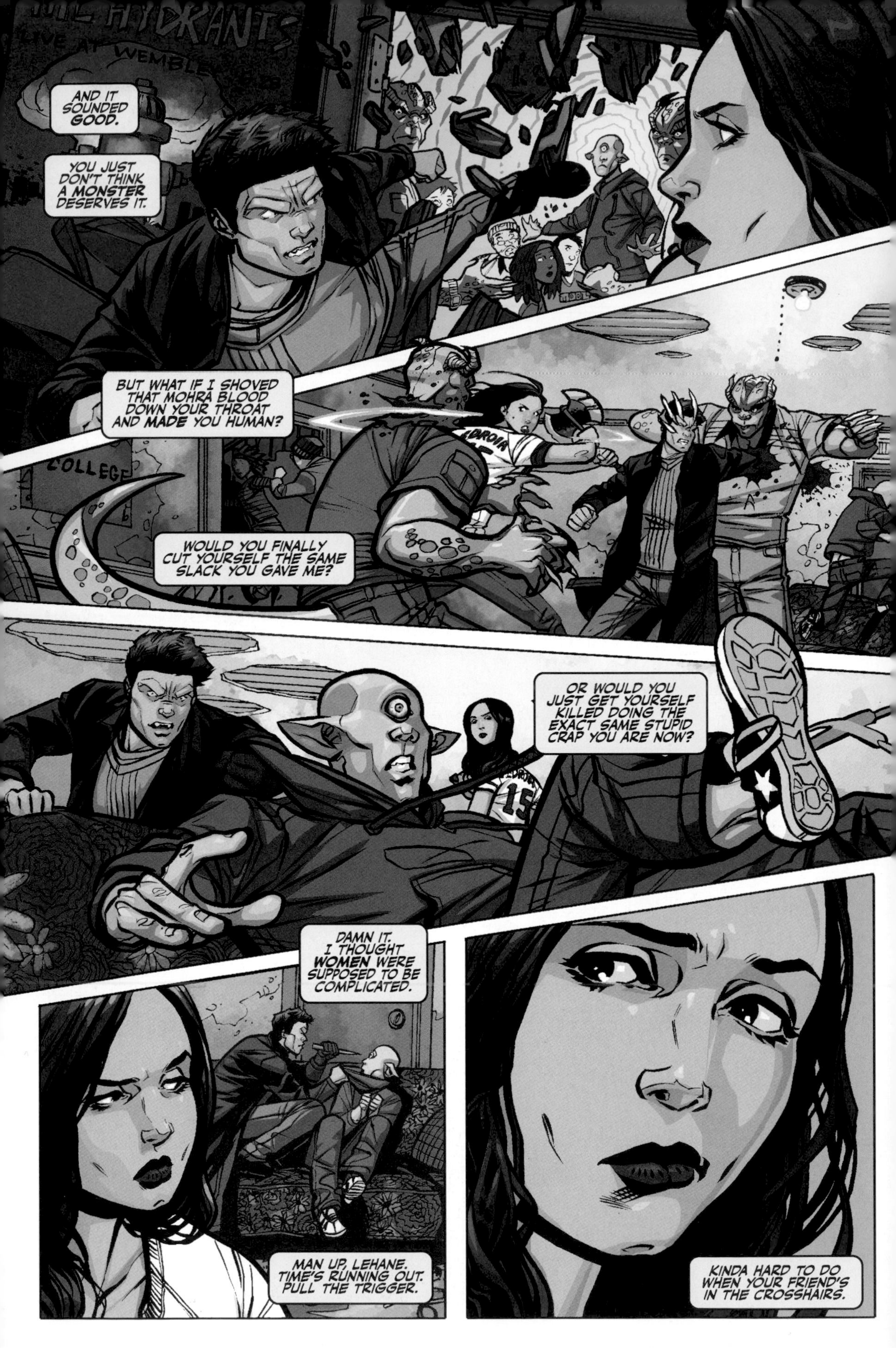

THE HYDRANTS
LIVE AT WEMBLEY
AND IT SOUNDED GOOD.
YOU JUST DON'T THINK A MONSTER DESERVES IT.
BUT WHAT IF I SHOVED THAT MOHRA BLOOD DOWN YOUR THROAT AND MADE YOU HUMAN?
COLLEGE
WOULD YOU FINALLY CUT YOURSELF THE SAME SLACK YOU GAVE ME?
OR WOULD YOU JUST GET YOURSELF KILLED DOING THE EXACT SAME STUPID CRAP YOU ARE NOW?
DAMN IT. I THOUGHT WOMEN WERE SUPPOSED TO BE COMPLICATED.
MAN UP, LEHANE. TIME'S RUNNING OUT. PULL THE TRIGGER.
KINDA HARD TO DO WHEN YOUR FRIEND'S IN THE CROSSHAIRS.

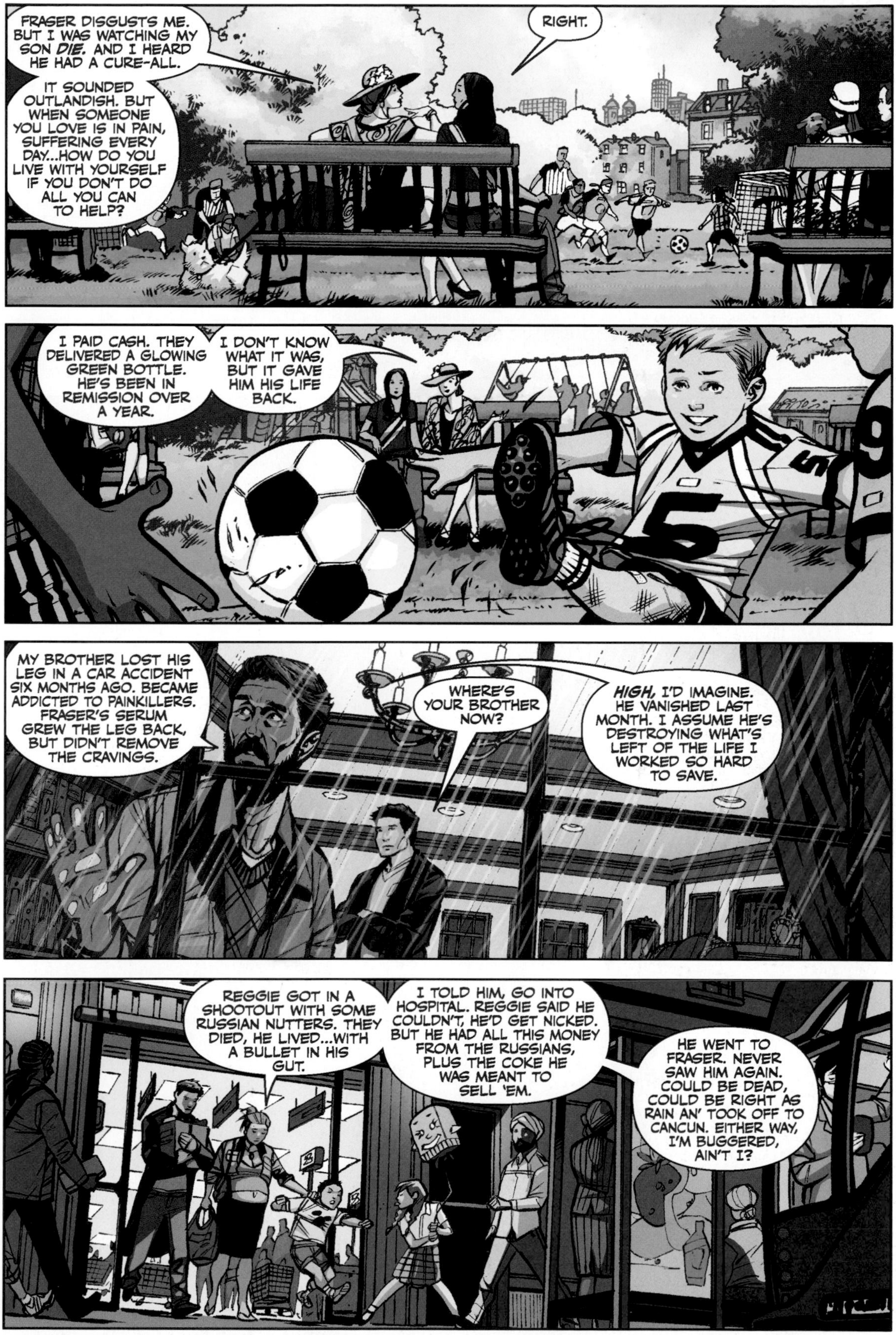
FRASER DISGUSTS ME. BUT I WAS WATCHING MY SON *DIE.* AND I HEARD HE HAD A CURE-ALL.
IT SOUNDED OUTLANDISH. BUT WHEN SOMEONE YOU LOVE IS IN PAIN, SUFFERING EVERY DAY...HOW DO YOU LIVE WITH YOURSELF IF YOU DON'T DO ALL YOU CAN TO HELP?
RIGHT.
I PAID CASH. THEY DELIVERED A GLOWING GREEN BOTTLE. HE'S BEEN IN REMISSION OVER A YEAR.
I DON'T KNOW WHAT IT WAS, BUT IT GAVE HIM HIS LIFE BACK.
MY BROTHER LOST HIS LEG IN A CAR ACCIDENT SIX MONTHS AGO. BECAME ADDICTED TO PAINKILLERS. FRASER'S SERUM GREW THE LEG BACK, BUT DIDN'T REMOVE THE CRAVINGS.
WHERE'S YOUR BROTHER NOW?
HIGH, I'D IMAGINE. HE VANISHED LAST MONTH. I ASSUME HE'S DESTROYING WHAT'S LEFT OF THE LIFE I WORKED SO HARD TO SAVE.
REGGIE GOT IN A SHOOTOUT WITH SOME RUSSIAN NUTTERS. THEY DIED, HE LIVED...WITH A BULLET IN HIS GUT.
I TOLD HIM, GO INTO HOSPITAL. REGGIE SAID HE COULDN'T, HE'D GET NICKED. BUT HE HAD ALL THIS MONEY FROM THE RUSSIANS, PLUS THE COKE HE WAS MEANT TO SELL 'EM.
HE WENT TO FRASER. NEVER SAW HIM AGAIN. COULD BE DEAD, COULD BE RIGHT AS RAIN AN' TOOK OFF TO CANCUN. EITHER WAY, I'M BUGGERED, AIN'T I?

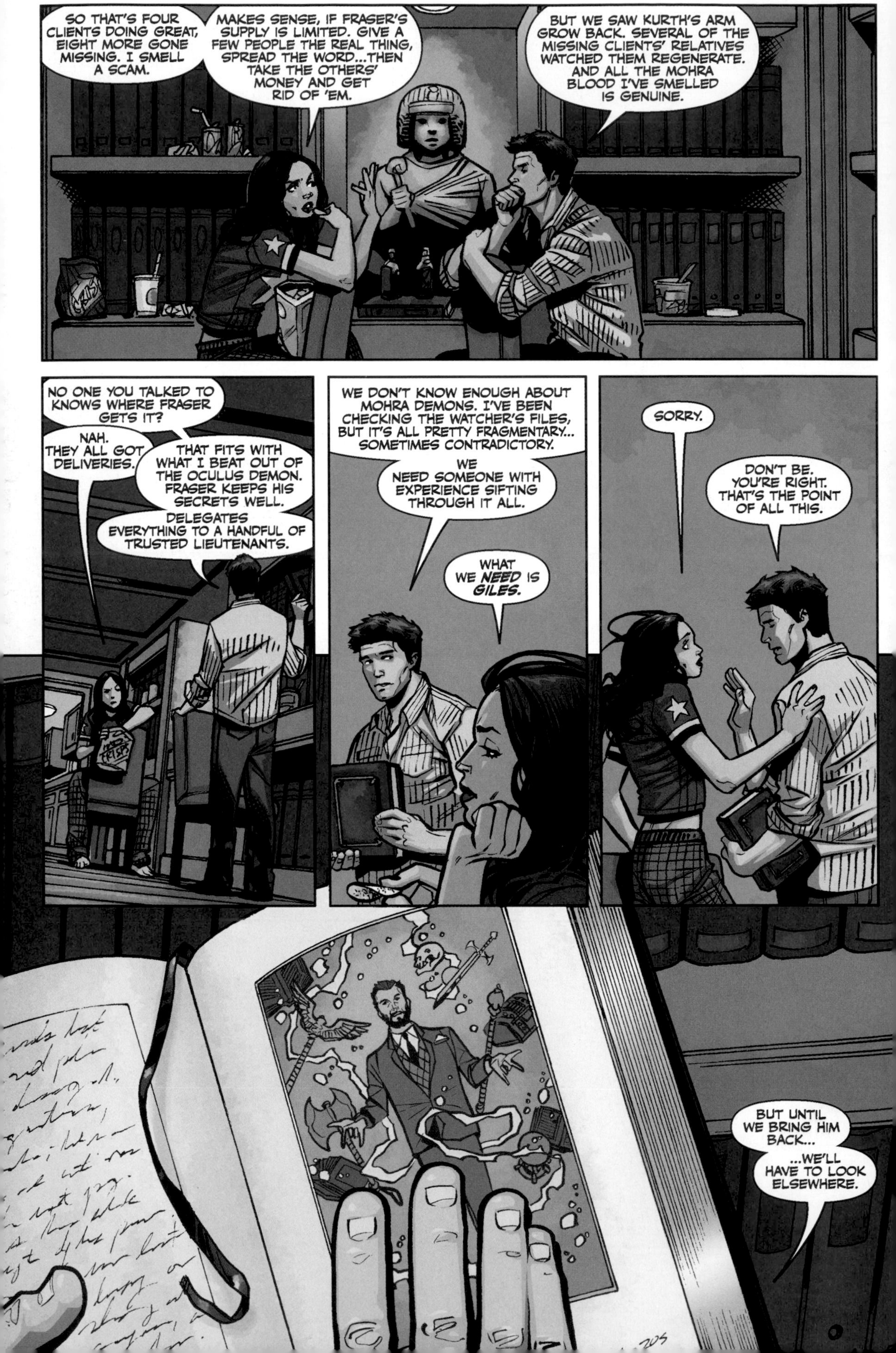
SO THAT'S FOUR CLIENTS DOING GREAT, EIGHT MORE GONE MISSING. I SMELL A SCAM.
MAKES SENSE, IF FRASER'S SUPPLY IS LIMITED. GIVE A FEW PEOPLE THE REAL THING, SPREAD THE WORD...THEN TAKE THE OTHERS' MONEY AND GET RID OF 'EM.
BUT WE SAW KURTH'S ARM GROW BACK. SEVERAL OF THE MISSING CLIENTS' RELATIVES WATCHED THEM REGENERATE. AND ALL THE MOHRA BLOOD I'VE SMELLED IS GENUINE.
NO ONE YOU TALKED TO KNOWS WHERE FRASER GETS IT?
NAH. THEY ALL GOT DELIVERIES.
THAT FITS WITH WHAT I BEAT OUT OF THE OCULUS DEMON. FRASER KEEPS HIS SECRETS WELL.
DELEGATES EVERYTHING TO A HANDFUL OF TRUSTED LIEUTENANTS.
WE DON'T KNOW ENOUGH ABOUT MOHRA DEMONS. I'VE BEEN CHECKING THE WATCHER'S FILES, BUT IT'S ALL PRETTY FRAGMENTARY... SOMETIMES CONTRADICTORY.
WE NEED SOMEONE WITH EXPERIENCE SIFTING THROUGH IT ALL.
WHAT WE *NEED* IS *GILES.*
SORRY.
DON'T BE. YOU'RE RIGHT. THAT'S THE POINT OF ALL THIS.
BUT UNTIL WE BRING HIM BACK...
...WE'LL HAVE TO LOOK ELSEWHERE.

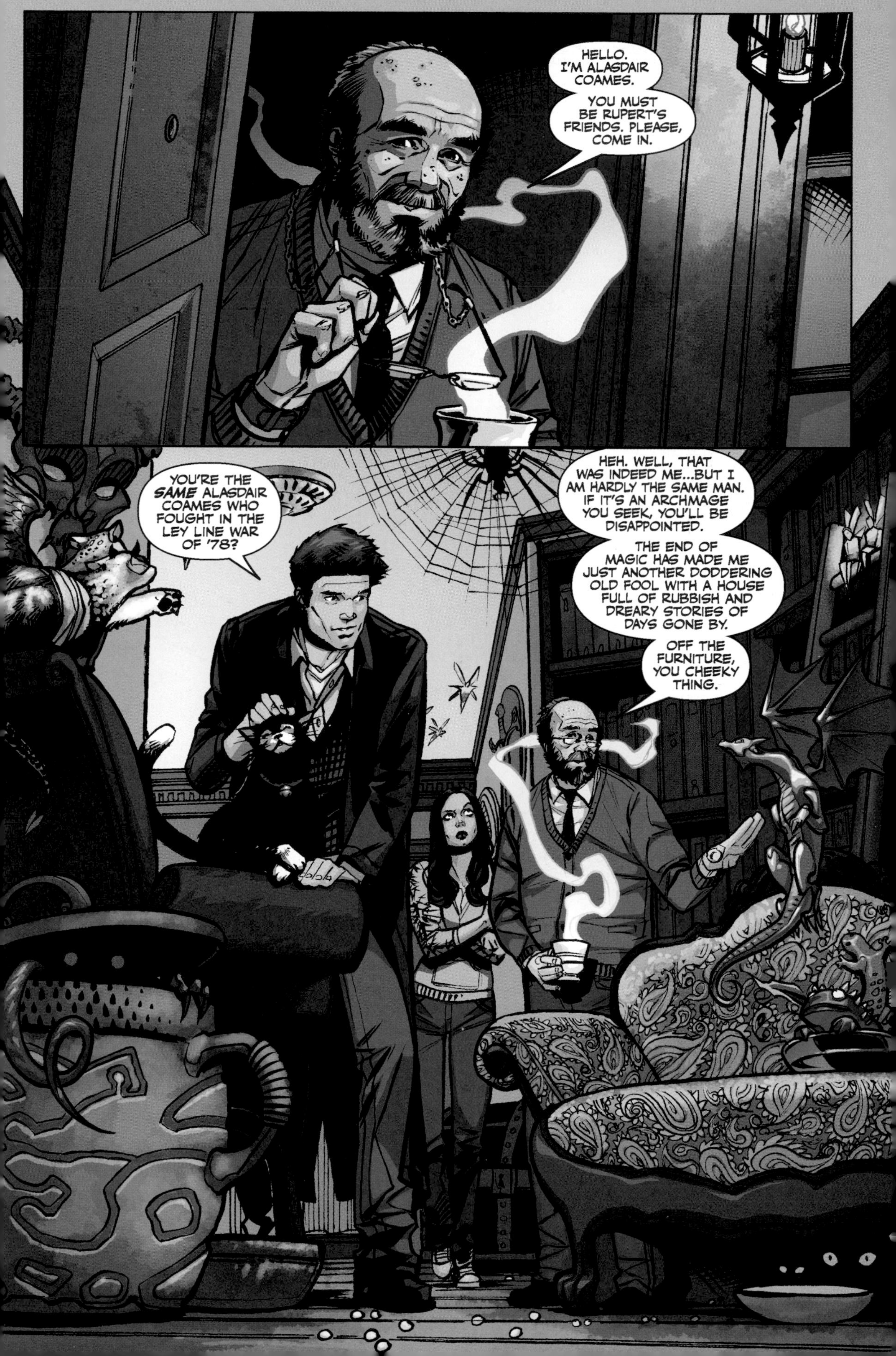
HELLO. I'M ALASDAIR COAMES.
YOU MUST BE RUPERT'S FRIENDS. PLEASE, COME IN.
YOU'RE THE SAME ALASDAIR COAMES WHO FOUGHT IN THE LEY LINE WAR OF '78?
HEH. WELL, THAT WAS INDEED ME...BUT I AM HARDLY THE SAME MAN. IF IT'S AN ARCHMAGE YOU SEEK, YOU'LL BE DISAPPOINTED.
THE END OF MAGIC HAS MADE ME JUST ANOTHER DODDERING OLD FOOL WITH A HOUSE FULL OF RUBBISH AND DREARY STORIES OF DAYS GONE BY.
OFF THE FURNITURE, YOU CHEEKY THING.

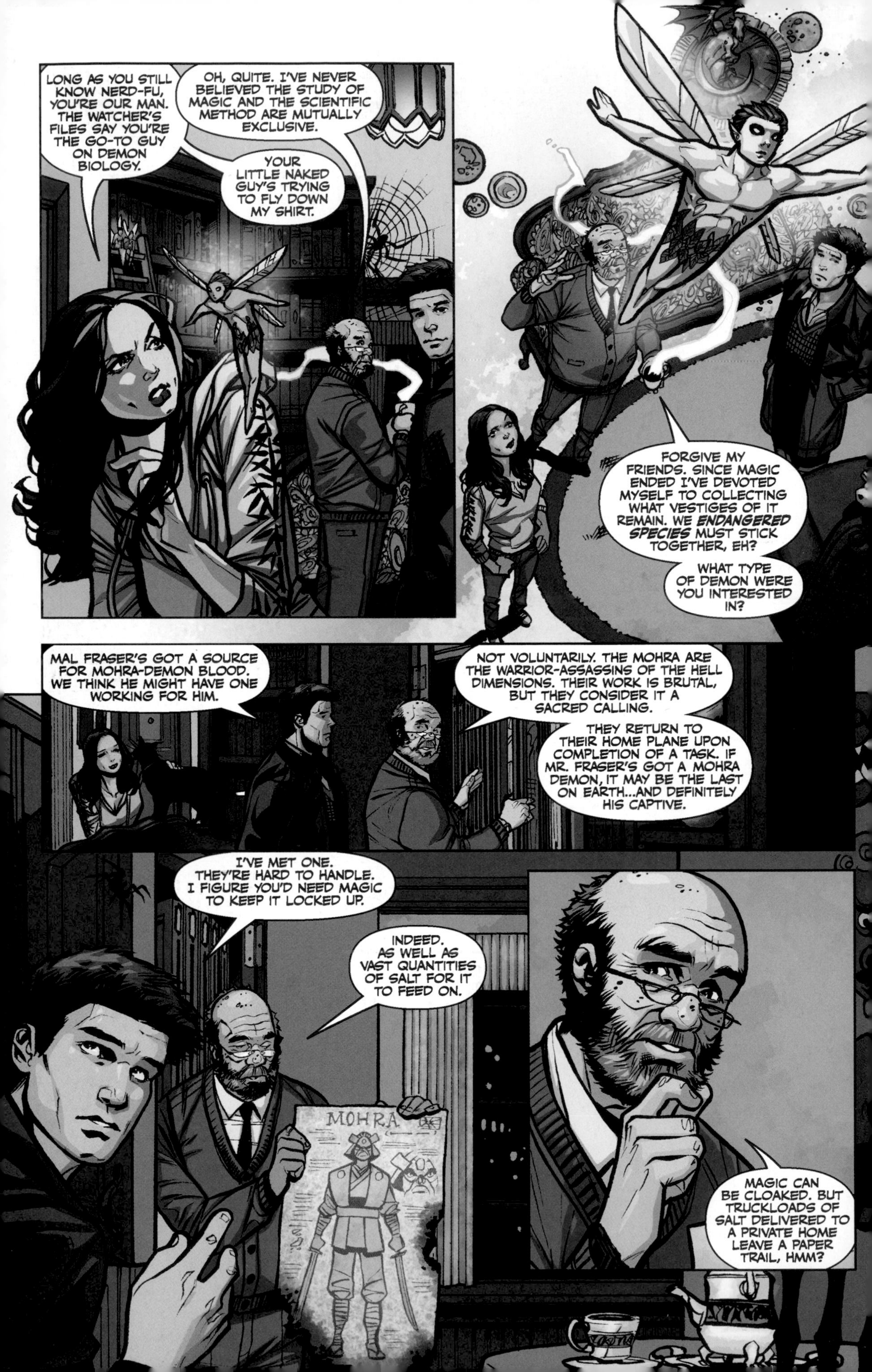
LONG AS YOU STILL KNOW NERD-FU, YOU'RE OUR MAN. THE WATCHER'S FILES SAY YOU'RE THE GO-TO GUY ON DEMON BIOLOGY.
OH, QUITE. I'VE NEVER BELIEVED THE STUDY OF MAGIC AND THE SCIENTIFIC METHOD ARE MUTUALLY EXCLUSIVE.
YOUR LITTLE NAKED GUY'S TRYING TO FLY DOWN MY SHIRT.
FORGIVE MY FRIENDS. SINCE MAGIC ENDED I'VE DEVOTED MYSELF TO COLLECTING WHAT VESTIGES OF IT REMAIN. WE *ENDANGERED SPECIES* MUST STICK TOGETHER, EH?
WHAT TYPE OF DEMON WERE YOU INTERESTED IN?
MAL FRASER'S GOT A SOURCE FOR MOHRA-DEMON BLOOD. WE THINK HE MIGHT HAVE ONE WORKING FOR HIM.
NOT VOLUNTARILY. THE MOHRA ARE THE WARRIOR-ASSASSINS OF THE HELL DIMENSIONS. THEIR WORK IS BRUTAL, BUT THEY CONSIDER IT A SACRED CALLING.
THEY RETURN TO THEIR HOME PLANE UPON COMPLETION OF A TASK. IF MR. FRASER'S GOT A MOHRA DEMON, IT MAY BE THE LAST ON EARTH...AND DEFINITELY HIS CAPTIVE.
I'VE MET ONE. THEY'RE HARD TO HANDLE. I FIGURE YOU'D NEED MAGIC TO KEEP IT LOCKED UP.
INDEED. AS WELL AS VAST QUANTITIES OF SALT FOR IT TO FEED ON.
MOHRA
MAGIC CAN BE CLOAKED. BUT TRUCKLOADS OF SALT DELIVERED TO A PRIVATE HOME LEAVE A PAPER TRAIL, HMM?

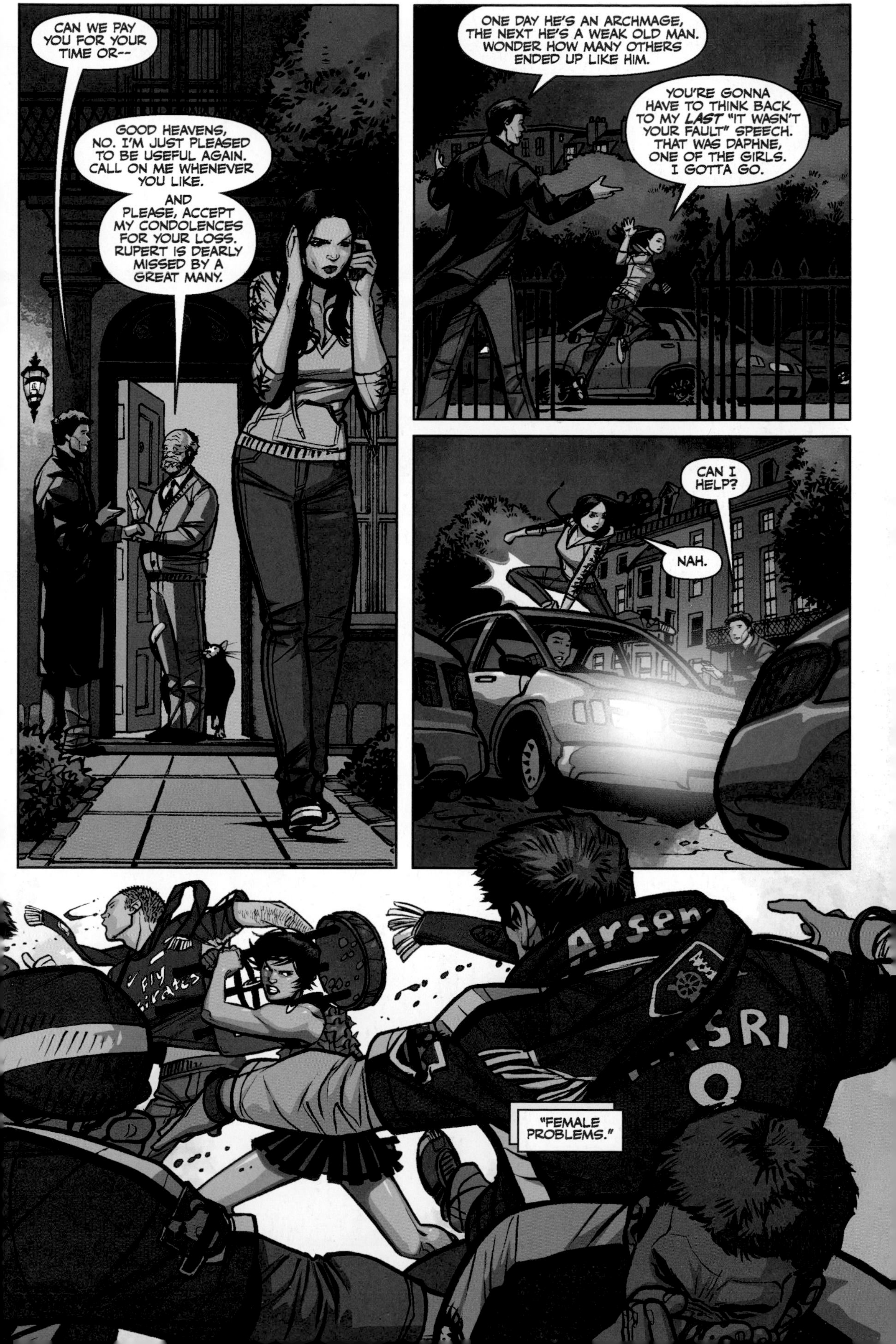
CAN WE PAY YOU FOR YOUR TIME OR--
GOOD HEAVENS, NO. I'M JUST PLEASED TO BE USEFUL AGAIN. CALL ON ME WHENEVER YOU LIKE.
AND PLEASE, ACCEPT MY CONDOLENCES FOR YOUR LOSS. RUPERT IS DEARLY MISSED BY A GREAT MANY.
ONE DAY HE'S AN ARCHMAGE, THE NEXT HE'S A WEAK OLD MAN. WONDER HOW MANY OTHERS ENDED UP LIKE HIM.
YOU'RE GONNA HAVE TO THINK BACK TO MY *LAST* "IT WASN'T YOUR FAULT" SPEECH. THAT WAS DAPHNE, ONE OF THE GIRLS. I GOTTA GO.
CAN I HELP?
NAH.
Arsen
SRI
"FEMALE PROBLEMS."

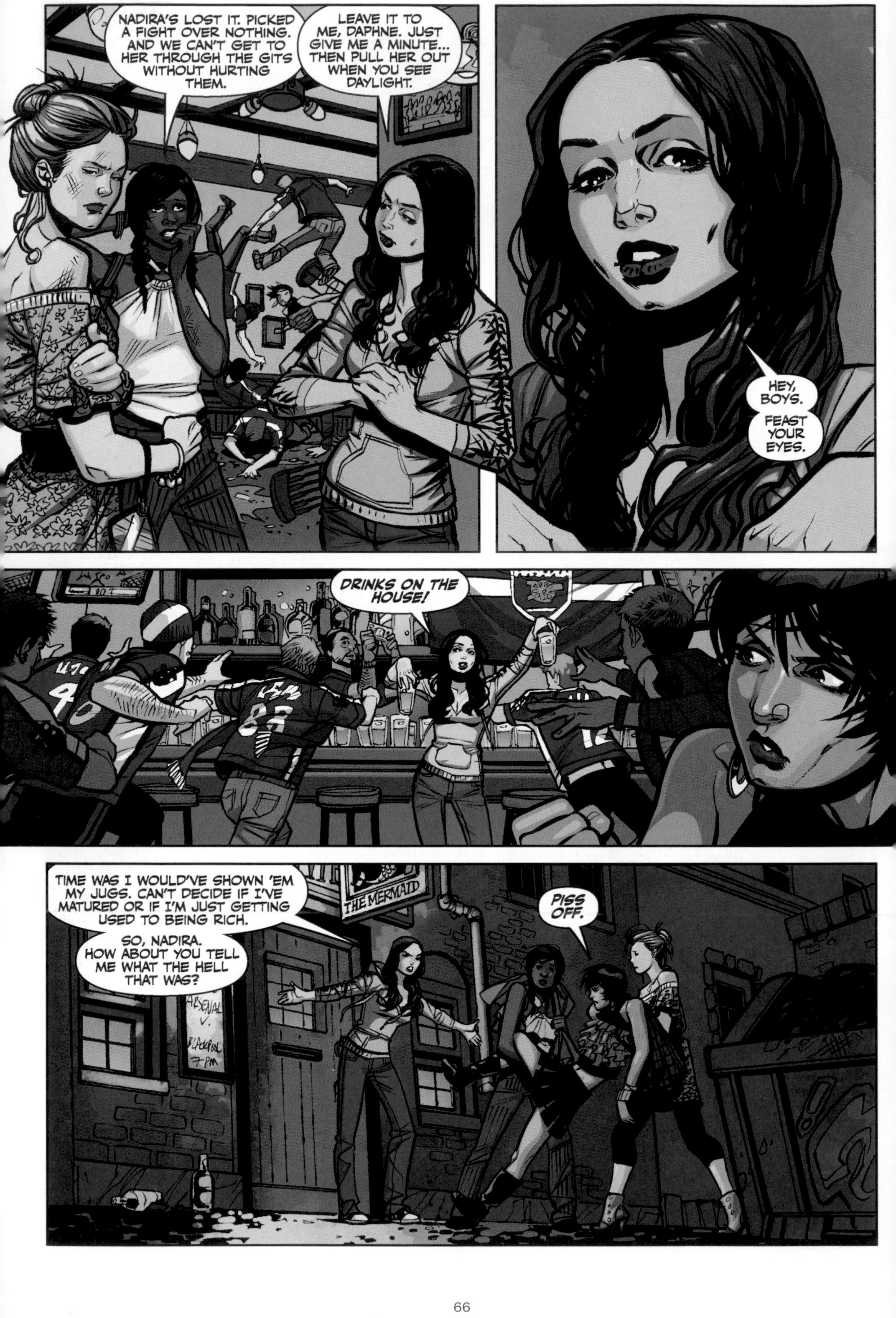
NADIRA'S LOST IT. PICKED A FIGHT OVER NOTHING. AND WE CAN'T GET TO HER THROUGH THE GITS WITHOUT HURTING THEM.
LEAVE IT TO ME, DAPHNE. JUST GIVE ME A MINUTE... THEN PULL HER OUT WHEN YOU SEE DAYLIGHT.
HEY, BOYS.
FEAST YOUR EYES.
DRINKS ON THE HOUSE!
THE MERMAID
TIME WAS I WOULD'VE SHOWN 'EM MY JUGS. CAN'T DECIDE IF I'VE MATURED OR IF I'M JUST GETTING USED TO BEING RICH.
SO, NADIRA. HOW ABOUT YOU TELL ME WHAT THE HELL THAT WAS?
PISS OFF.
ARSENAL V. BLACKPOOL 7PM

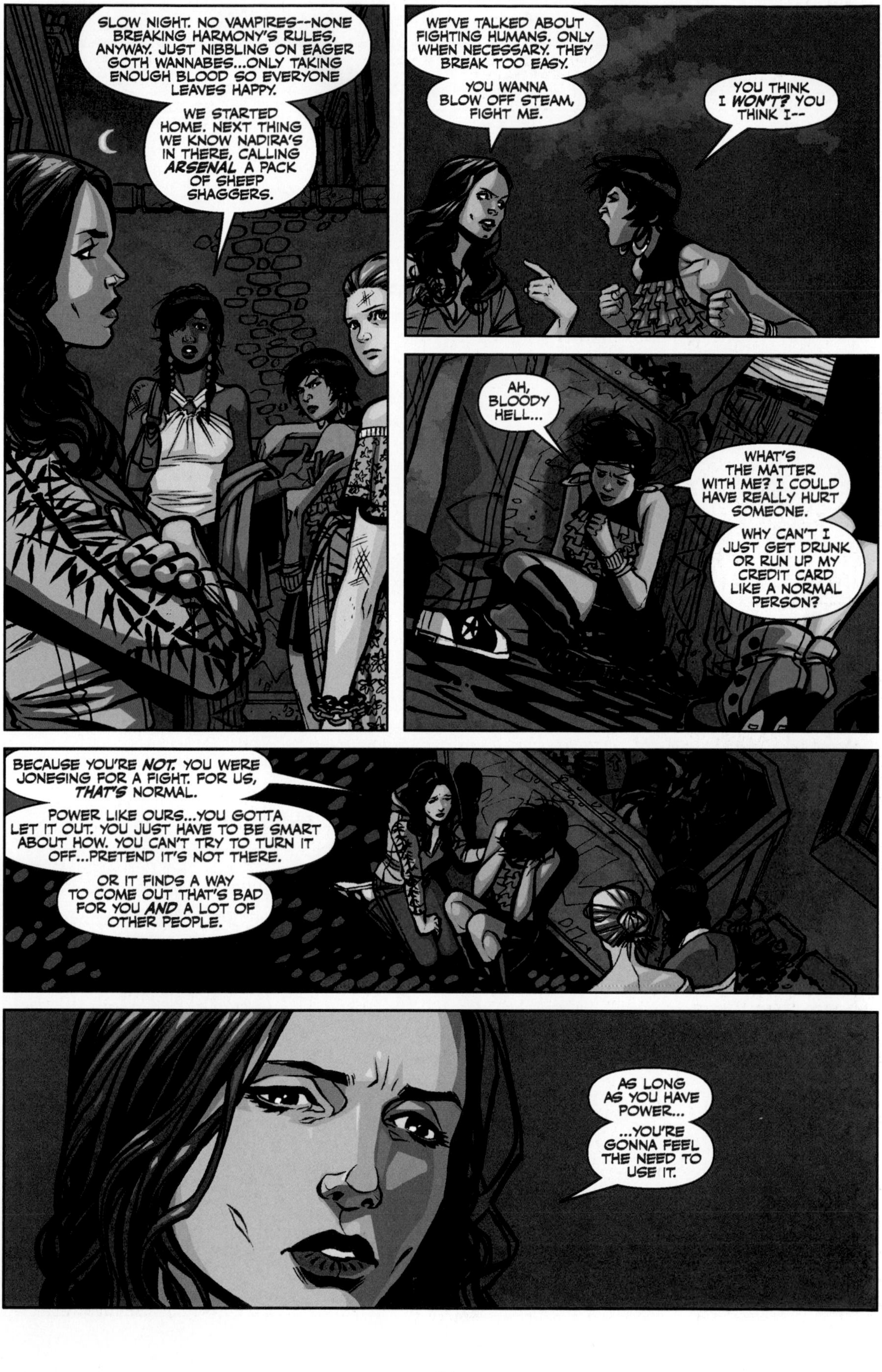
SLOW NIGHT. NO VAMPIRES--NONE BREAKING HARMONY'S RULES, ANYWAY. JUST NIBBLING ON EAGER GOTH WANNABES...ONLY TAKING ENOUGH BLOOD SO EVERYONE LEAVES HAPPY.
WE STARTED HOME. NEXT THING WE KNOW NADIRA'S IN THERE, CALLING *ARSENAL* A PACK OF SHEEP SHAGGERS.
WE'VE TALKED ABOUT FIGHTING HUMANS. ONLY WHEN NECESSARY. THEY BREAK TOO EASY.
YOU WANNA BLOW OFF STEAM, FIGHT ME.
YOU THINK I *WON'T?* YOU THINK I--
AH, BLOODY HELL...
WHAT'S THE MATTER WITH ME? I COULD HAVE REALLY HURT SOMEONE.
WHY CAN'T I JUST GET DRUNK OR RUN UP MY CREDIT CARD LIKE A NORMAL PERSON?
BECAUSE YOU'RE *NOT.* YOU WERE JONESING FOR A FIGHT. FOR US, *THAT'S* NORMAL.
POWER LIKE OURS...YOU GOTTA LET IT OUT. YOU JUST HAVE TO BE SMART ABOUT HOW. YOU CAN'T TRY TO TURN IT OFF...PRETEND IT'S NOT THERE.
OR IT FINDS A WAY TO COME OUT THAT'S BAD FOR YOU *AND* A LOT OF OTHER PEOPLE.
AS LONG AS YOU HAVE POWER...
...YOU'RE GONNA FEEL THE NEED TO USE IT.

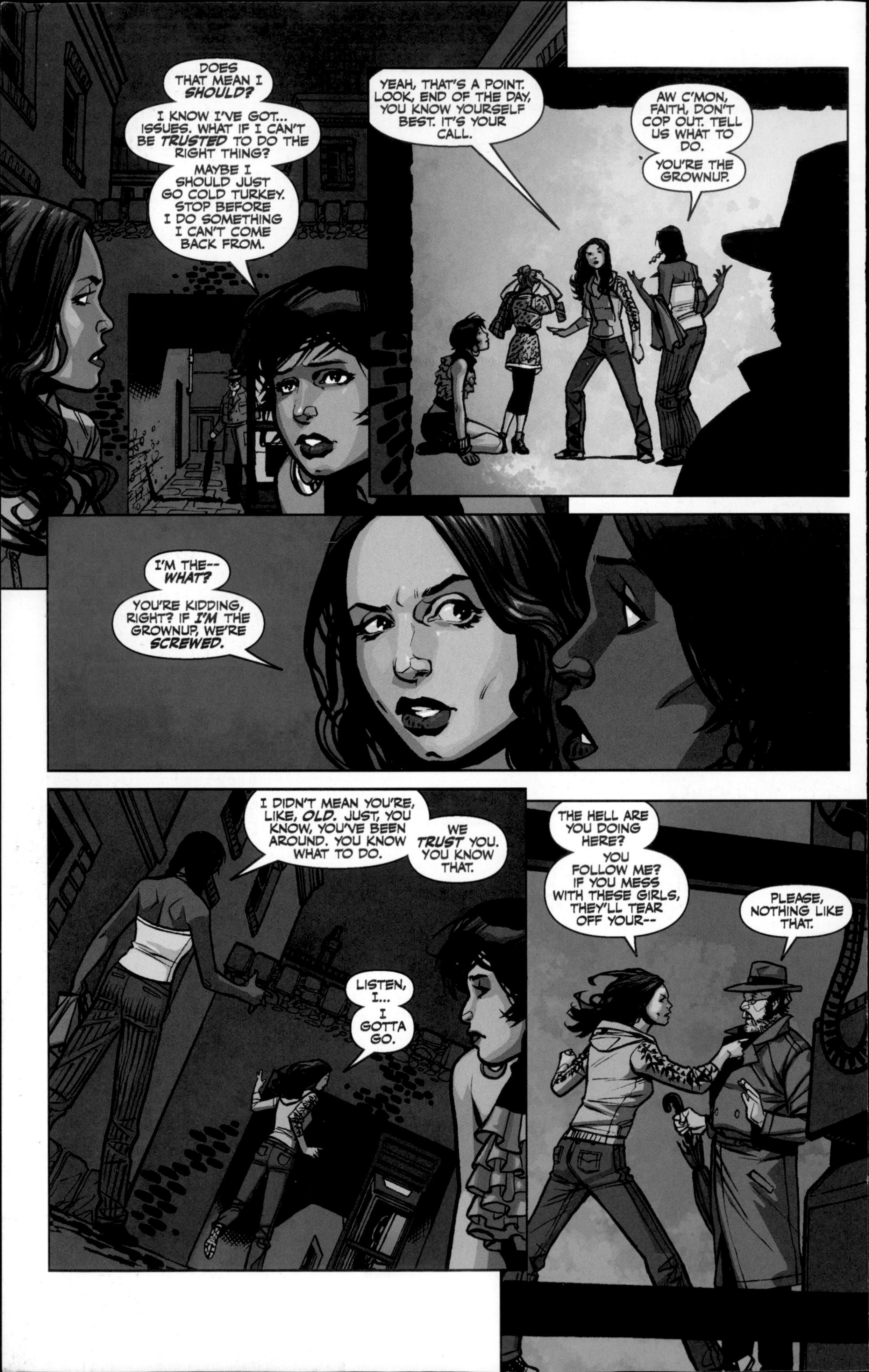
DOES THAT MEAN I *SHOULD?*
I KNOW I'VE GOT... ISSUES. WHAT IF I CAN'T BE *TRUSTED* TO DO THE RIGHT THING?
MAYBE I SHOULD JUST GO COLD TURKEY. STOP BEFORE I DO SOMETHING I CAN'T COME BACK FROM.
YEAH, THAT'S A POINT. LOOK, END OF THE DAY, YOU KNOW YOURSELF BEST. IT'S YOUR CALL.
AW C'MON, FAITH, DON'T COP OUT. TELL US WHAT TO DO.
YOU'RE THE GROWNUP.
I'M THE-- *WHAT?*
YOU'RE KIDDING, RIGHT? IF *I'M* THE GROWNUP, WE'RE *SCREWED.*
I DIDN'T MEAN YOU'RE, LIKE, *OLD.* JUST, YOU KNOW, YOU'VE BEEN AROUND. YOU KNOW WHAT TO DO.
WE *TRUST* YOU. YOU KNOW THAT.
LISTEN, I... I GOTTA GO.
THE HELL ARE YOU DOING HERE?
YOU FOLLOW ME? IF YOU MESS WITH THESE GIRLS, THEY'LL TEAR OFF YOUR--
PLEASE, NOTHING LIKE THAT.

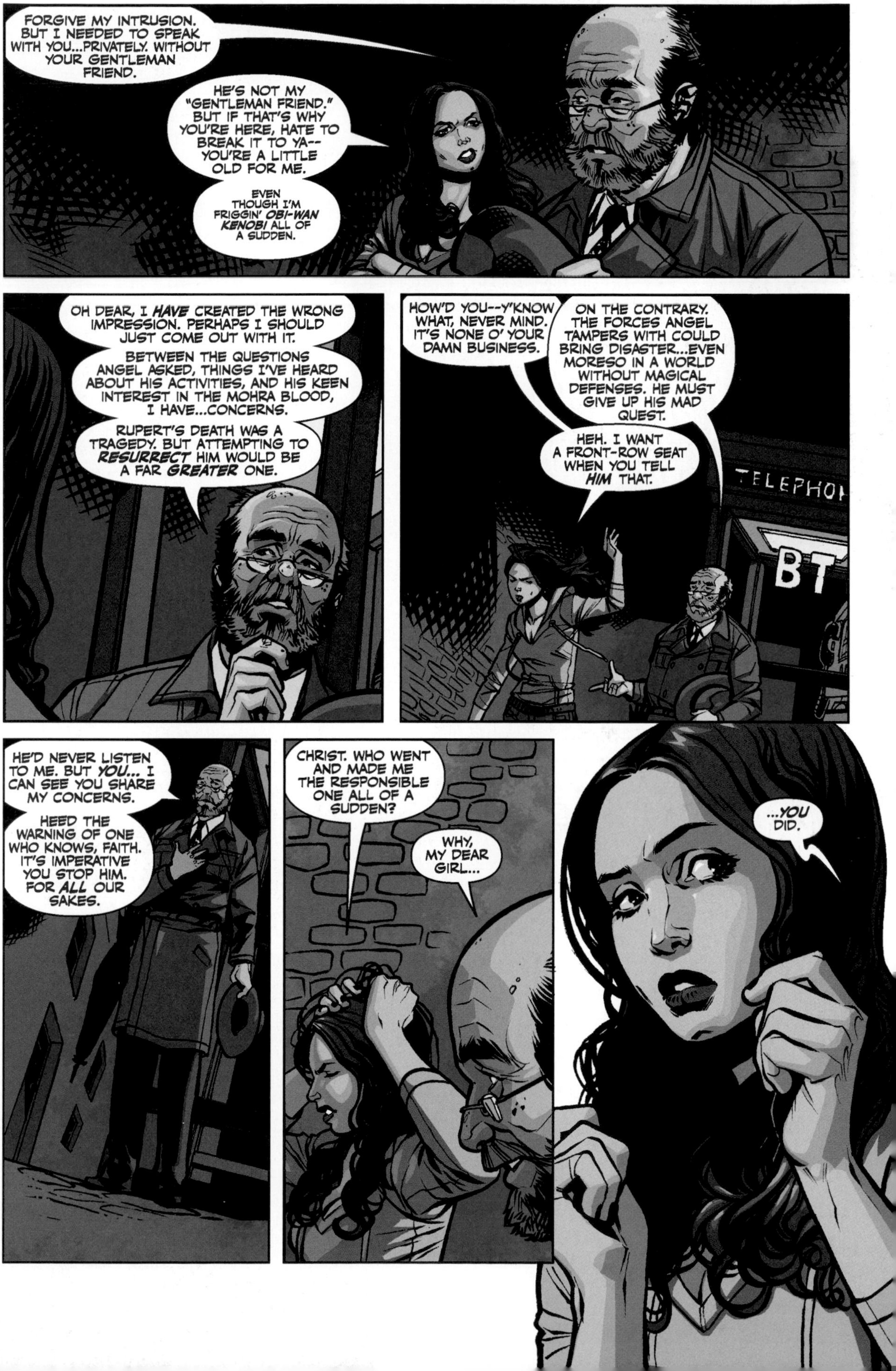
FORGIVE MY INTRUSION. BUT I NEEDED TO SPEAK WITH YOU...PRIVATELY. WITHOUT YOUR GENTLEMAN FRIEND.
HE'S NOT MY "GENTLEMAN FRIEND." BUT IF THAT'S WHY YOU'RE HERE, HATE TO BREAK IT TO YA--YOU'RE A LITTLE OLD FOR ME.
EVEN THOUGH I'M FRIGGIN' OBI-WAN KENOBI ALL OF A SUDDEN.
OH DEAR, I HAVE CREATED THE WRONG IMPRESSION. PERHAPS I SHOULD JUST COME OUT WITH IT.
BETWEEN THE QUESTIONS ANGEL ASKED, THINGS I'VE HEARD ABOUT HIS ACTIVITIES, AND HIS KEEN INTEREST IN THE MOHRA BLOOD, I HAVE...CONCERNS.
RUPERT'S DEATH WAS A TRAGEDY. BUT ATTEMPTING TO RESURRECT HIM WOULD BE A FAR GREATER ONE.
HOW'D YOU--Y'KNOW WHAT, NEVER MIND. IT'S NONE O' YOUR DAMN BUSINESS.
ON THE CONTRARY. THE FORCES ANGEL TAMPERS WITH COULD BRING DISASTER...EVEN MORESO IN A WORLD WITHOUT MAGICAL DEFENSES. HE MUST GIVE UP HIS MAD QUEST.
HEH. I WANT A FRONT-ROW SEAT WHEN YOU TELL HIM THAT.
TELEPHO
BT
HE'D NEVER LISTEN TO ME. BUT YOU... I CAN SEE YOU SHARE MY CONCERNS.
HEED THE WARNING OF ONE WHO KNOWS, FAITH. IT'S IMPERATIVE YOU STOP HIM. FOR ALL OUR SAKES.
CHRIST. WHO WENT AND MADE ME THE RESPONSIBLE ONE ALL OF A SUDDEN?
WHY, MY DEAR GIRL...
...YOU DID.

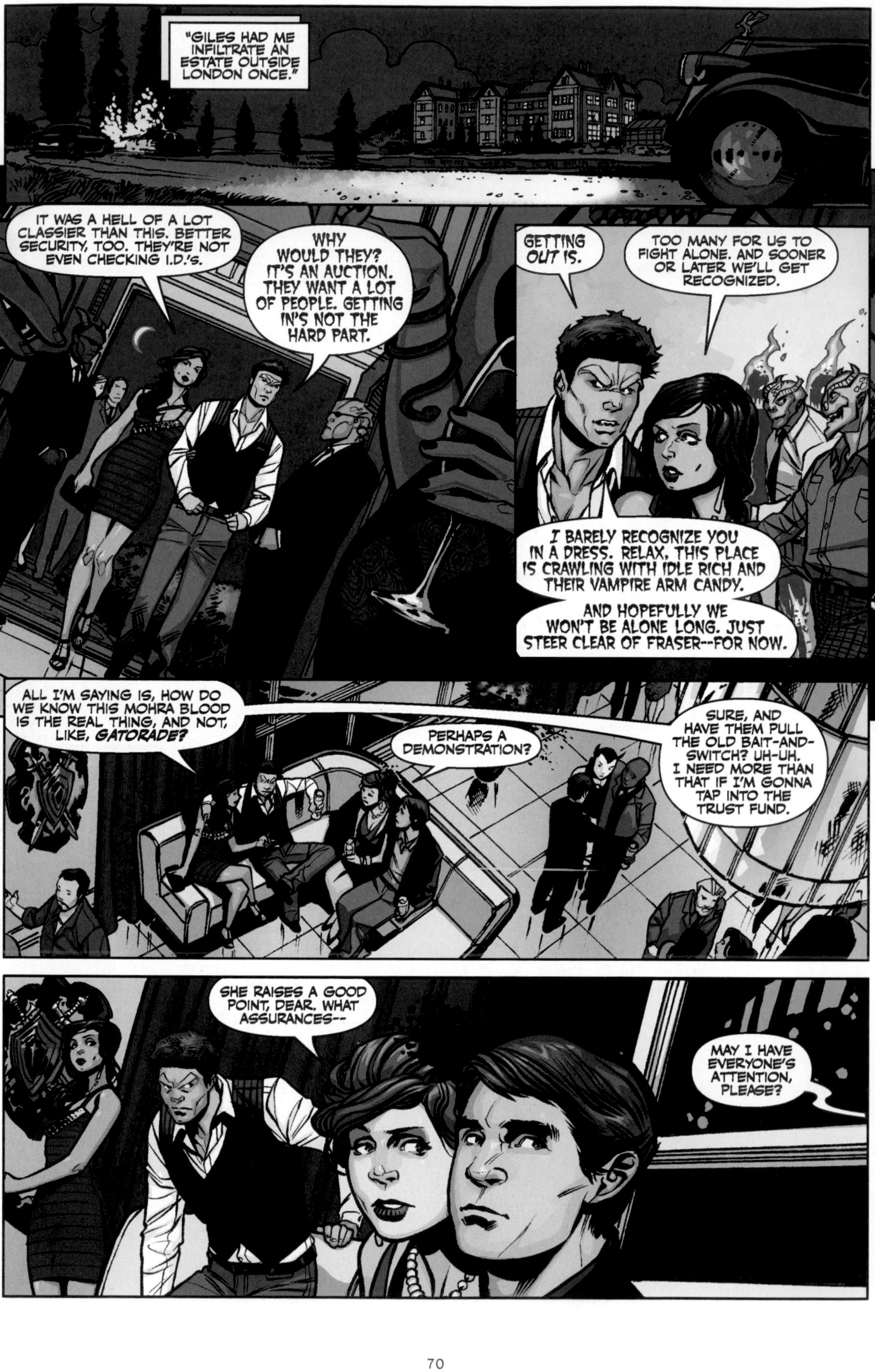
"GILES HAD ME INFILTRATE AN ESTATE OUTSIDE LONDON ONCE."
IT WAS A HELL OF A LOT CLASSIER THAN THIS. BETTER SECURITY, TOO. THEY'RE NOT EVEN CHECKING I.D.'S.
WHY WOULD THEY? IT'S AN AUCTION. THEY WANT A LOT OF PEOPLE. GETTING IN'S NOT THE HARD PART.
GETTING *OUT* IS.
TOO MANY FOR US TO FIGHT ALONE. AND SOONER OR LATER WE'LL GET RECOGNIZED.
I BARELY RECOGNIZE YOU IN A DRESS. RELAX, THIS PLACE IS CRAWLING WITH IDLE RICH AND THEIR VAMPIRE ARM CANDY.
AND HOPEFULLY WE WON'T BE ALONE LONG. JUST STEER CLEAR OF FRASER--FOR NOW.
ALL I'M SAYING IS, HOW DO WE KNOW THIS MOHRA BLOOD IS THE REAL THING, AND NOT, LIKE, *GATORADE?*
PERHAPS A DEMONSTRATION?
SURE, AND HAVE THEM PULL THE OLD BAIT-AND-SWITCH? UH-UH. I NEED MORE THAN THAT IF I'M GONNA TAP INTO THE TRUST FUND.
SHE RAISES A GOOD POINT, DEAR. WHAT ASSURANCES--
MAY I HAVE EVERYONE'S ATTENTION, PLEASE?

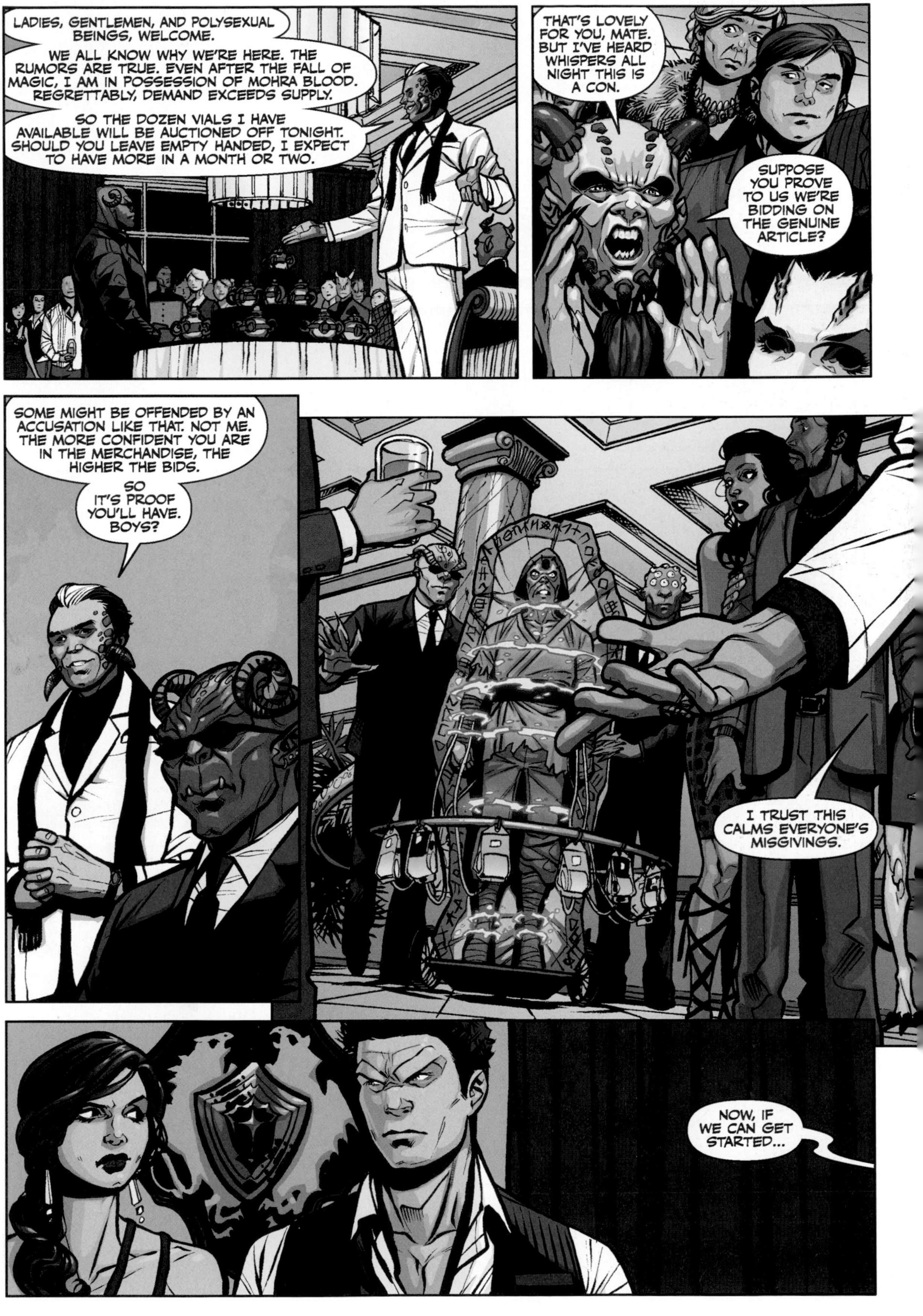

LADIES, GENTLEMEN, AND POLYSEXUAL BEINGS, WELCOME.
WE ALL KNOW WHY WE'RE HERE. THE RUMORS ARE TRUE. EVEN AFTER THE FALL OF MAGIC, I AM IN POSSESSION OF MOHRA BLOOD. REGRETTABLY, DEMAND EXCEEDS SUPPLY.
SO THE DOZEN VIALS I HAVE AVAILABLE WILL BE AUCTIONED OFF TONIGHT. SHOULD YOU LEAVE EMPTY HANDED, I EXPECT TO HAVE MORE IN A MONTH OR TWO.
THAT'S LOVELY FOR YOU, MATE. BUT I'VE HEARD WHISPERS ALL NIGHT THIS IS A CON.
SUPPOSE YOU PROVE TO US WE'RE BIDDING ON THE GENUINE ARTICLE?
SOME MIGHT BE OFFENDED BY AN ACCUSATION LIKE THAT. NOT ME. THE MORE CONFIDENT YOU ARE IN THE MERCHANDISE, THE HIGHER THE BIDS.
SO IT'S PROOF YOU'LL HAVE. BOYS?
I TRUST THIS CALMS EVERYONE'S MISGIVINGS.
NOW, IF WE CAN GET STARTED...

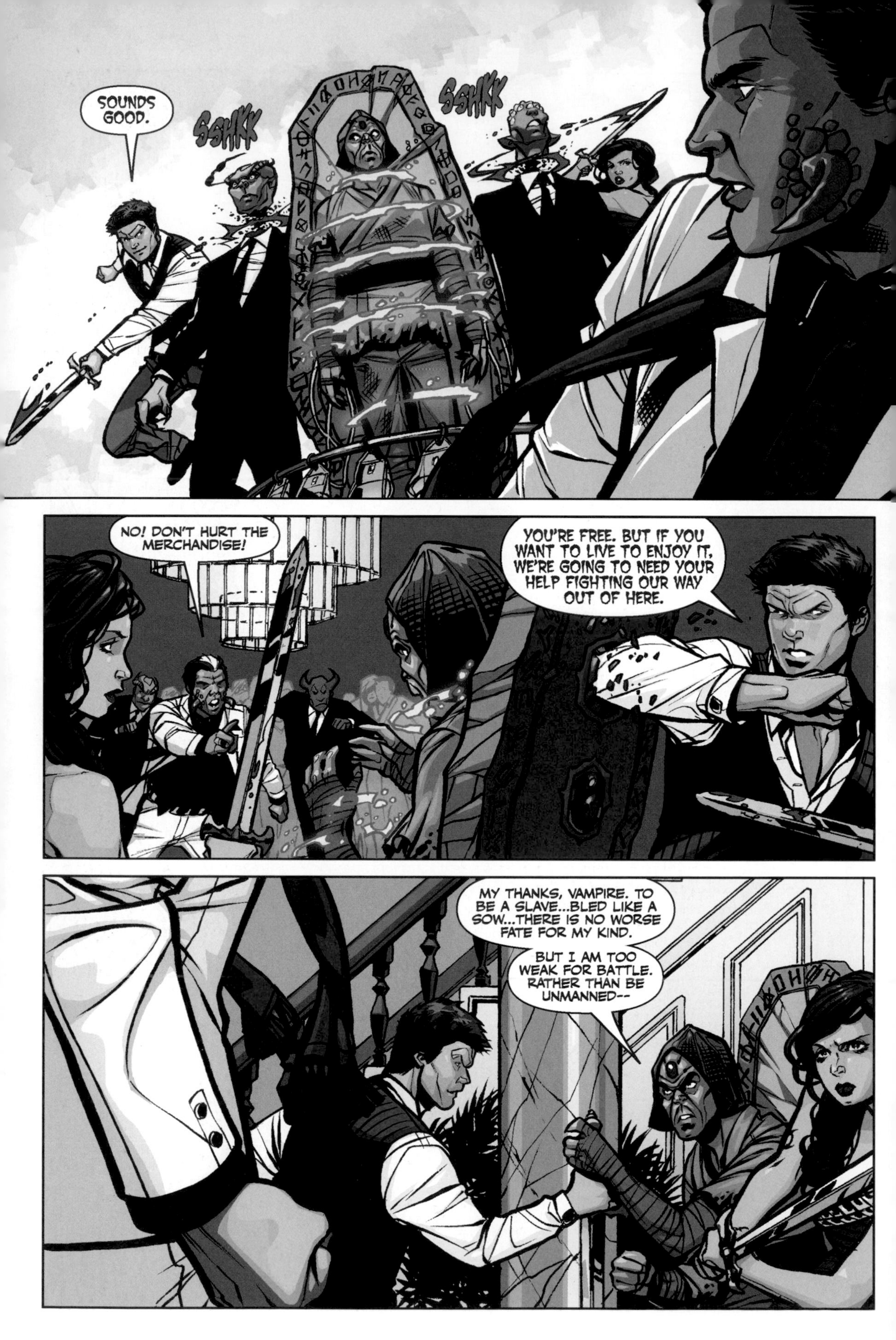
SOUNDS GOOD.
SSHKK
SSHKK
NO! DON'T HURT THE MERCHANDISE!
YOU'RE FREE. BUT IF YOU WANT TO LIVE TO ENJOY IT, WE'RE GOING TO NEED YOUR HELP FIGHTING OUR WAY OUT OF HERE.
MY THANKS, VAMPIRE. TO BE A SLAVE...BLED LIKE A SOW...THERE IS NO WORSE FATE FOR MY KIND.
BUT I AM TOO WEAK FOR BATTLE. RATHER THAN BE UNMANNED--

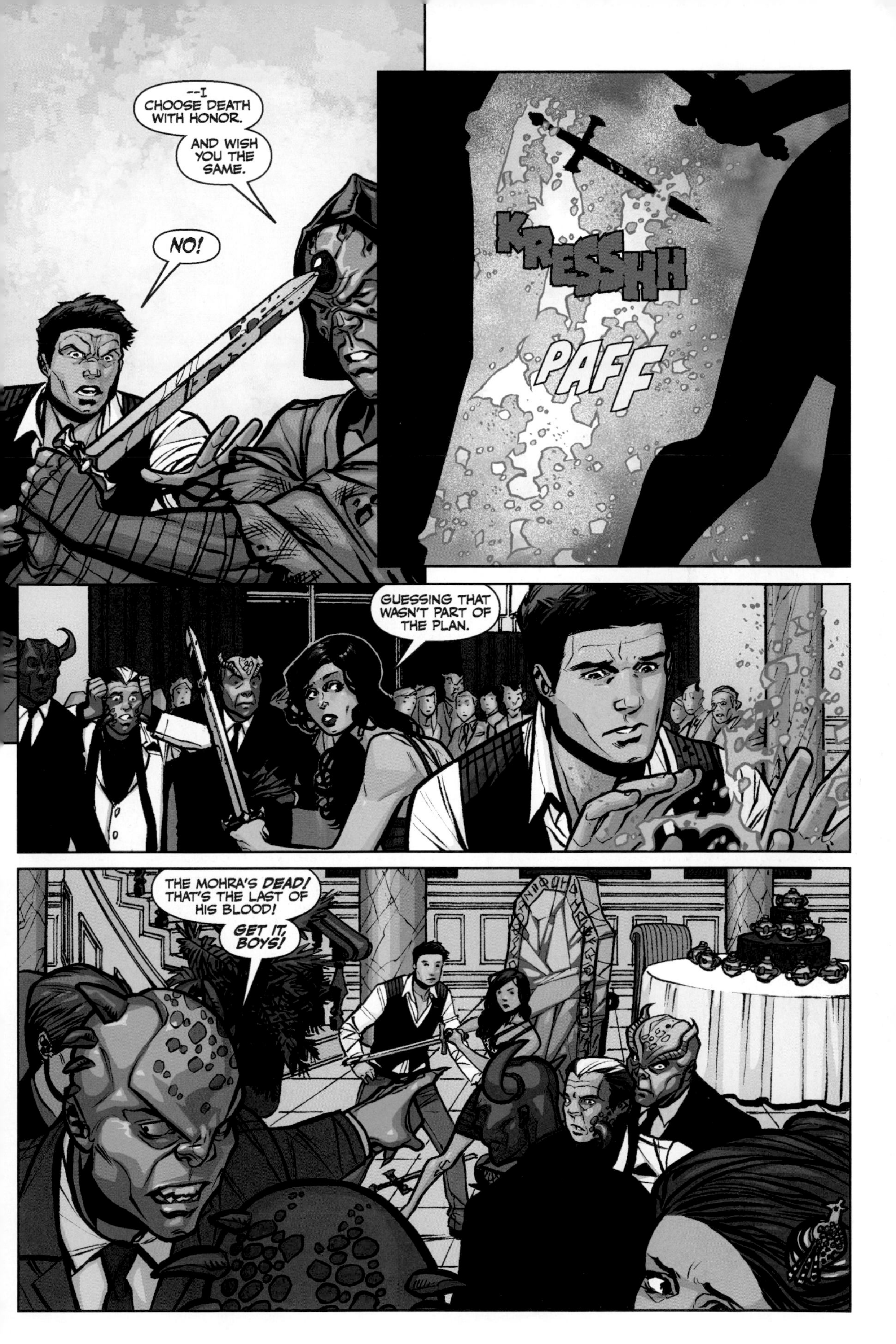
--I CHOOSE DEATH WITH HONOR.
AND WISH YOU THE SAME.
NO!
KRESSHH
PAFF
GUESSING THAT WASN'T PART OF THE PLAN.
THE MOHRA'S DEAD! THAT'S THE LAST OF HIS BLOOD!
GET IT, BOYS!

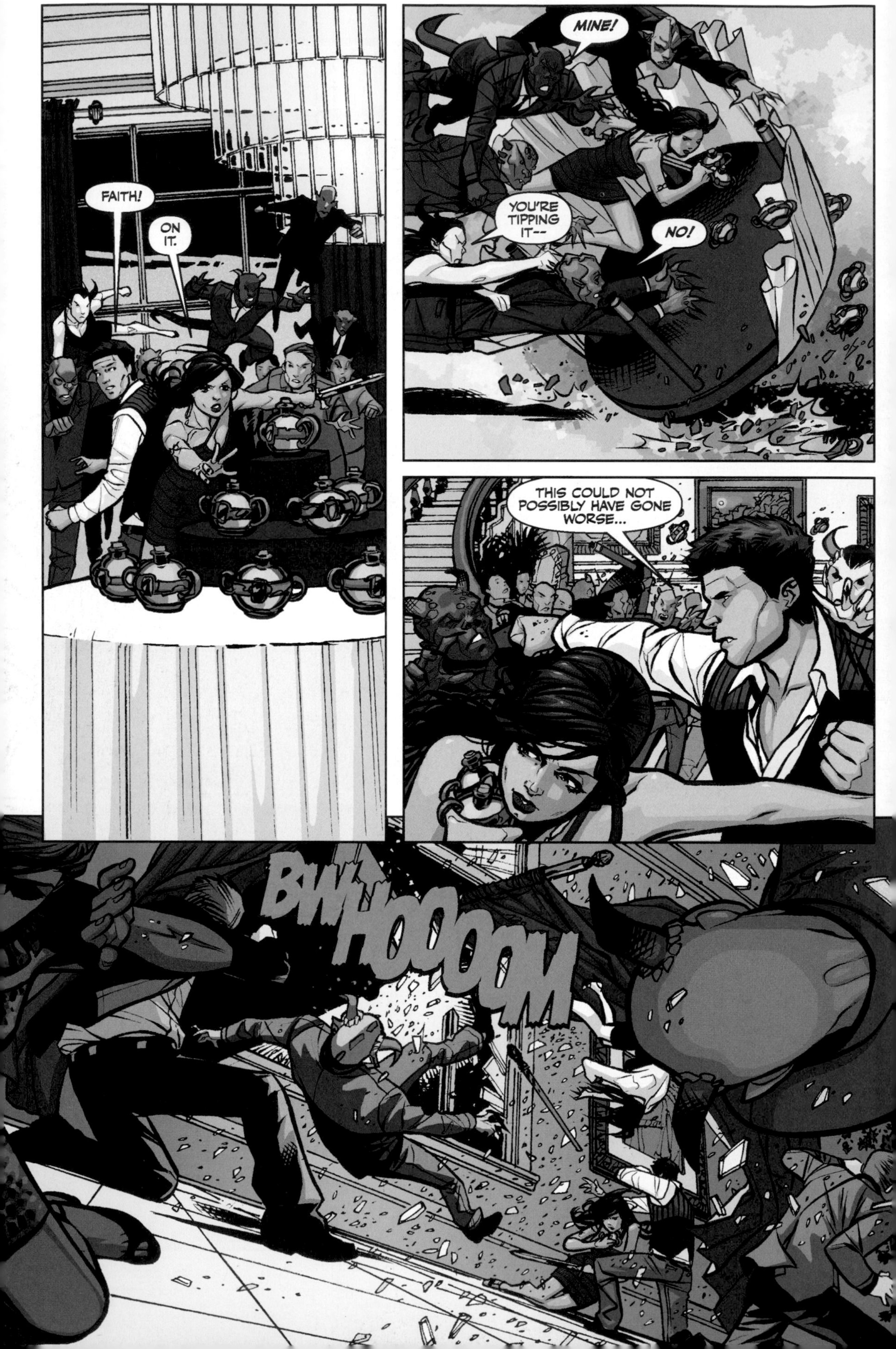
FAITH!
ON IT.
MINE!
YOU'RE TIPPING IT--
NO!
THIS COULD NOT POSSIBLY HAVE GONE WORSE...
BWHOOOOM

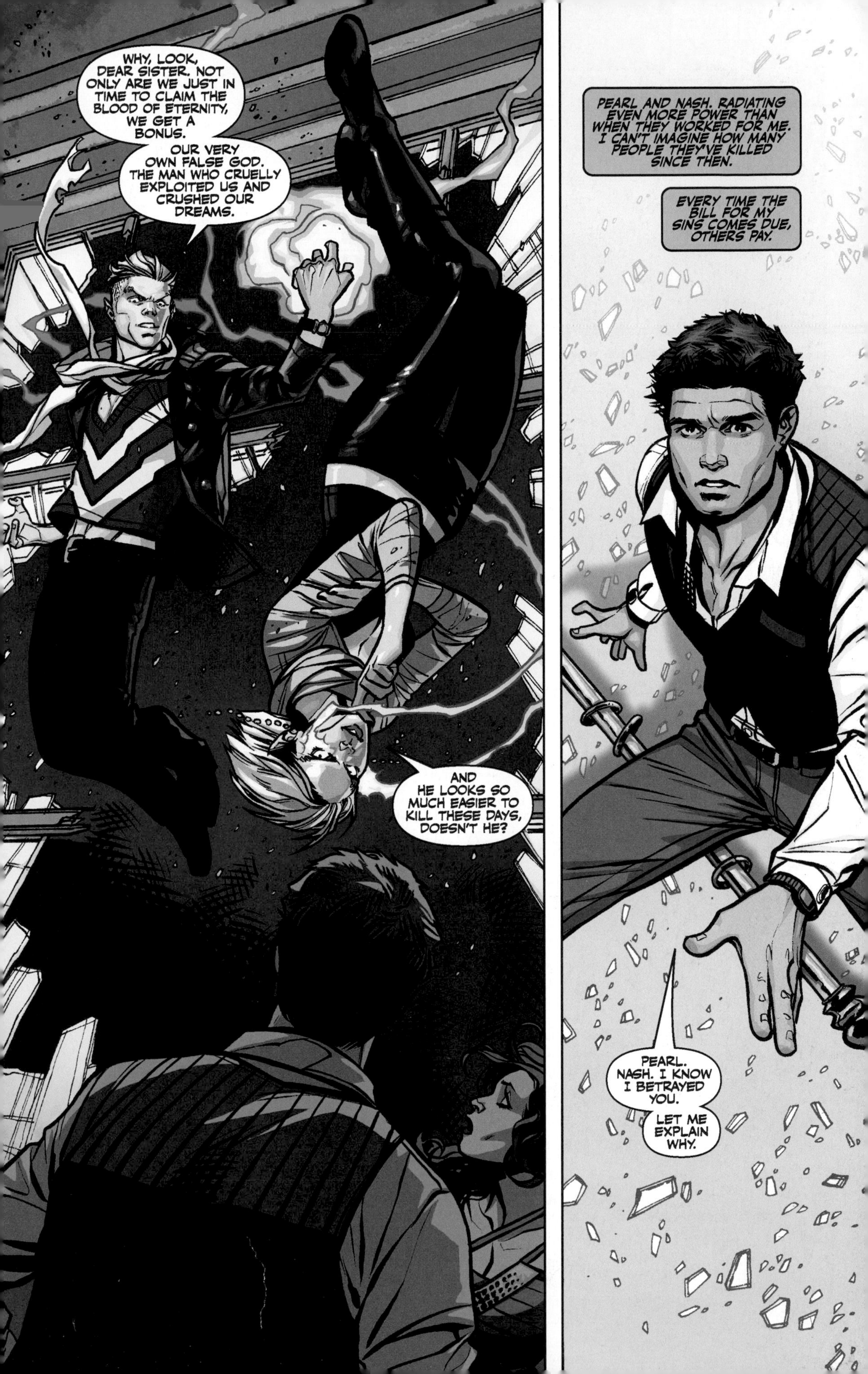
WHY, LOOK, DEAR SISTER. NOT ONLY ARE WE JUST IN TIME TO CLAIM THE BLOOD OF ETERNITY, WE GET A BONUS.
OUR VERY OWN FALSE GOD. THE MAN WHO CRUELLY EXPLOITED US AND CRUSHED OUR DREAMS.
AND HE LOOKS SO MUCH EASIER TO KILL THESE DAYS, DOESN'T HE?
PEARL AND NASH. RADIATING EVEN MORE POWER THAN WHEN THEY WORKED FOR ME. I CAN'T IMAGINE HOW MANY PEOPLE THEY'VE KILLED SINCE THEN.
EVERY TIME THE BILL FOR MY SINS COMES DUE, OTHERS PAY.
PEARL. NASH. I KNOW I BETRAYED YOU.
LET ME EXPLAIN WHY.

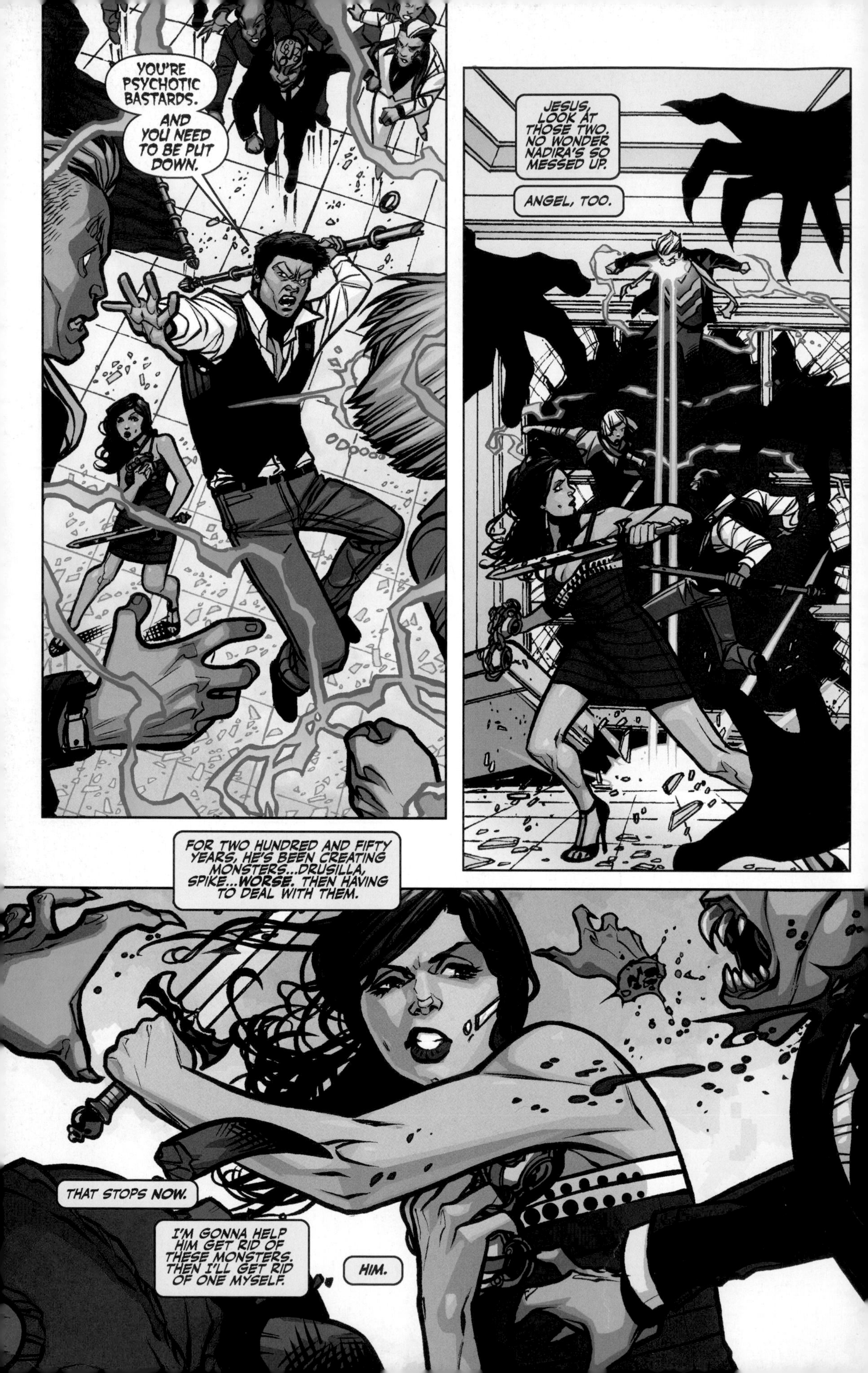
YOU'RE PSYCHOTIC BASTARDS.
AND YOU NEED TO BE PUT DOWN.
JESUS, LOOK AT THOSE TWO. NO WONDER NADIRA'S SO MESSED UP.
ANGEL, TOO.
FOR TWO HUNDRED AND FIFTY YEARS, HE'S BEEN CREATING MONSTERS...DRUSILLA, SPIKE...WORSE. THEN HAVING TO DEAL WITH THEM.
THAT STOPS NOW.
I'M GONNA HELP HIM GET RID OF THESE MONSTERS. THEN I'LL GET RID OF ONE MYSELF.
HIM.

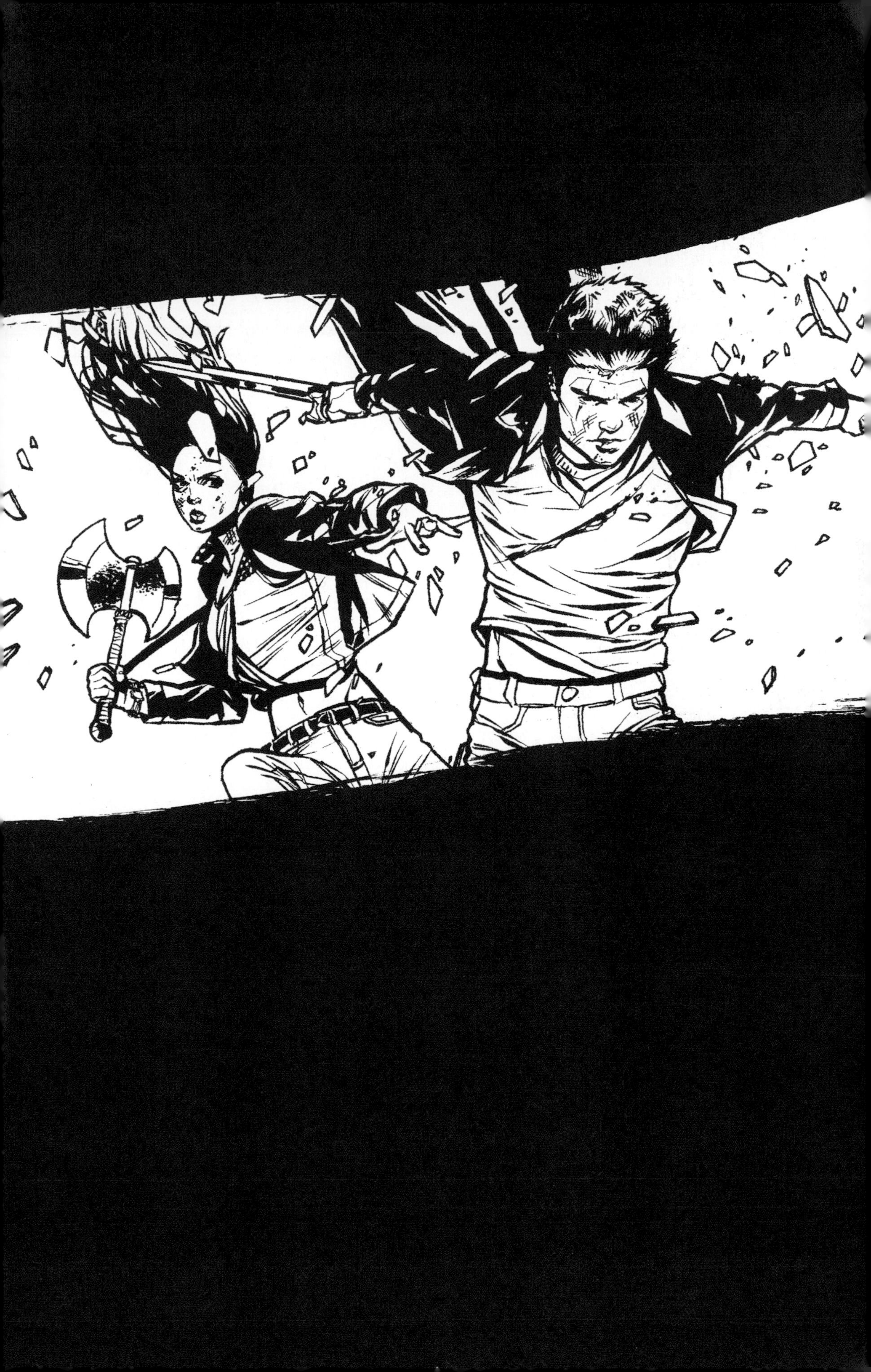

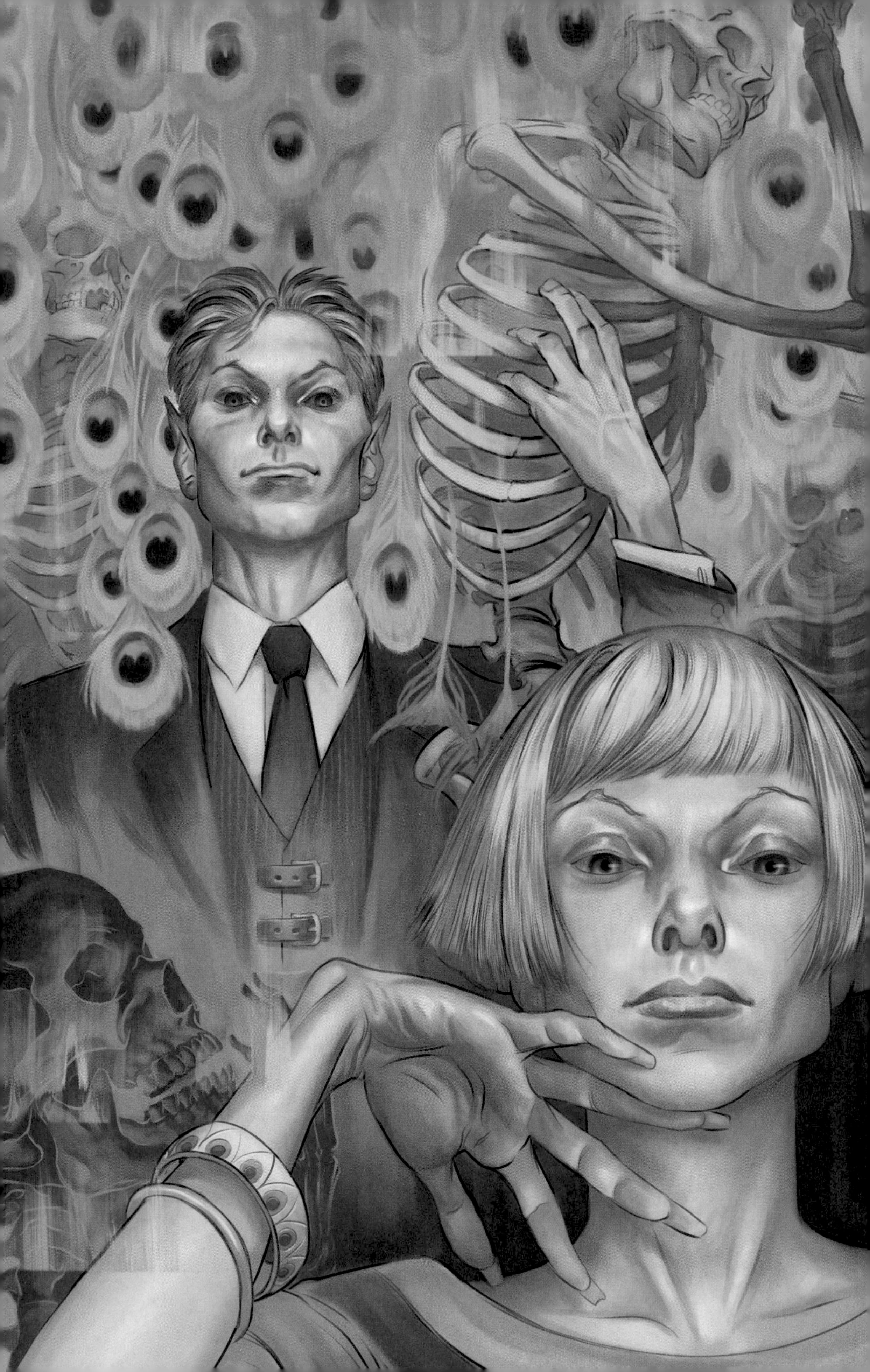

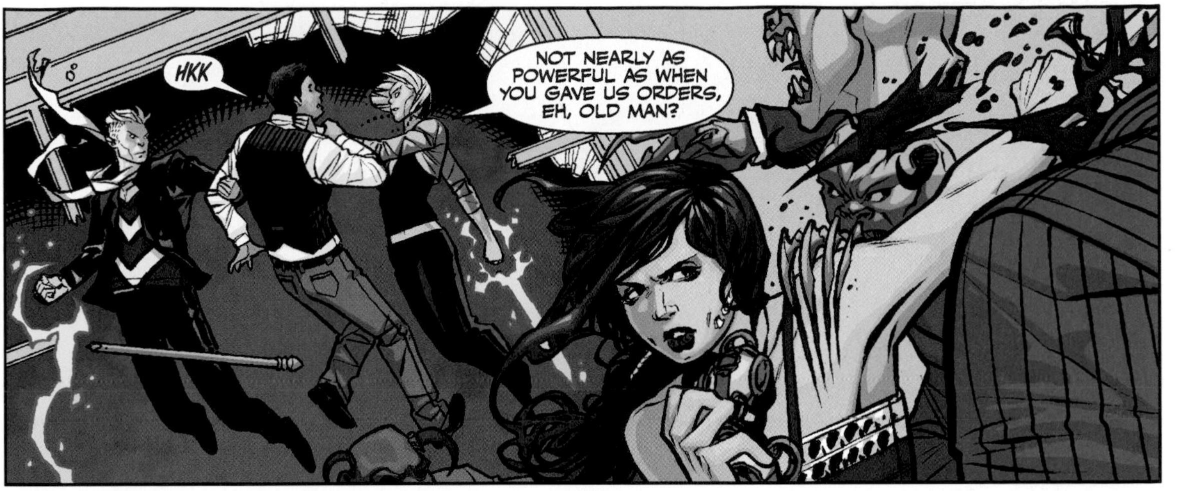
HKK
NOT NEARLY AS POWERFUL AS WHEN YOU GAVE US ORDERS, EH, OLD MAN?

LIVE THROUGH THIS PART FOUR

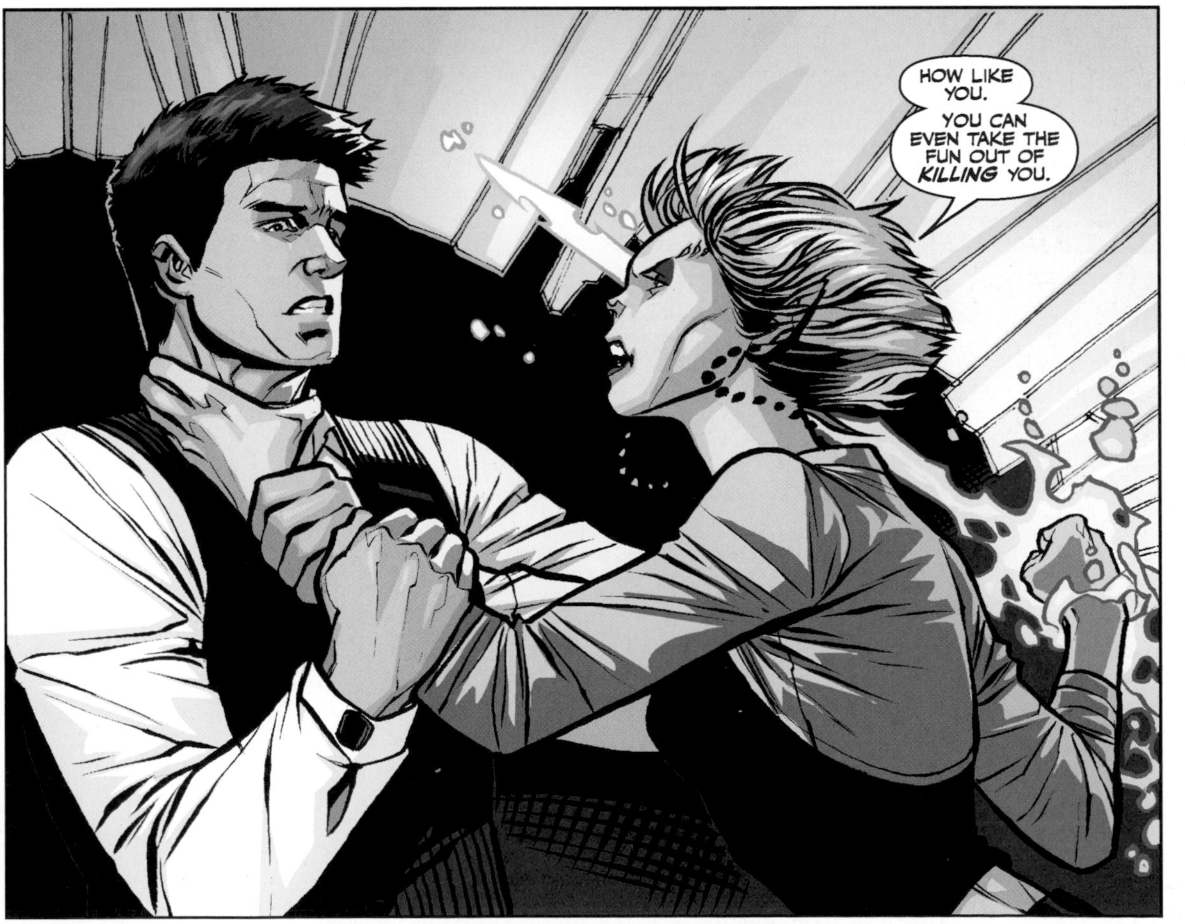
HOW LIKE YOU.
YOU CAN EVEN TAKE THE FUN OUT OF *KILLING* YOU.

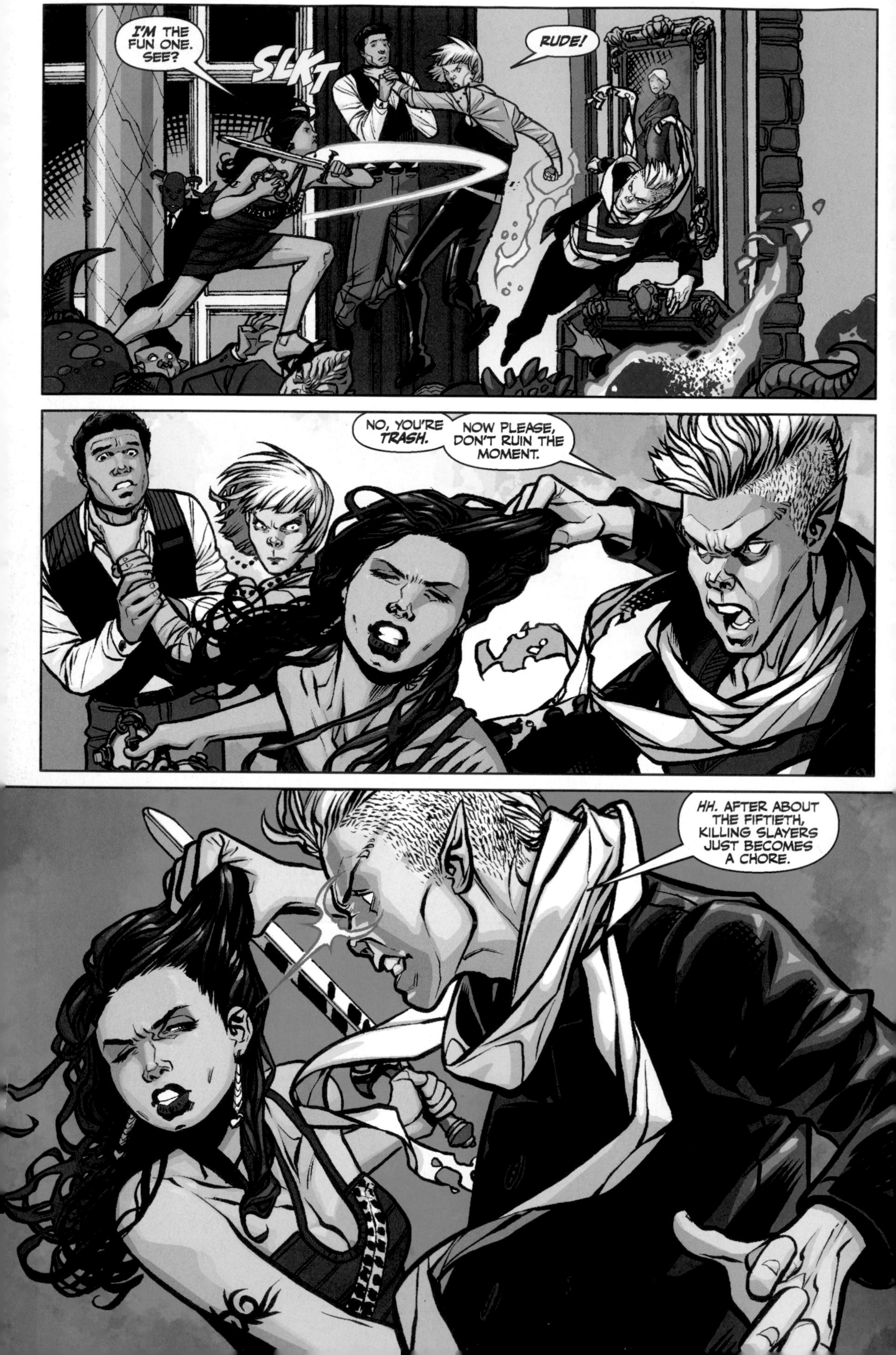

I'M THE FUN ONE. SEE?
SLKT
RUDE!
NO, YOU'RE TRASH.
NOW PLEASE, DON'T RUIN THE MOMENT.
HH. AFTER ABOUT THE FIFTIETH, KILLING SLAYERS JUST BECOMES A CHORE.

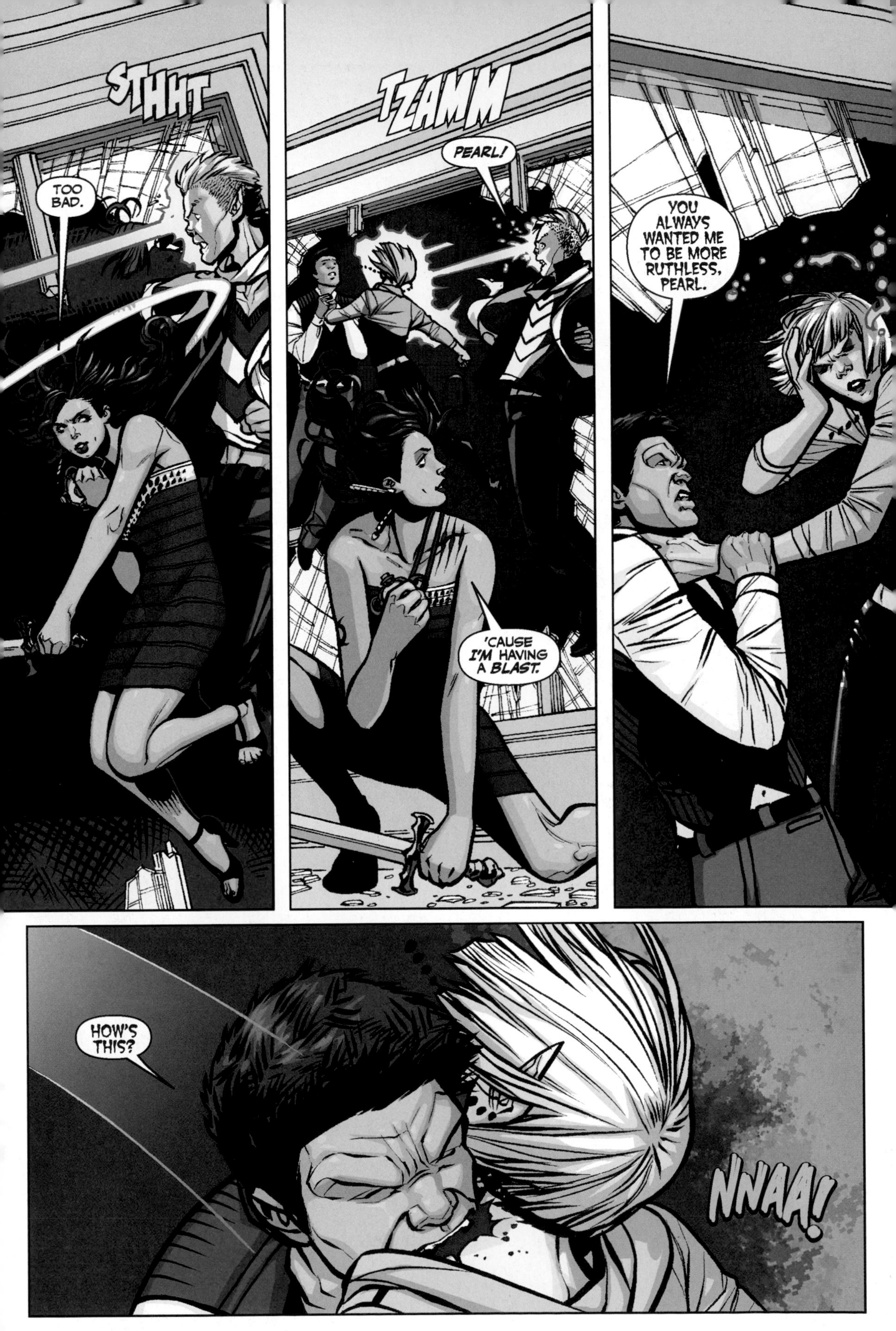
STHHT
TOO BAD.
TZAMM
PEARL!
'CAUSE I'M HAVING A BLAST.
YOU ALWAYS WANTED ME TO BE MORE RUTHLESS, PEARL.
HOW'S THIS?
NNAA!

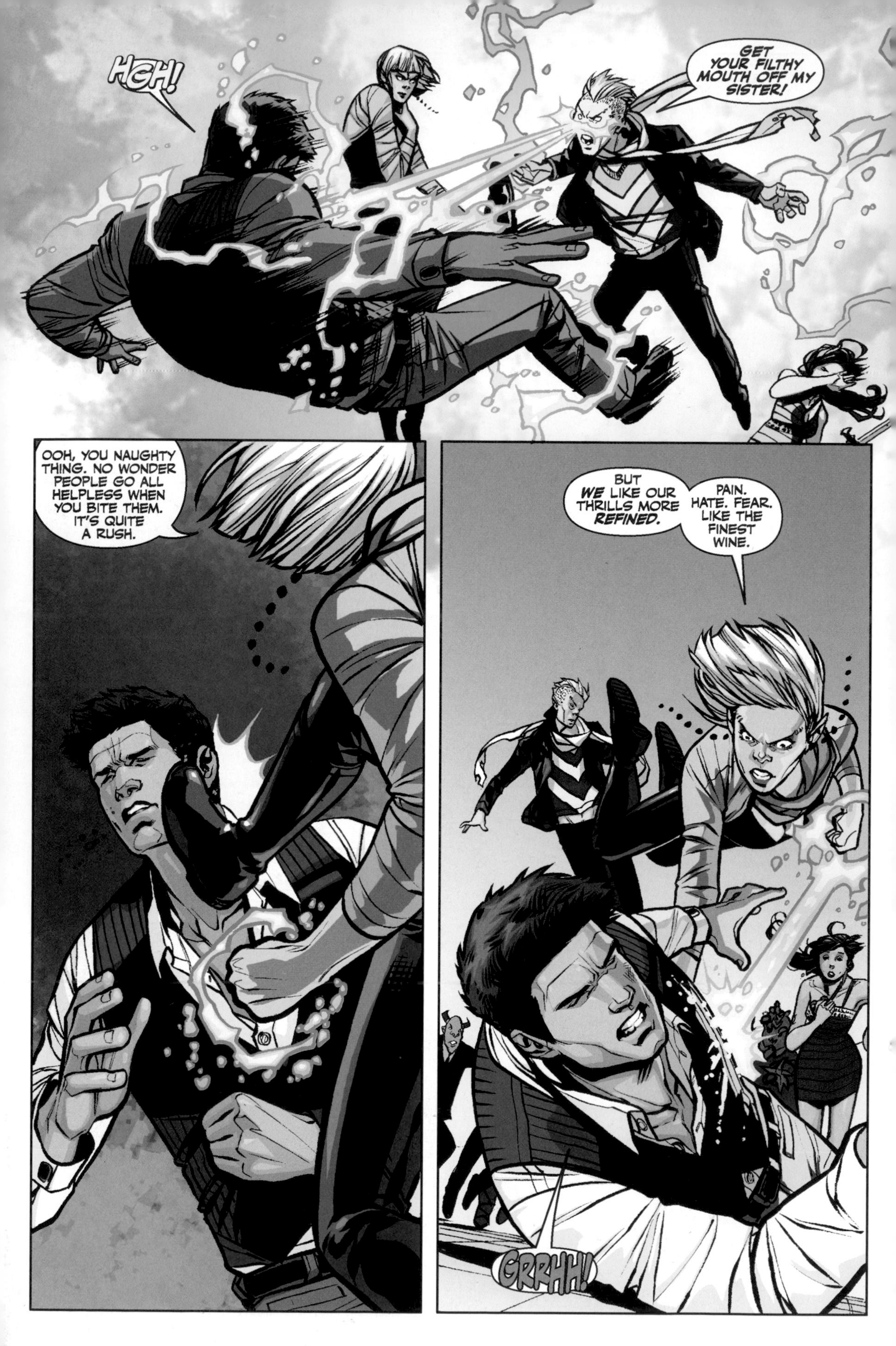
HGH!
GET YOUR FILTHY MOUTH OFF MY SISTER!
OOH, YOU NAUGHTY THING. NO WONDER PEOPLE GO ALL HELPLESS WHEN YOU BITE THEM. IT'S QUITE A RUSH.
BUT *WE* LIKE OUR THRILLS MORE *REFINED.*
PAIN. HATE. FEAR. LIKE THE FINEST WINE.
GRRHH!

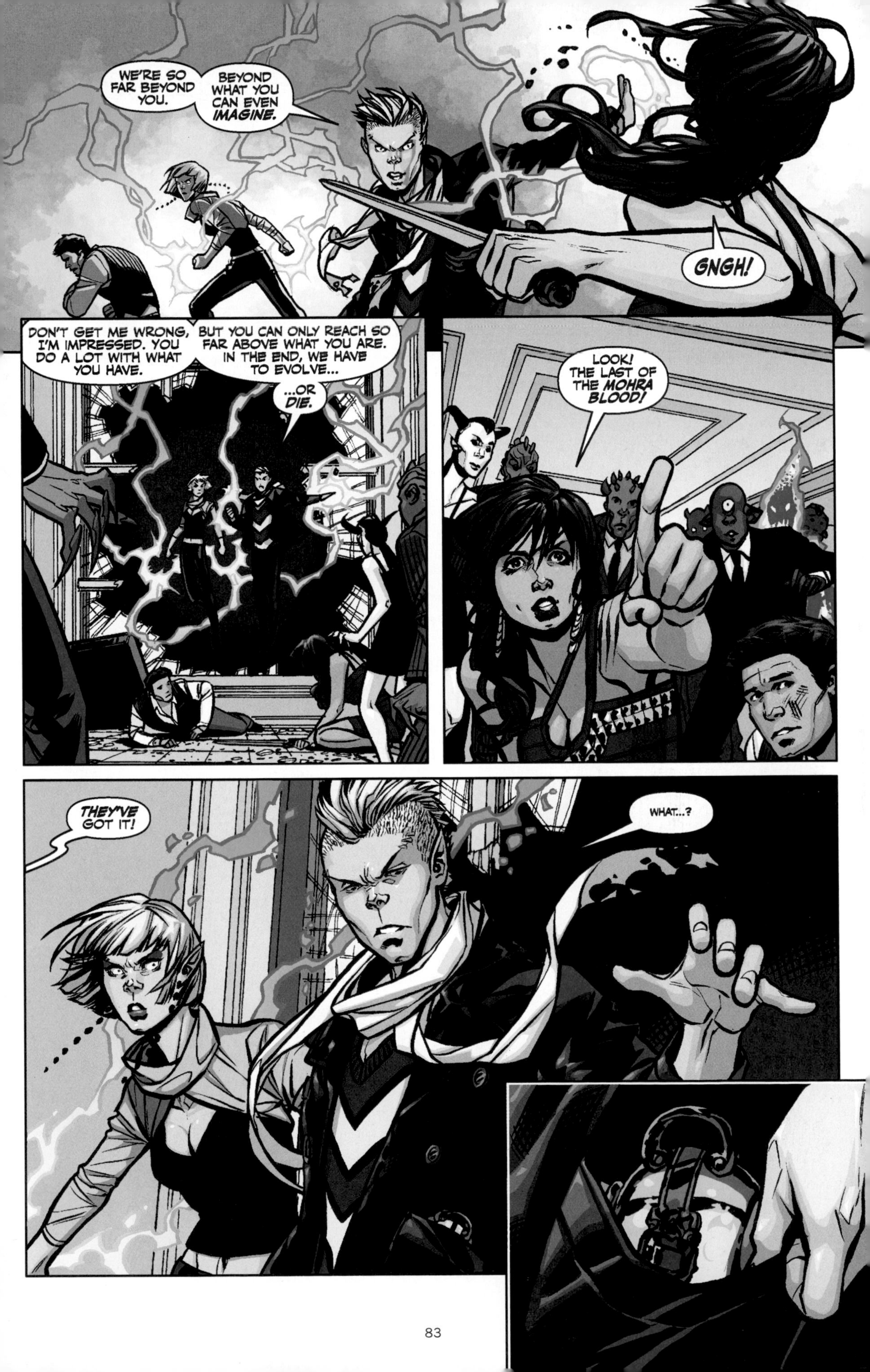
WE'RE SO FAR BEYOND YOU.
BEYOND WHAT YOU CAN EVEN IMAGINE.
GNGH!
DON'T GET ME WRONG, I'M IMPRESSED. YOU DO A LOT WITH WHAT YOU HAVE.
BUT YOU CAN ONLY REACH SO FAR ABOVE WHAT YOU ARE. IN THE END, WE HAVE TO EVOLVE...
...OR DIE.
LOOK! THE LAST OF THE MOHRA BLOOD!
THEY'VE GOT IT!
WHAT...?

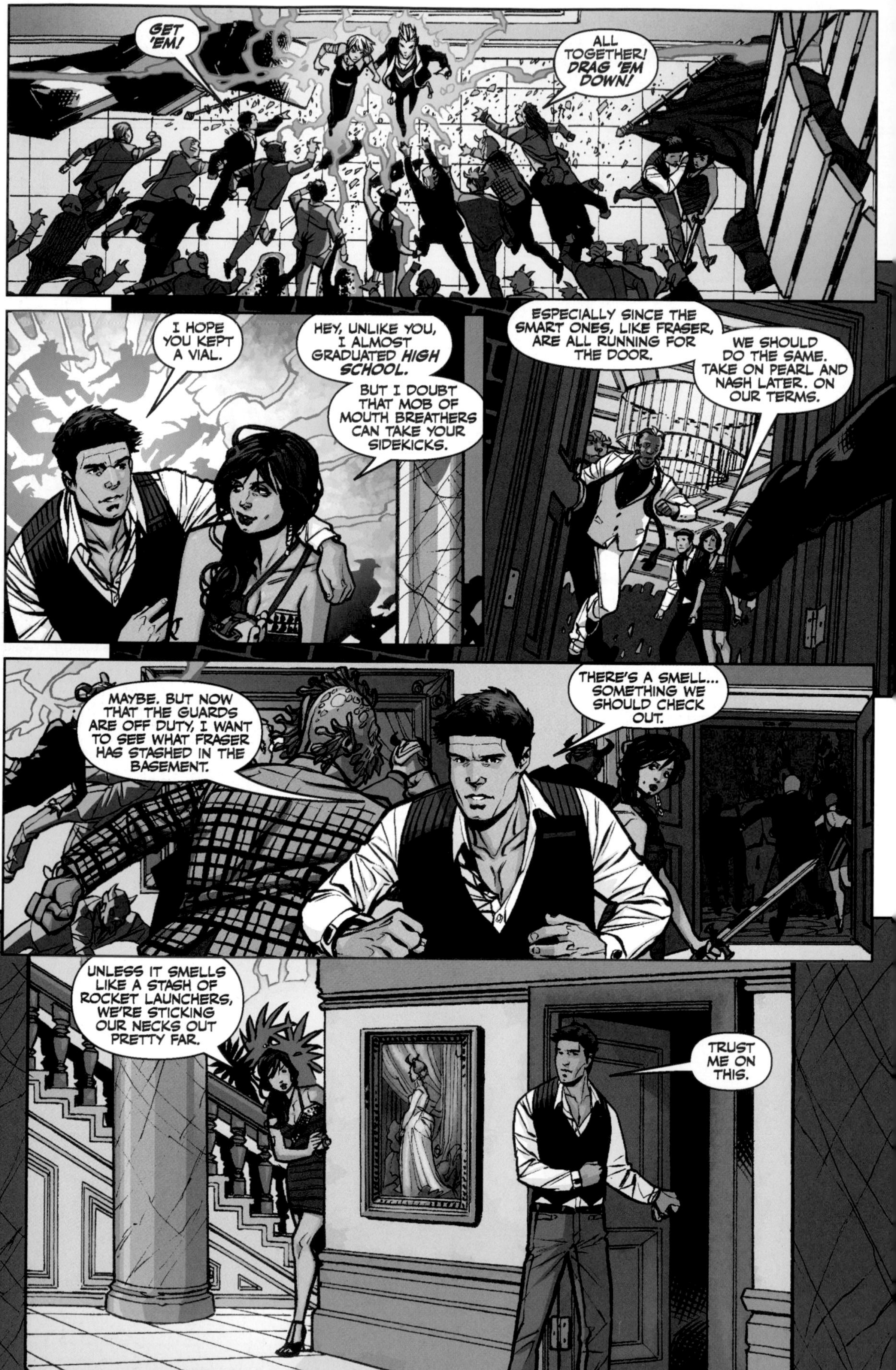
GET 'EM!
ALL TOGETHER! DRAG 'EM DOWN!
I HOPE YOU KEPT A VIAL.
HEY, UNLIKE YOU, I ALMOST GRADUATED HIGH SCHOOL.
BUT I DOUBT THAT MOB OF MOUTH BREATHERS CAN TAKE YOUR SIDEKICKS.
ESPECIALLY SINCE THE SMART ONES, LIKE FRASER, ARE ALL RUNNING FOR THE DOOR.
WE SHOULD DO THE SAME. TAKE ON PEARL AND NASH LATER. ON OUR TERMS.
MAYBE. BUT NOW THAT THE GUARDS ARE OFF DUTY, I WANT TO SEE WHAT FRASER HAS STASHED IN THE BASEMENT.
THERE'S A SMELL... SOMETHING WE SHOULD CHECK OUT.
UNLESS IT SMELLS LIKE A STASH OF ROCKET LAUNCHERS, WE'RE STICKING OUR NECKS OUT PRETTY FAR.
TRUST ME ON THIS.

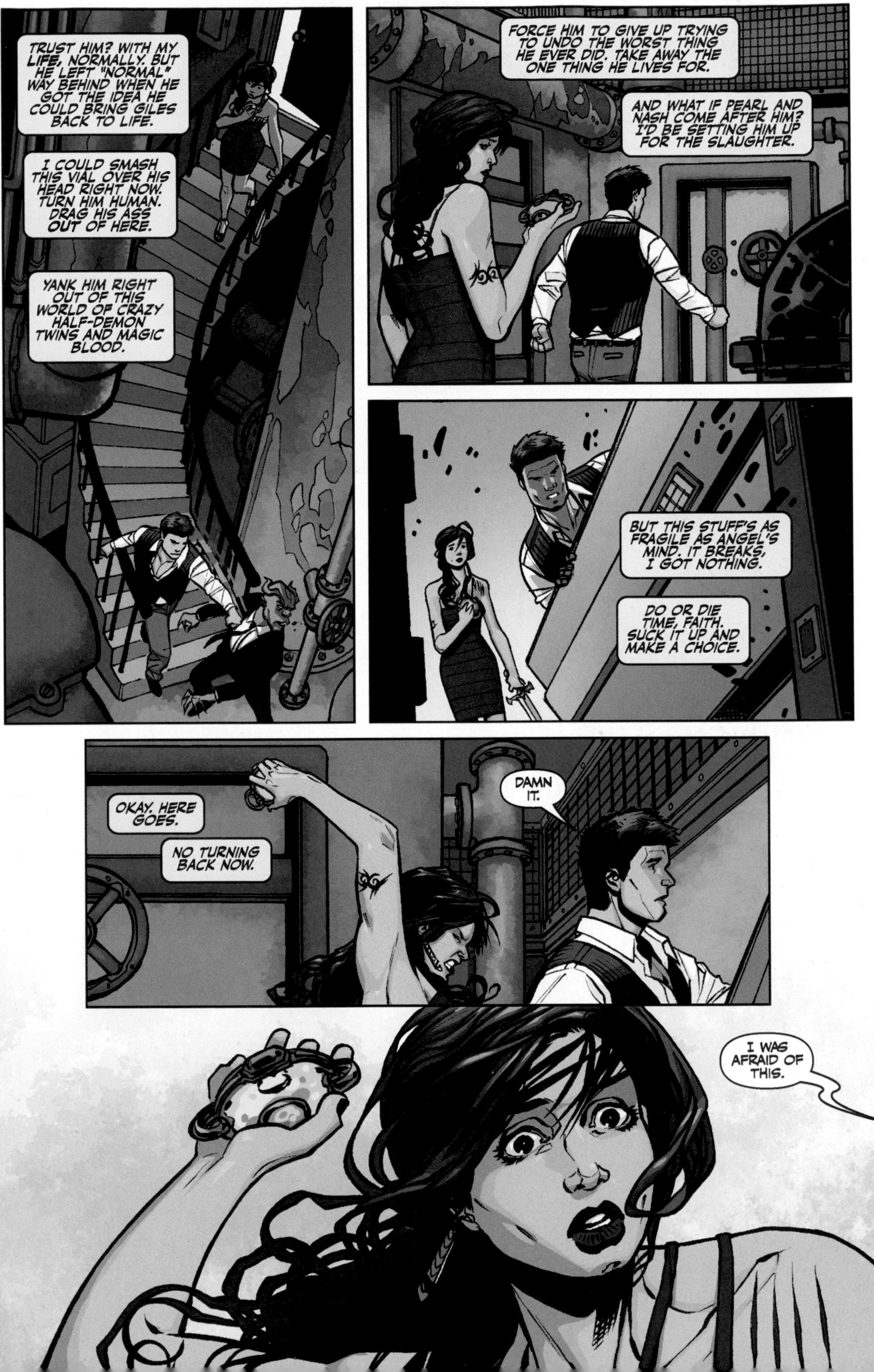
TRUST HIM? WITH MY LIFE, NORMALLY. BUT HE LEFT "NORMAL" WAY BEHIND WHEN HE GOT THE IDEA HE COULD BRING GILES BACK TO LIFE.
I COULD SMASH THIS VIAL OVER HIS HEAD RIGHT NOW. TURN HIM HUMAN. DRAG HIS ASS OUT OF HERE.
YANK HIM RIGHT OUT OF THIS WORLD OF CRAZY HALF-DEMON TWINS AND MAGIC BLOOD.
FORCE HIM TO GIVE UP TRYING TO UNDO THE WORST THING HE EVER DID. TAKE AWAY THE ONE THING HE LIVES FOR.
AND WHAT IF PEARL AND NASH COME AFTER HIM? I'D BE SETTING HIM UP FOR THE SLAUGHTER.
BUT THIS STUFF'S AS FRAGILE AS ANGEL'S MIND. IT BREAKS, I GOT NOTHING.
DO OR DIE TIME, FAITH. SUCK IT UP AND MAKE A CHOICE.
OKAY. HERE GOES.
NO TURNING BACK NOW.
DAMN IT.
I WAS AFRAID OF THIS.

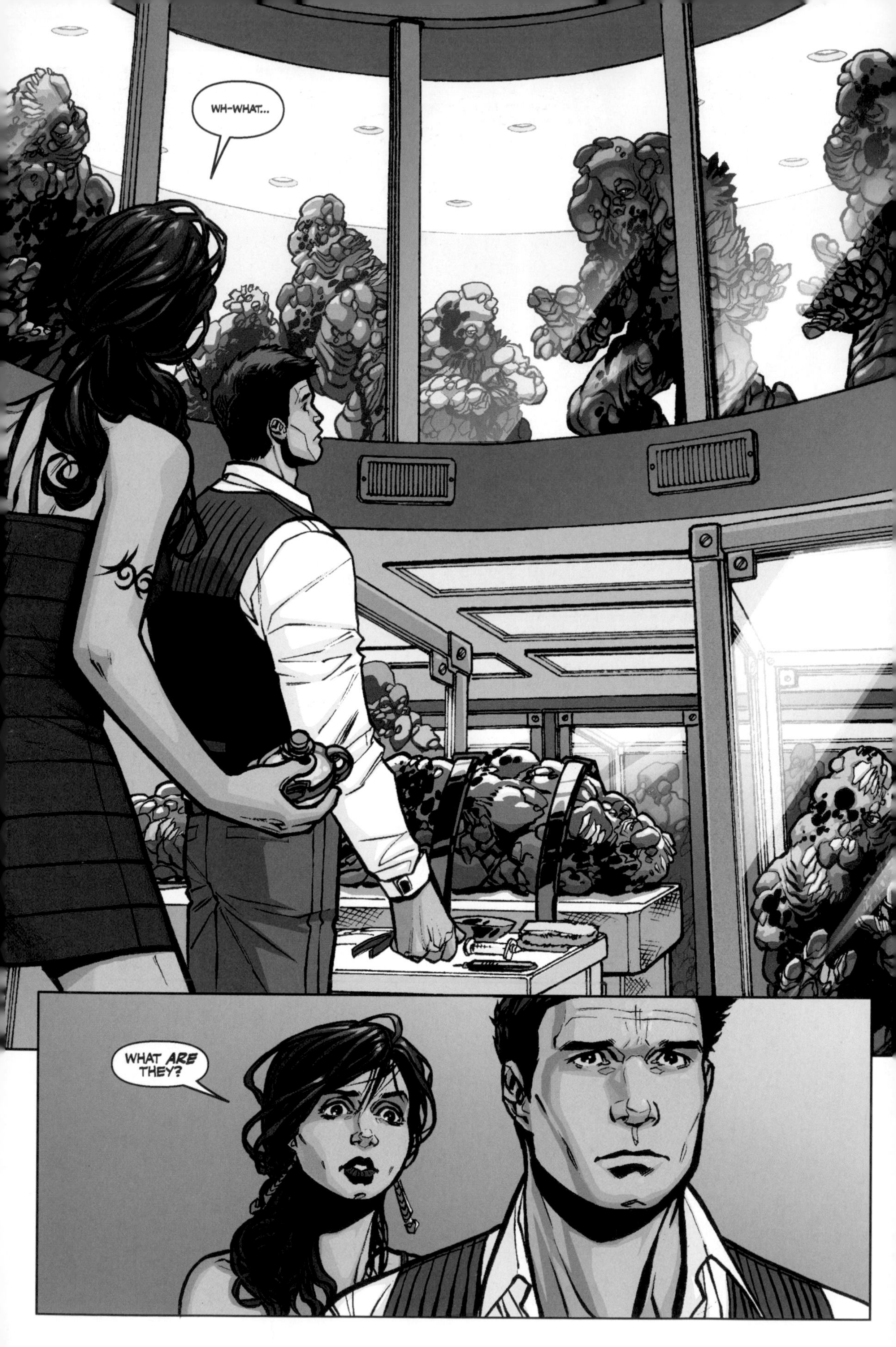
WH-WHAT...
WHAT ARE THEY?

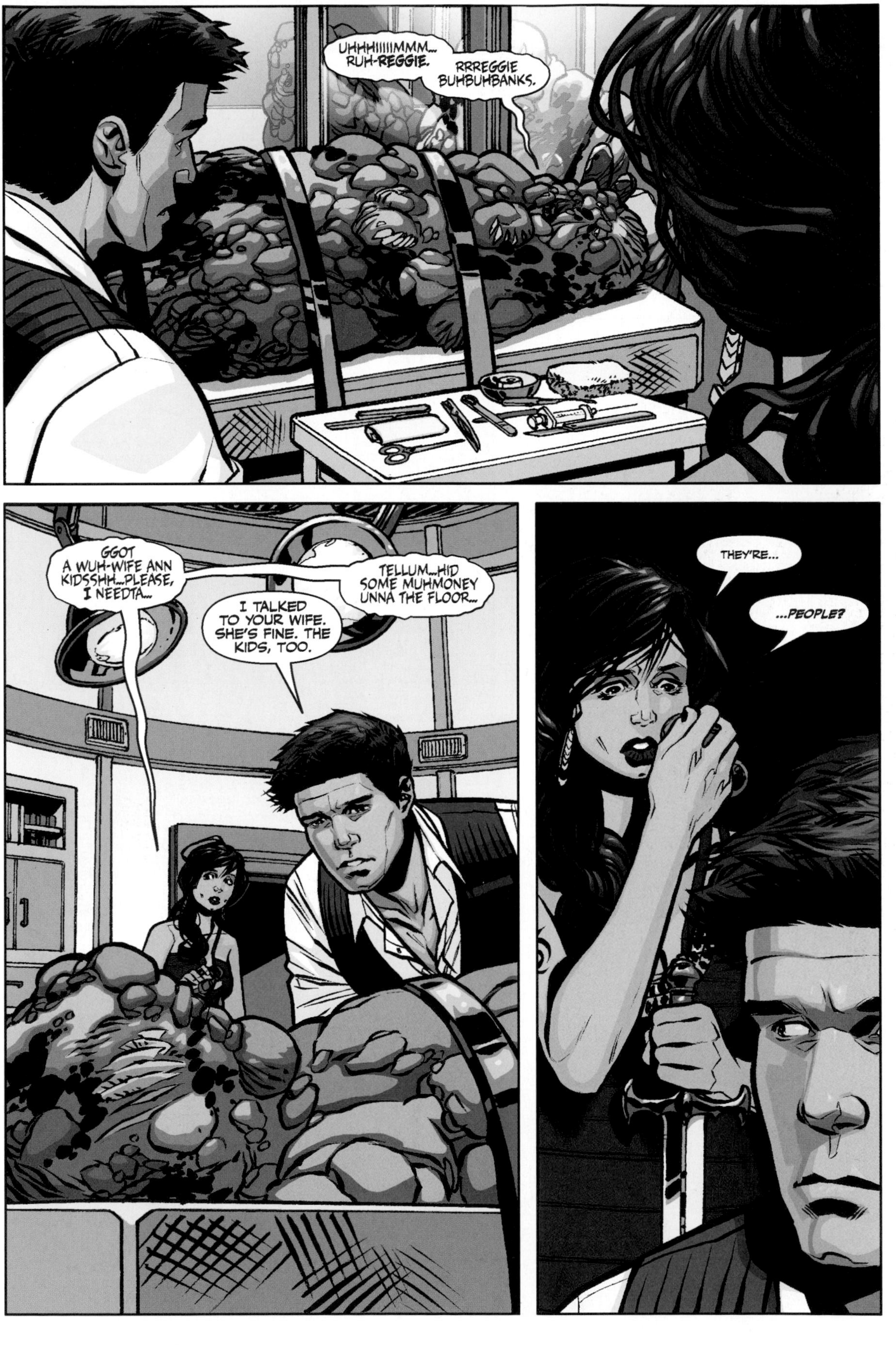
UHHHIIIIIMMM... RUH-REGGIE.
RRREGGIE BUHBUHBANKS.
GGOT A WUH-WIFE ANN KIDSSHH...PLEASE, I NEEDTA...
TELLUM...HID SOME MUHMONEY UNNA THE FLOOR...
I TALKED TO YOUR WIFE. SHE'S FINE. THE KIDS, TOO.
THEY'RE...
...PEOPLE?

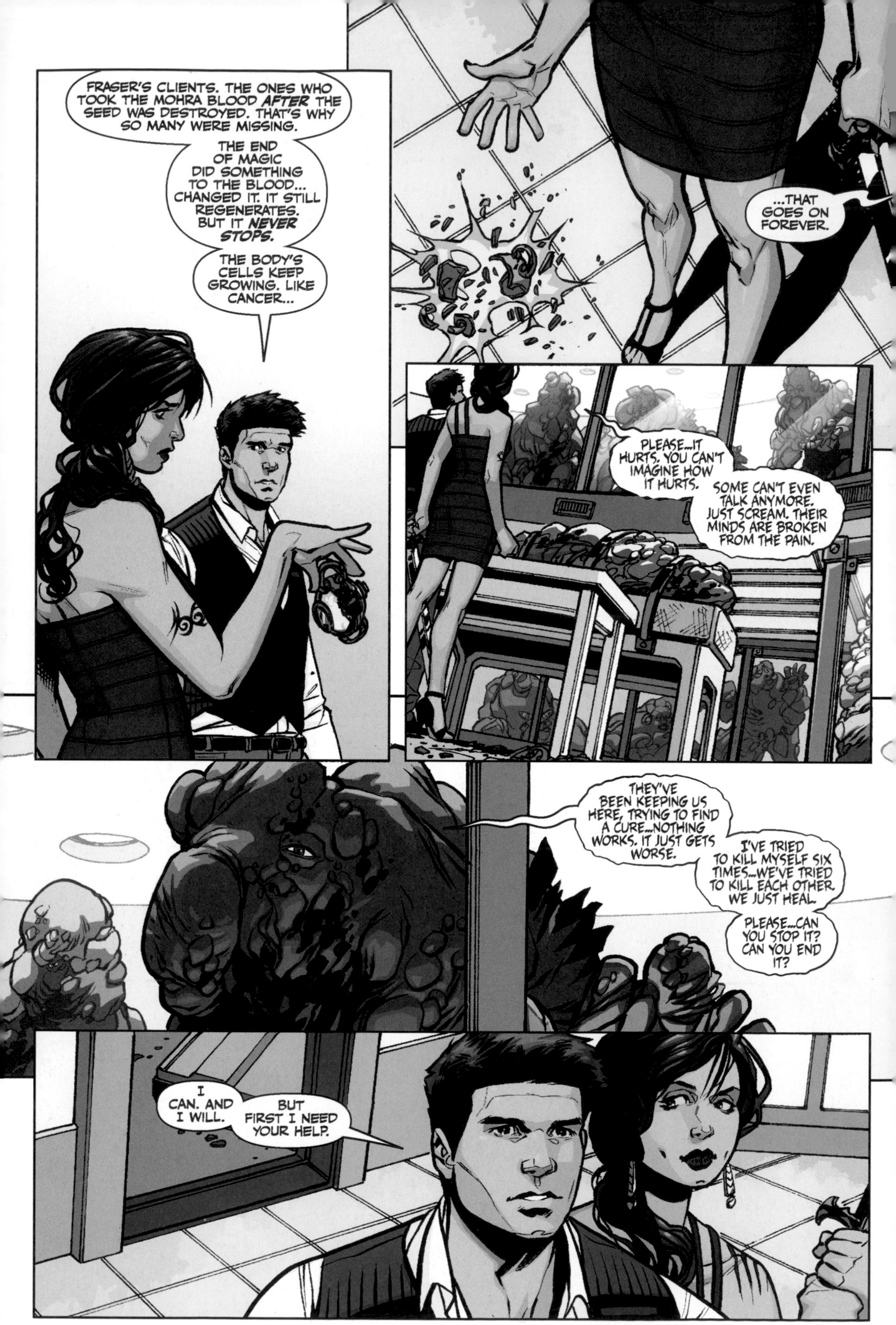

FRASER'S CLIENTS. THE ONES WHO TOOK THE MOHRA BLOOD *AFTER* THE SEED WAS DESTROYED. THAT'S WHY SO MANY WERE MISSING.
THE END OF MAGIC DID SOMETHING TO THE BLOOD... CHANGED IT. IT STILL REGENERATES. BUT IT *NEVER STOPS.*
THE BODY'S CELLS KEEP GROWING. LIKE CANCER...
...THAT GOES ON FOREVER.
PLEASE...IT HURTS. YOU CAN'T IMAGINE HOW IT HURTS.
SOME CAN'T EVEN TALK ANYMORE. JUST SCREAM. THEIR MINDS ARE BROKEN FROM THE PAIN.
THEY'VE BEEN KEEPING US HERE, TRYING TO FIND A CURE...NOTHING WORKS. IT JUST GETS WORSE.
I'VE TRIED TO KILL MYSELF SIX TIMES...WE'VE TRIED TO KILL EACH OTHER. WE JUST HEAL.
PLEASE...CAN YOU STOP IT? CAN YOU END IT?
I CAN. AND I WILL.
BUT FIRST I NEED YOUR HELP.

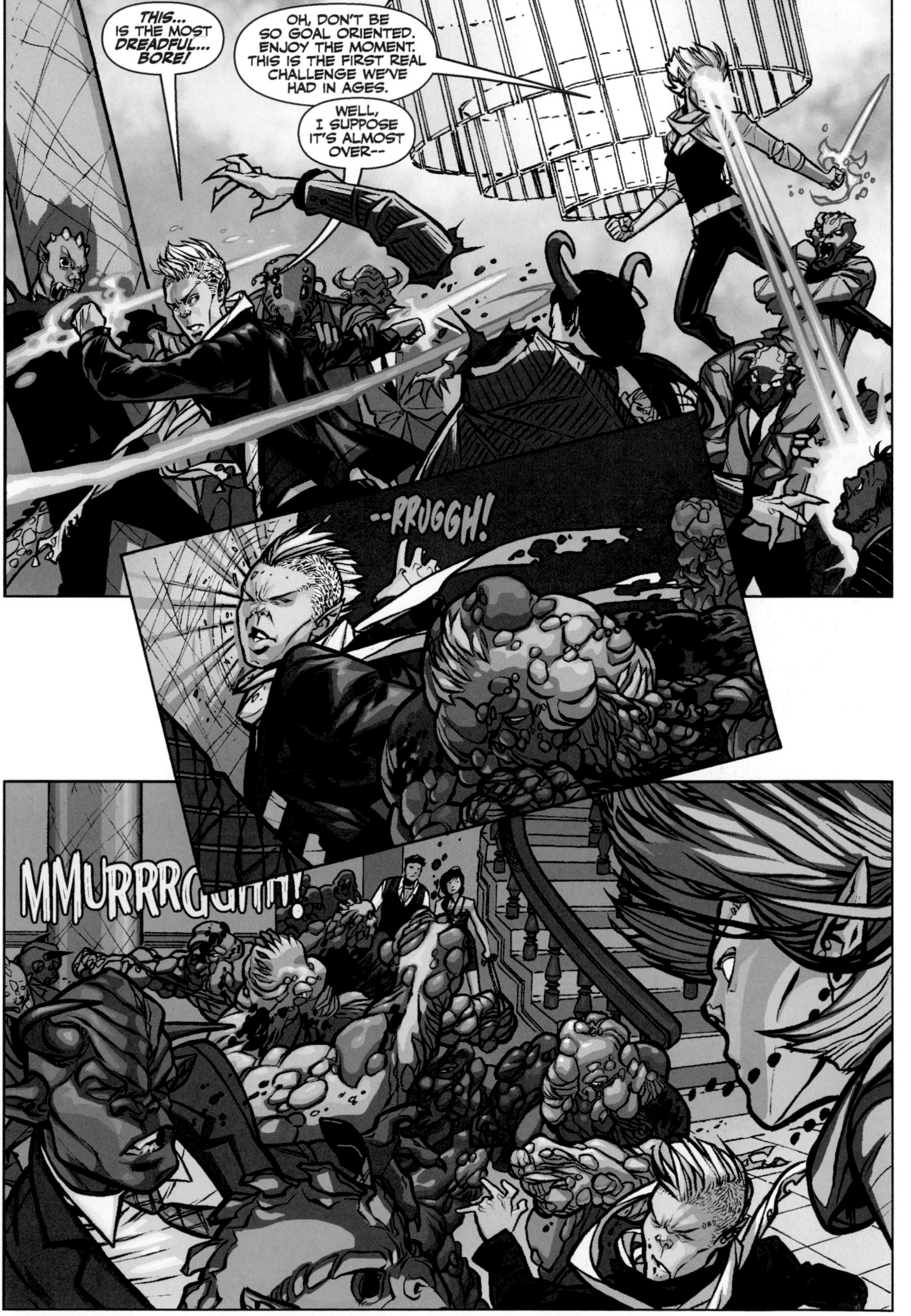
THIS... IS THE MOST DREADFUL... BORE!
OH, DON'T BE SO GOAL ORIENTED. ENJOY THE MOMENT. THIS IS THE FIRST REAL CHALLENGE WE'VE HAD IN AGES.
WELL, I SUPPOSE IT'S ALMOST OVER--
--RRUGGH!
MMURRRRGHHH!

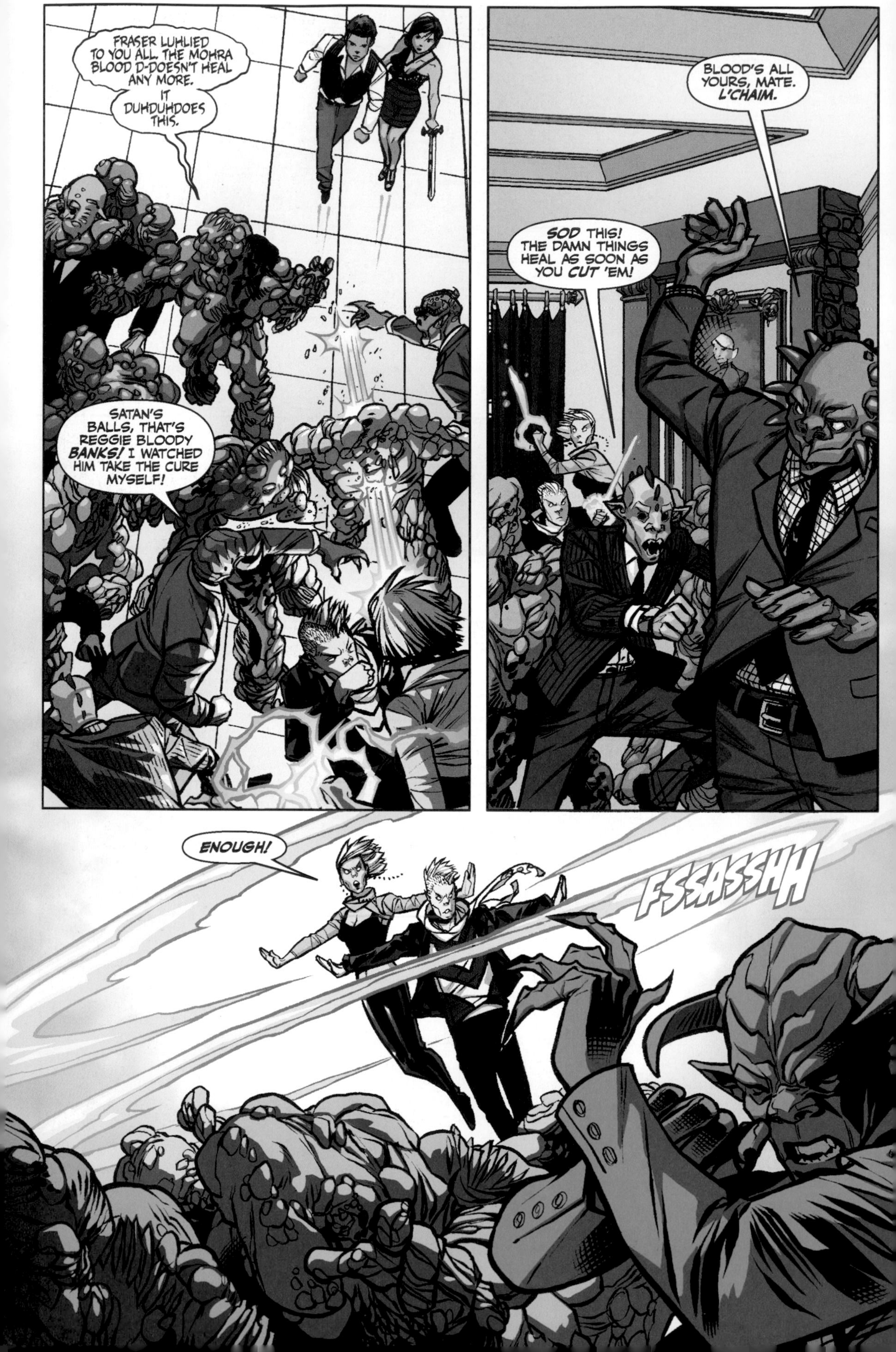
FRASER LUHLIED TO YOU ALL. THE MOHRA BLOOD D-DOESN'T HEAL ANY MORE.
IT DUHDUHDOES THIS.
SATAN'S BALLS, THAT'S REGGIE BLOODY BANKS! I WATCHED HIM TAKE THE CURE MYSELF!
BLOOD'S ALL YOURS, MATE. L'CHAIM.
SOD THIS! THE DAMN THINGS HEAL AS SOON AS YOU CUT 'EM!
ENOUGH!
FSSASSHH

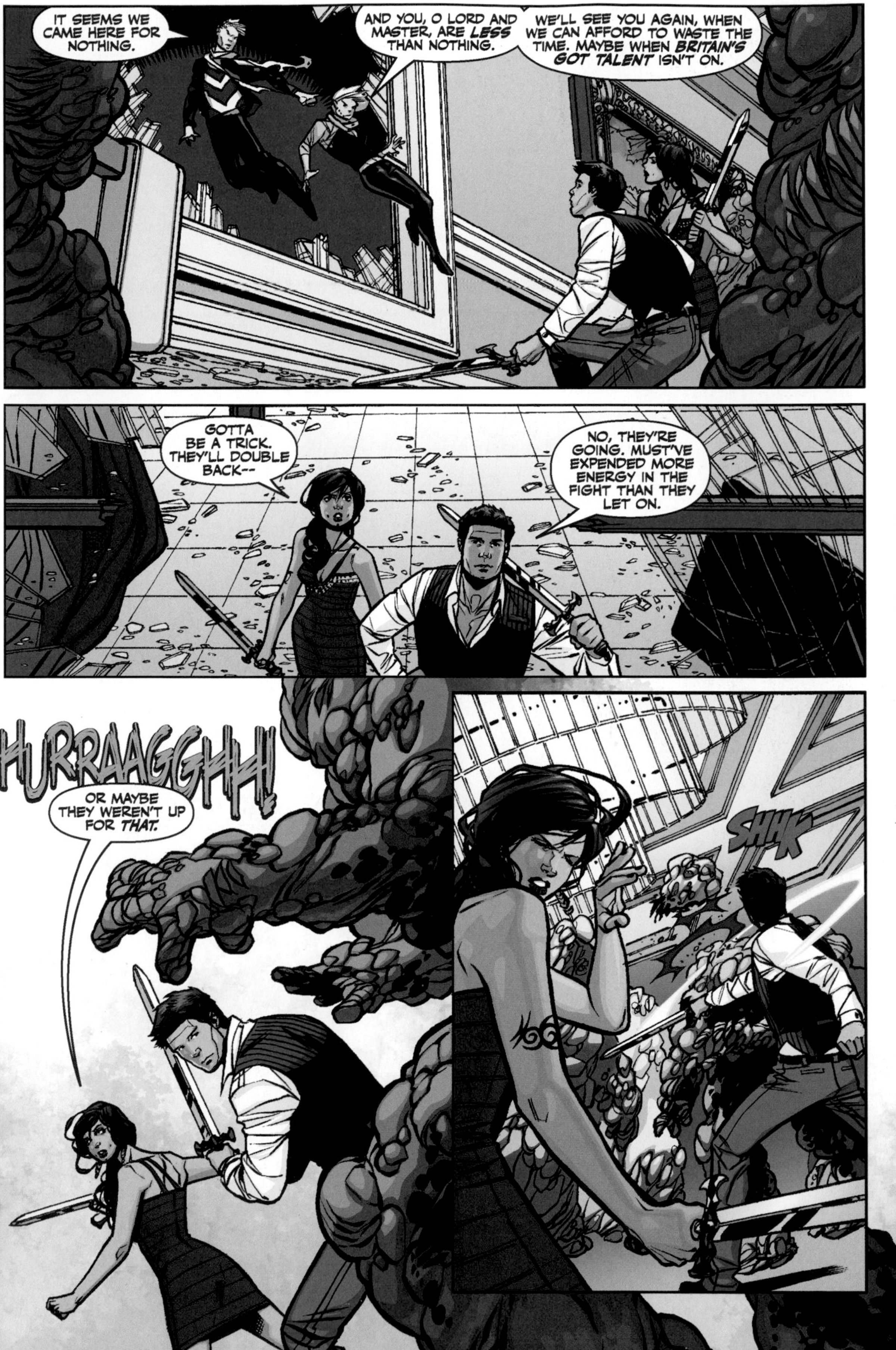
IT SEEMS WE CAME HERE FOR NOTHING.
AND YOU, O LORD AND MASTER, ARE LESS THAN NOTHING.
WE'LL SEE YOU AGAIN, WHEN WE CAN AFFORD TO WASTE THE TIME. MAYBE WHEN BRITAIN'S GOT TALENT ISN'T ON.
GOTTA BE A TRICK. THEY'LL DOUBLE BACK--
NO, THEY'RE GOING. MUST'VE EXPENDED MORE ENERGY IN THE FIGHT THAN THEY LET ON.
HURRAAGGHH!
OR MAYBE THEY WEREN'T UP FOR THAT.
SHHK

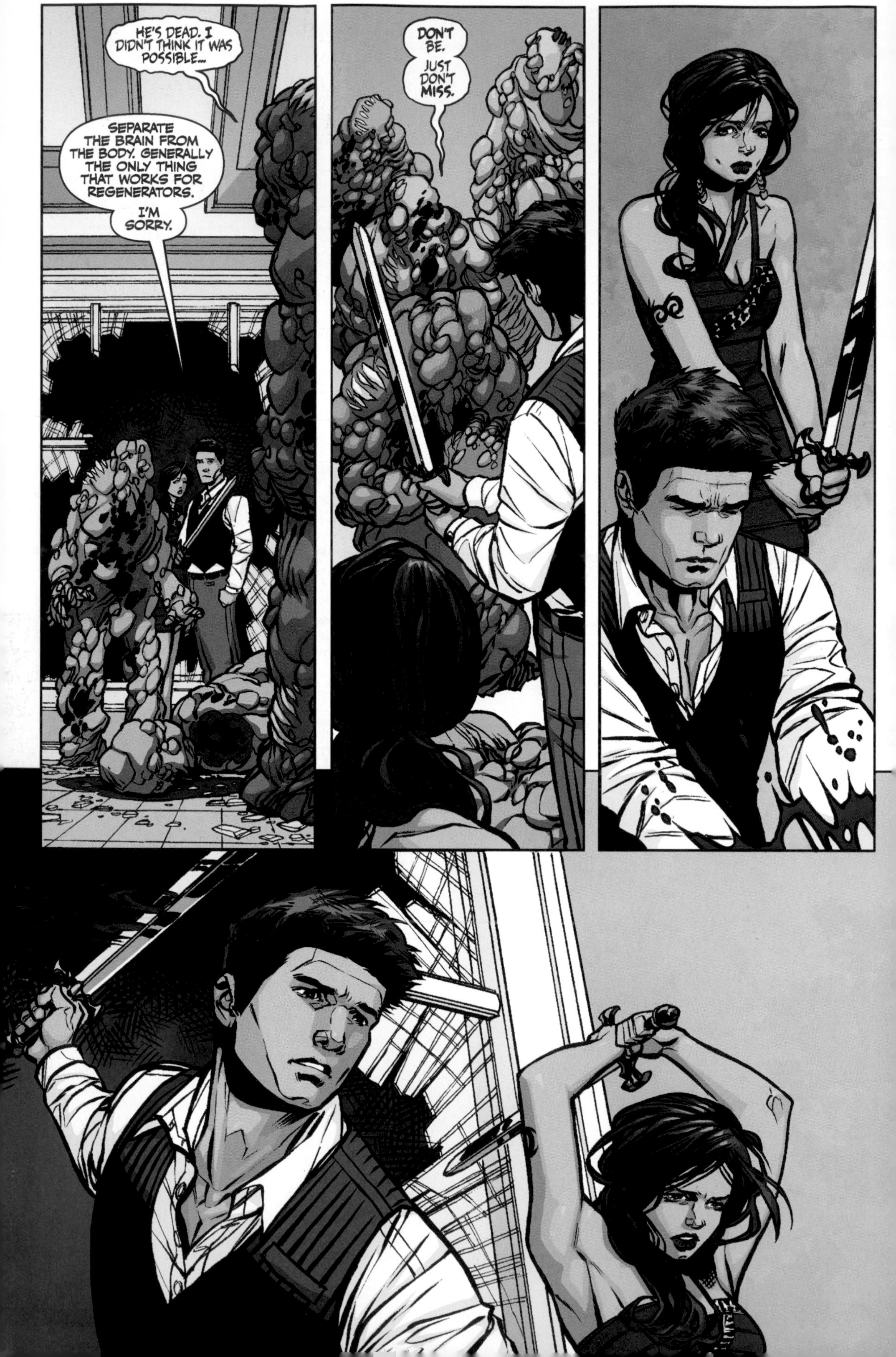
HE'S DEAD. I DIDN'T THINK IT WAS POSSIBLE...
SEPARATE THE BRAIN FROM THE BODY. GENERALLY THE ONLY THING THAT WORKS FOR REGENERATORS.
I'M SORRY.
DON'T BE.
JUST DON'T MISS.

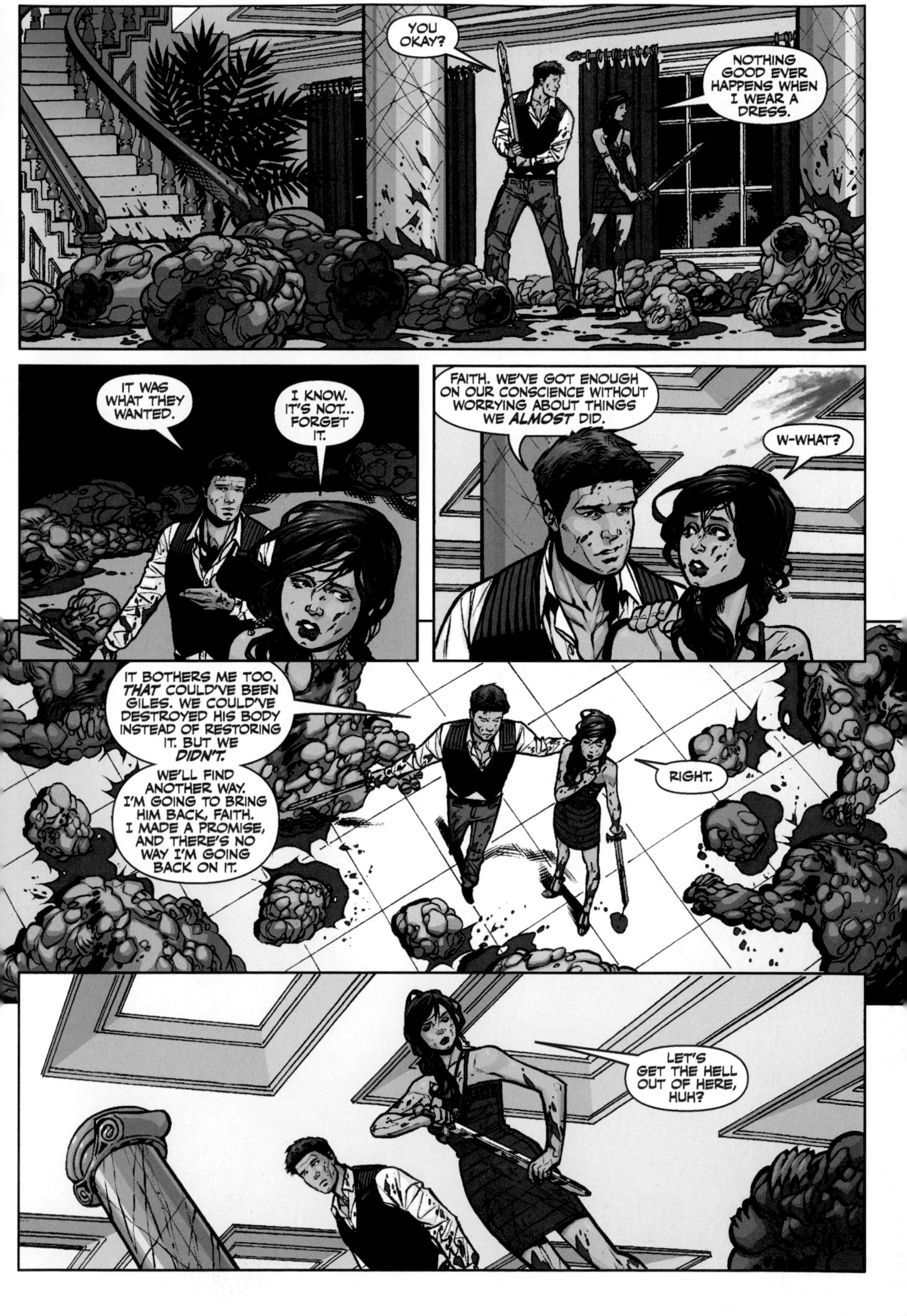
YOU OKAY?
NOTHING GOOD EVER HAPPENS WHEN I WEAR A DRESS.
IT WAS WHAT THEY WANTED.
I KNOW. IT'S NOT... FORGET IT.
FAITH. WE'VE GOT ENOUGH ON OUR CONSCIENCE WITHOUT WORRYING ABOUT THINGS WE *ALMOST* DID.
W-WHAT?
IT BOTHERS ME TOO. *THAT* COULD'VE BEEN GILES. WE COULD'VE DESTROYED HIS BODY INSTEAD OF RESTORING IT. BUT WE *DIDN'T.*
WE'LL FIND ANOTHER WAY. I'M GOING TO BRING HIM BACK, FAITH. I MADE A PROMISE, AND THERE'S NO WAY I'M GOING BACK ON IT.
RIGHT.
LET'S GET THE HELL OUT OF HERE, HUH?

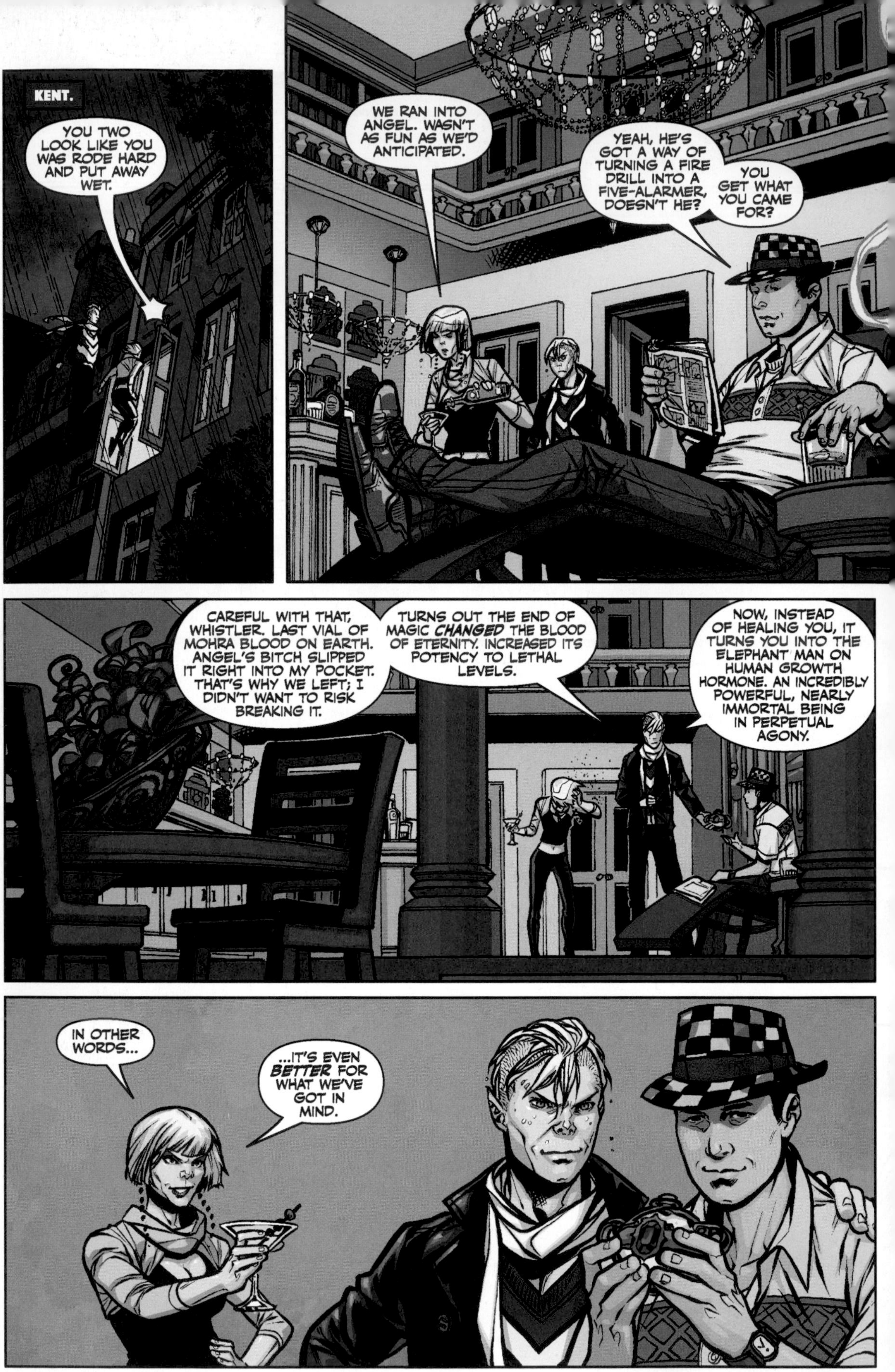
KENT.
YOU TWO LOOK LIKE YOU WAS RODE HARD AND PUT AWAY WET.
WE RAN INTO ANGEL. WASN'T AS FUN AS WE'D ANTICIPATED.
YEAH, HE'S GOT A WAY OF TURNING A FIRE DRILL INTO A FIVE-ALARMER, DOESN'T HE?
YOU GET WHAT YOU CAME FOR?
CAREFUL WITH THAT, WHISTLER. LAST VIAL OF MOHRA BLOOD ON EARTH. ANGEL'S BITCH SLIPPED IT RIGHT INTO MY POCKET. THAT'S WHY WE LEFT; I DIDN'T WANT TO RISK BREAKING IT.
TURNS OUT THE END OF MAGIC *CHANGED* THE BLOOD OF ETERNITY. INCREASED ITS POTENCY TO LETHAL LEVELS.
NOW, INSTEAD OF HEALING YOU, IT TURNS YOU INTO THE ELEPHANT MAN ON HUMAN GROWTH HORMONE. AN INCREDIBLY POWERFUL, NEARLY IMMORTAL BEING IN PERPETUAL AGONY.
IN OTHER WORDS...
...IT'S EVEN *BETTER* FOR WHAT WE'VE GOT IN MIND.

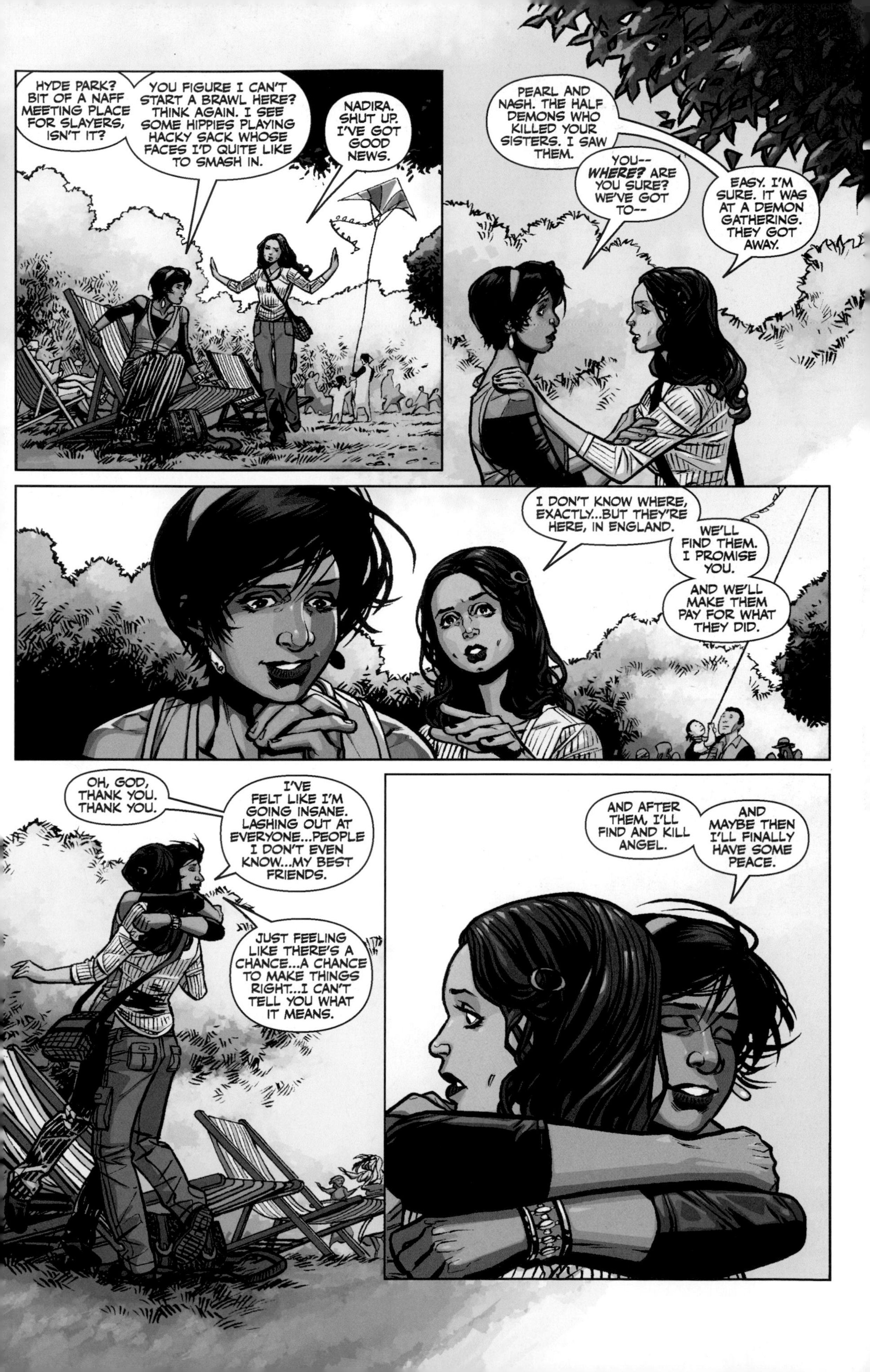
HYDE PARK? BIT OF A NAFF MEETING PLACE FOR SLAYERS, ISN'T IT?
YOU FIGURE I CAN'T START A BRAWL HERE? THINK AGAIN. I SEE SOME HIPPIES PLAYING HACKY SACK WHOSE FACES I'D QUITE LIKE TO SMASH IN.
NADIRA. SHUT UP. I'VE GOT GOOD NEWS.
PEARL AND NASH. THE HALF DEMONS WHO KILLED YOUR SISTERS. I SAW THEM.
YOU-- WHERE? ARE YOU SURE? WE'VE GOT TO--
EASY. I'M SURE. IT WAS AT A DEMON GATHERING. THEY GOT AWAY.
I DON'T KNOW WHERE, EXACTLY...BUT THEY'RE HERE, IN ENGLAND.
WE'LL FIND THEM. I PROMISE YOU.
AND WE'LL MAKE THEM PAY FOR WHAT THEY DID.
OH, GOD, THANK YOU. THANK YOU.
I'VE FELT LIKE I'M GOING INSANE. LASHING OUT AT EVERYONE...PEOPLE I DON'T EVEN KNOW...MY BEST FRIENDS.
JUST FEELING LIKE THERE'S A CHANCE...A CHANCE TO MAKE THINGS RIGHT...I CAN'T TELL YOU WHAT IT MEANS.
AND AFTER THEM, I'LL FIND AND KILL ANGEL.
AND MAYBE THEN I'LL FINALLY HAVE SOME PEACE.

HELLO, FAITH.

YOU AGAIN. *ALASDAIR,* RIGHT?

Y'KNOW, IF YOU'RE *NOT* A PERVERT, HANGING AROUND PUBLIC PARKS IN AN OVERCOAT ISN'T EXACTLY HELPING YOUR CASE.

I HEARD ABOUT THE INCIDENT WITH THE MOHRA BLOOD. TRAGIC. AND TYPICAL OF THE SORTS OF THINGS HAPPENING WITH MAGIC GONE FROM THE EARTH.

YOU SEE NOW THE DANGERS INHERENT IN PURSUING SOMETHING AS RECKLESS AS WHAT ANGEL INTENDS.

HAVE YOU GIVEN ANY THOUGHT TO OUR PREVIOUS DISCUSSION?

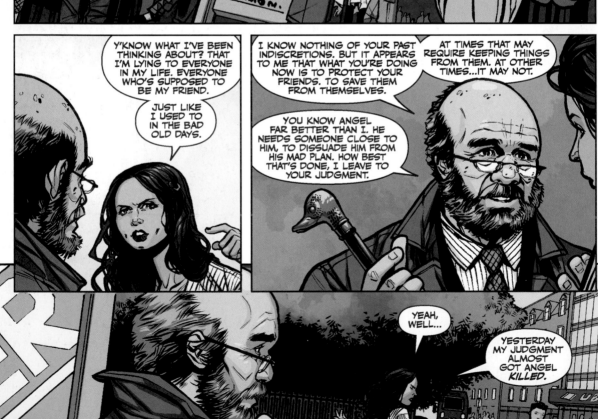

Y'KNOW WHAT I'VE BEEN THINKING ABOUT? THAT I'M LYING TO EVERYONE IN MY LIFE. EVERYONE WHO'S SUPPOSED TO BE MY FRIEND.

JUST LIKE I USED TO IN THE BAD OLD DAYS.

I KNOW NOTHING OF YOUR PAST INDISCRETIONS. BUT IT APPEARS TO ME THAT WHAT YOU'RE DOING NOW IS TO PROTECT YOUR FRIENDS. TO SAVE THEM FROM THEMSELVES.

AT TIMES THAT MAY REQUIRE KEEPING THINGS FROM THEM. AT OTHER TIMES...IT MAY NOT.

YOU KNOW ANGEL FAR BETTER THAN I. HE NEEDS SOMEONE CLOSE TO HIM, TO DISSUADE HIM FROM HIS MAD PLAN. HOW BEST THAT'S DONE, I LEAVE TO YOUR JUDGMENT.

YEAH, WELL...

YESTERDAY MY JUDGMENT ALMOST GOT ANGEL *KILLED.*

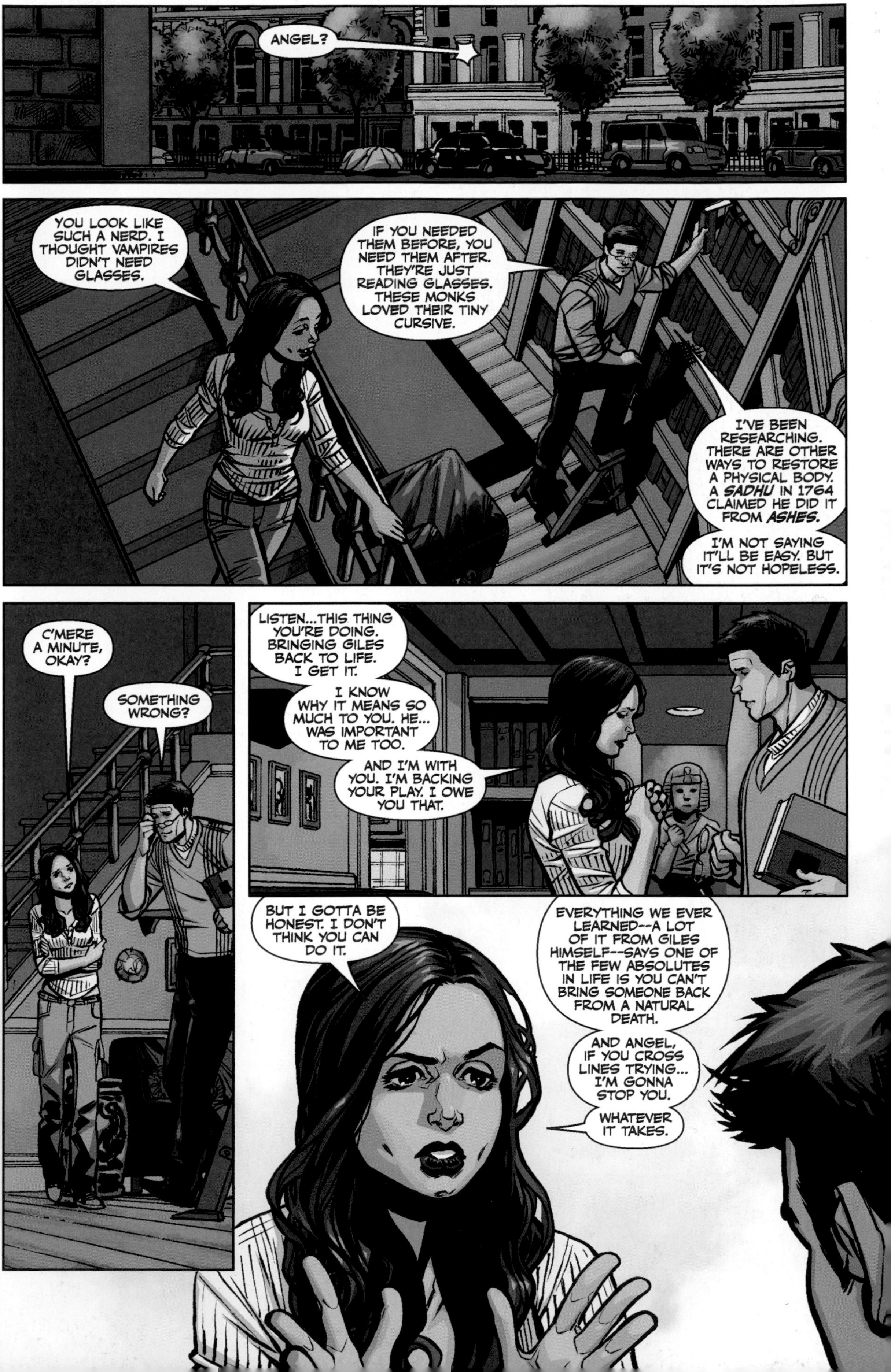
ANGEL?
YOU LOOK LIKE SUCH A NERD. I THOUGHT VAMPIRES DIDN'T NEED GLASSES.
IF YOU NEEDED THEM BEFORE, YOU NEED THEM AFTER. THEY'RE JUST READING GLASSES. THESE MONKS LOVED THEIR TINY CURSIVE.
I'VE BEEN RESEARCHING. THERE ARE OTHER WAYS TO RESTORE A PHYSICAL BODY. A SADHU IN 1764 CLAIMED HE DID IT FROM ASHES.
I'M NOT SAYING IT'LL BE EASY. BUT IT'S NOT HOPELESS.
C'MERE A MINUTE, OKAY?
SOMETHING WRONG?
LISTEN...THIS THING YOU'RE DOING. BRINGING GILES BACK TO LIFE. I GET IT.
I KNOW WHY IT MEANS SO MUCH TO YOU. HE... WAS IMPORTANT TO ME TOO.
AND I'M WITH YOU. I'M BACKING YOUR PLAY. I OWE YOU THAT.
BUT I GOTTA BE HONEST. I DON'T THINK YOU CAN DO IT.
EVERYTHING WE EVER LEARNED--A LOT OF IT FROM GILES HIMSELF--SAYS ONE OF THE FEW ABSOLUTES IN LIFE IS YOU CAN'T BRING SOMEONE BACK FROM A NATURAL DEATH.
AND ANGEL, IF YOU CROSS LINES TRYING... I'M GONNA STOP YOU.
WHATEVER IT TAKES.

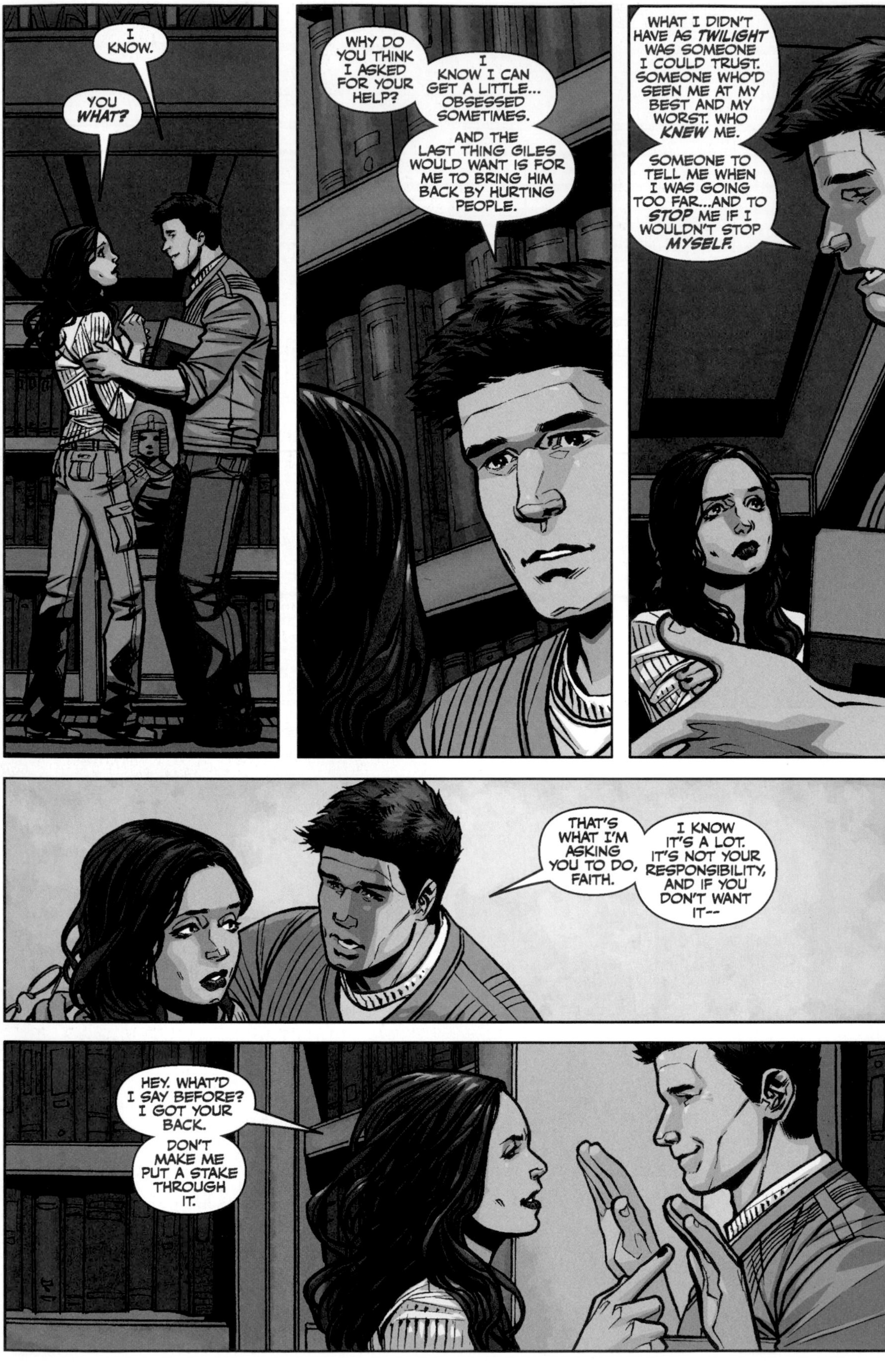
I KNOW.
YOU *WHAT?*
WHY DO YOU THINK I ASKED FOR YOUR HELP?
I KNOW I CAN GET A LITTLE... OBSESSED SOMETIMES.
AND THE LAST THING GILES WOULD WANT IS FOR ME TO BRING HIM BACK BY HURTING PEOPLE.
WHAT I DIDN'T HAVE AS *TWILIGHT* WAS SOMEONE I COULD TRUST. SOMEONE WHO'D SEEN ME AT MY BEST AND MY WORST. WHO *KNEW* ME.
SOMEONE TO TELL ME WHEN I WAS GOING TOO FAR...AND TO *STOP* ME IF I WOULDN'T STOP *MYSELF.*
THAT'S WHAT I'M ASKING YOU TO DO, FAITH.
I KNOW IT'S A LOT. IT'S NOT YOUR RESPONSIBILITY, AND IF YOU DON'T WANT IT--
HEY. WHAT'D I SAY BEFORE? I GOT YOUR BACK.
DON'T MAKE ME PUT A STAKE THROUGH IT.

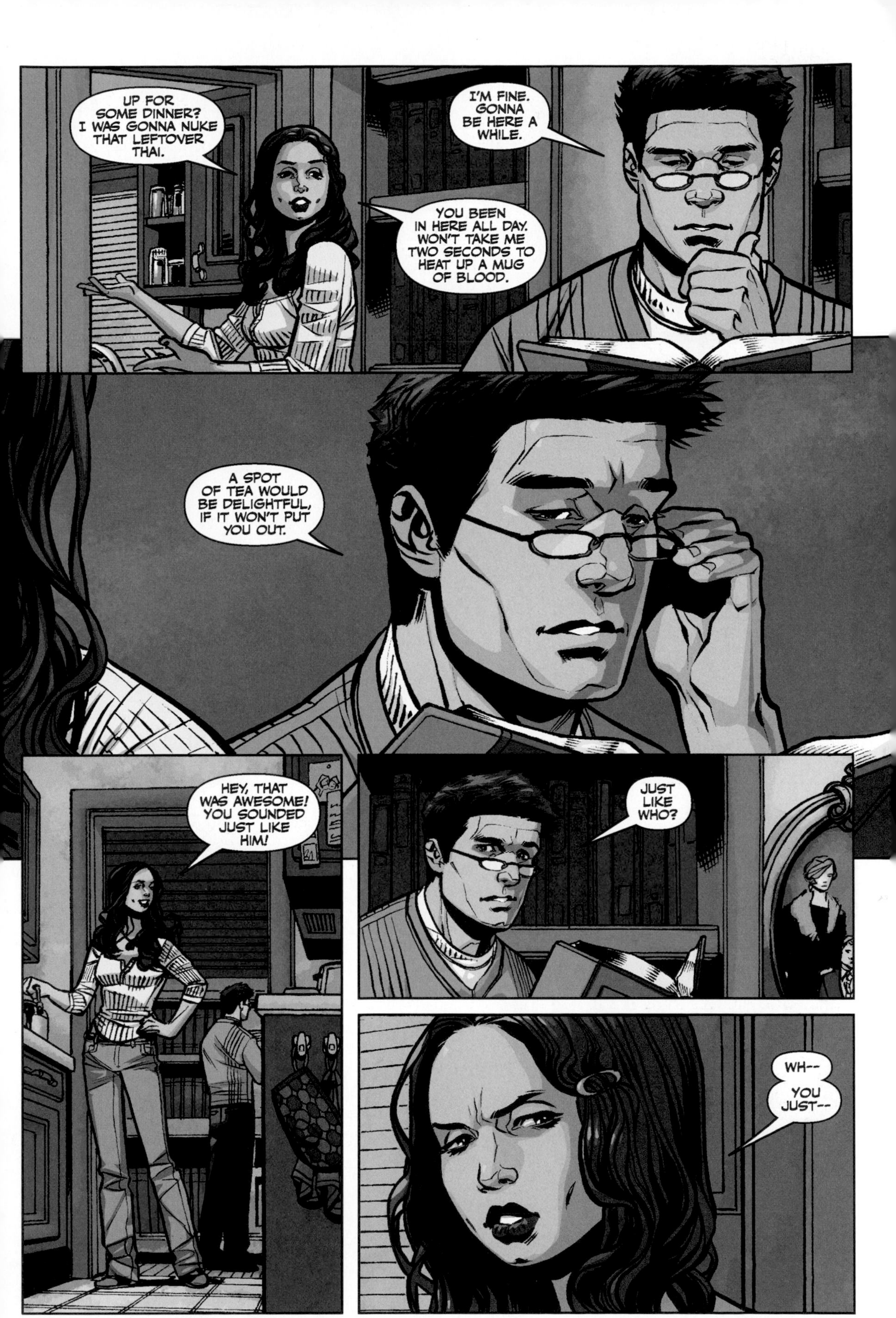
UP FOR SOME DINNER? I WAS GONNA NUKE THAT LEFTOVER THAI.
I'M FINE. GONNA BE HERE A WHILE.
YOU BEEN IN HERE ALL DAY. WON'T TAKE ME TWO SECONDS TO HEAT UP A MUG OF BLOOD.
A SPOT OF TEA WOULD BE DELIGHTFUL, IF IT WON'T PUT YOU OUT.
HEY, THAT WAS AWESOME! YOU SOUNDED JUST LIKE HIM!
JUST LIKE WHO?
WH--
YOU JUST--

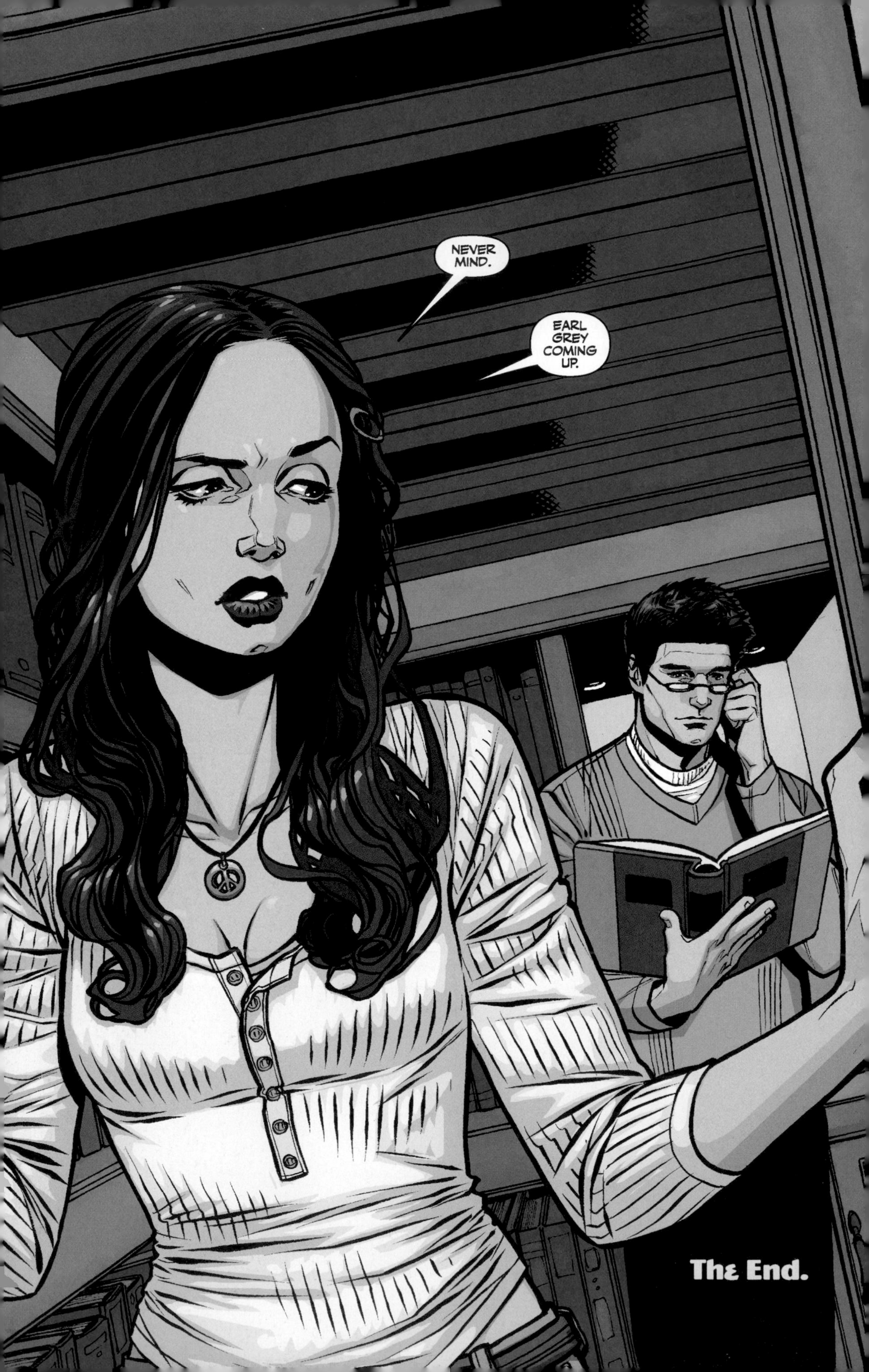
NEVER MIND.
EARL GREY COMING UP.
The End.

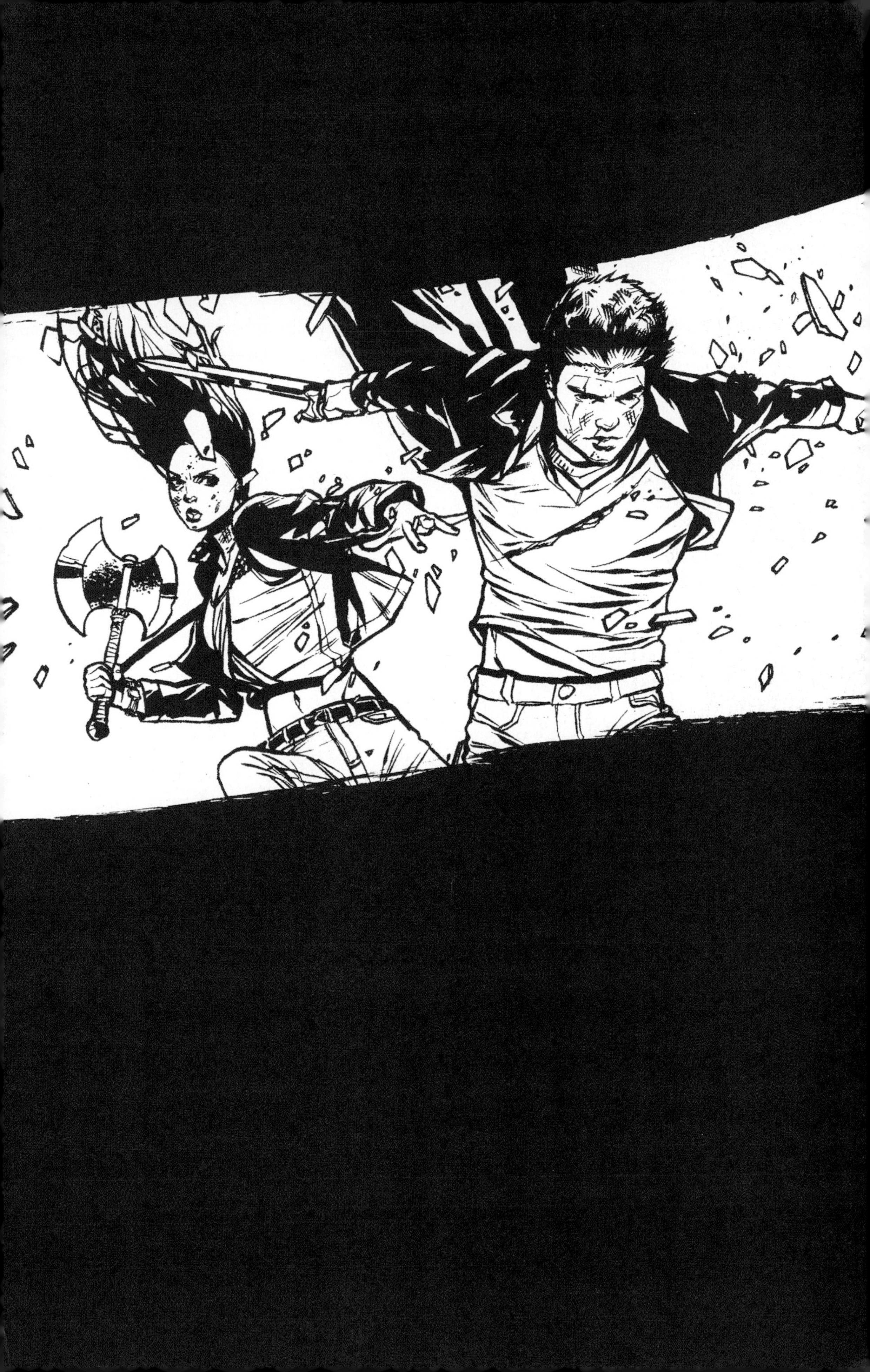

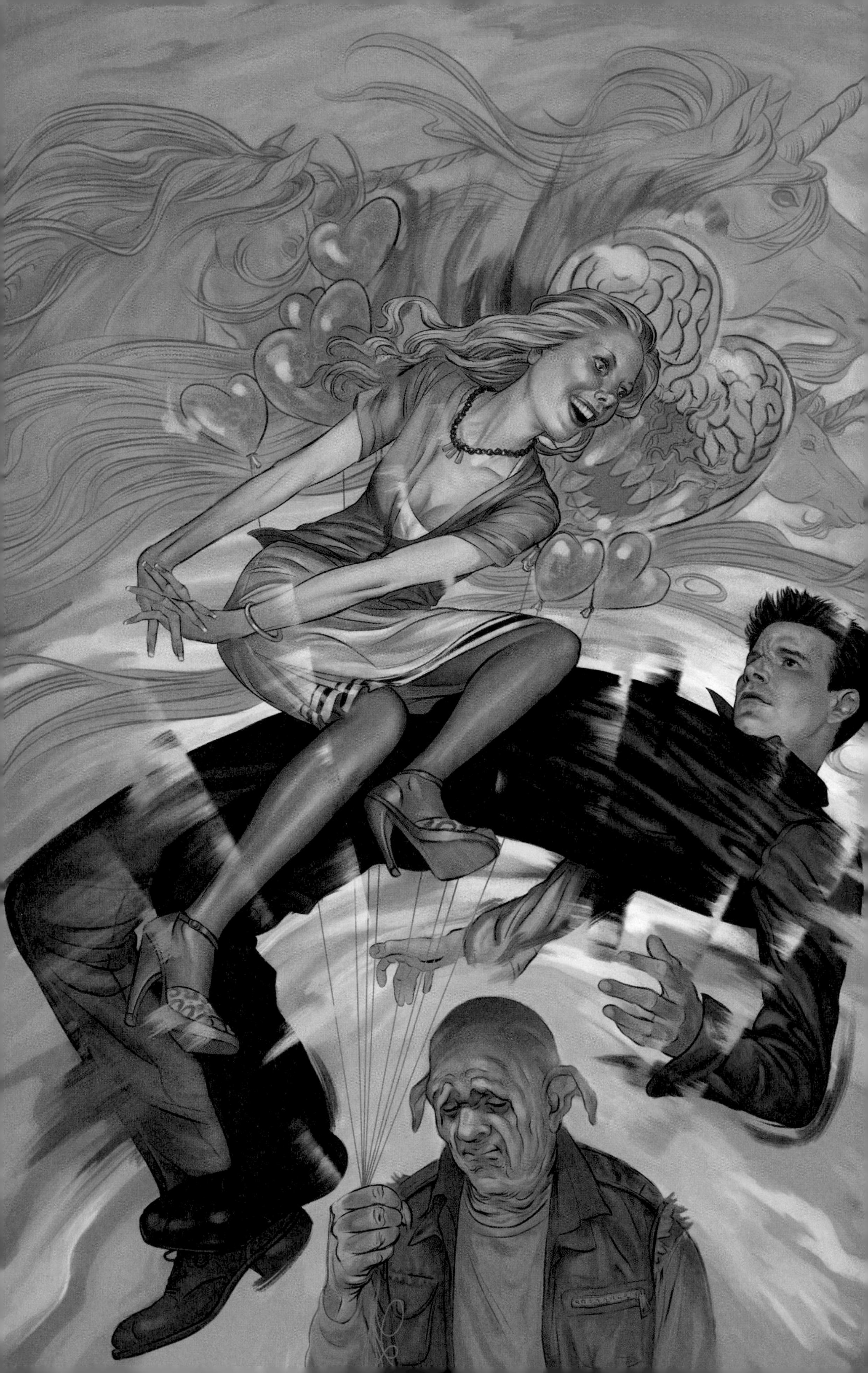

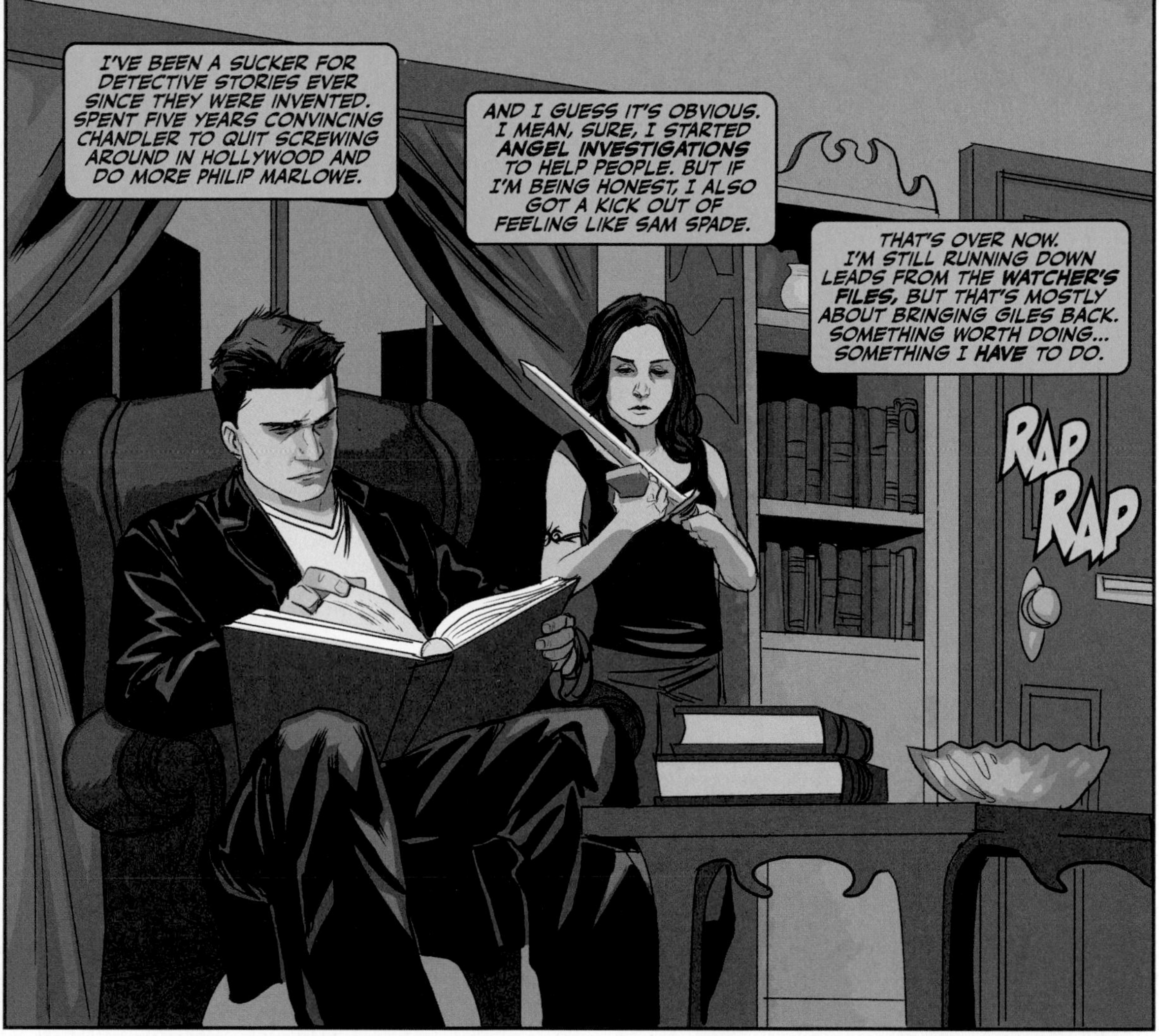
I'VE BEEN A SUCKER FOR DETECTIVE STORIES EVER SINCE THEY WERE INVENTED. SPENT FIVE YEARS CONVINCING CHANDLER TO QUIT SCREWING AROUND IN HOLLYWOOD AND DO MORE PHILIP MARLOWE.
AND I GUESS IT'S OBVIOUS. I MEAN, SURE, I STARTED **ANGEL INVESTIGATIONS** TO HELP PEOPLE. BUT IF I'M BEING HONEST, I ALSO GOT A KICK OUT OF FEELING LIKE SAM SPADE.
THAT'S OVER NOW. I'M STILL RUNNING DOWN LEADS FROM THE **WATCHER'S FILES,** BUT THAT'S MOSTLY ABOUT BRINGING GILES BACK. SOMETHING WORTH DOING... SOMETHING I **HAVE** TO DO.
RAP RAP

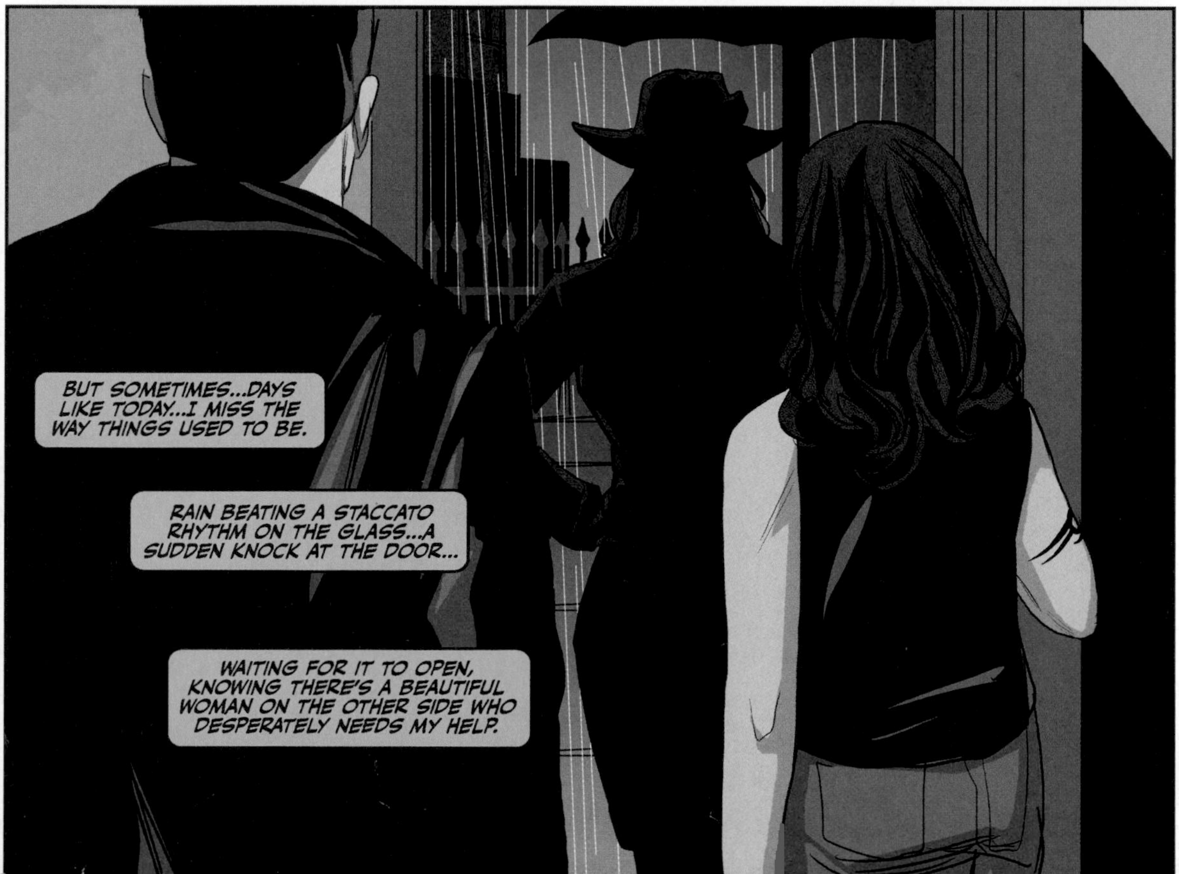
BUT SOMETIMES...DAYS LIKE TODAY...I MISS THE WAY THINGS USED TO BE.
RAIN BEATING A STACCATO RHYTHM ON THE GLASS...A SUDDEN KNOCK AT THE DOOR...
WAITING FOR IT TO OPEN, KNOWING THERE'S A BEAUTIFUL WOMAN ON THE OTHER SIDE WHO DESPERATELY NEEDS MY HELP.

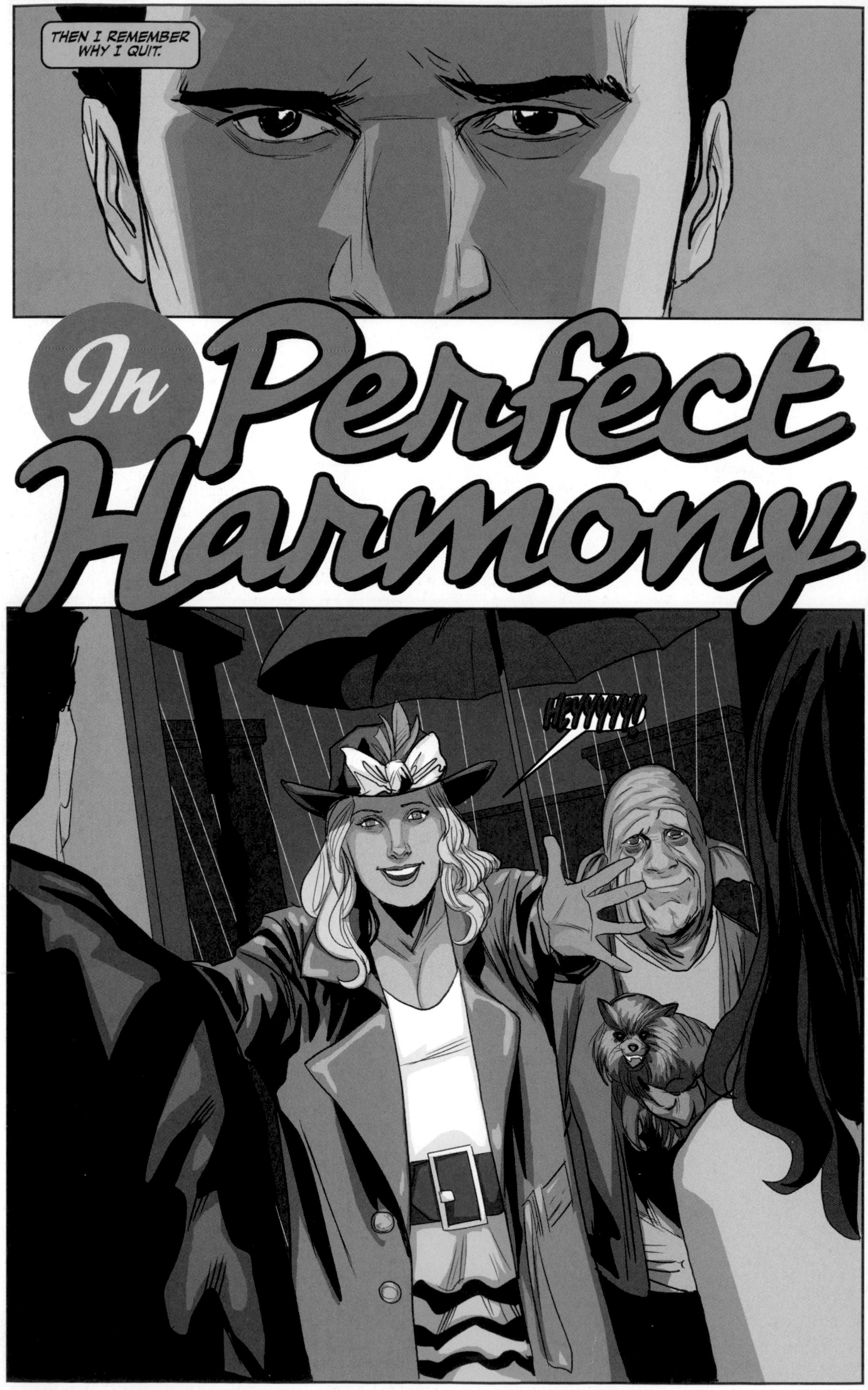
THEN I REMEMBER WHY I QUIT.
In Perfect Harmony
HEYYYYY!

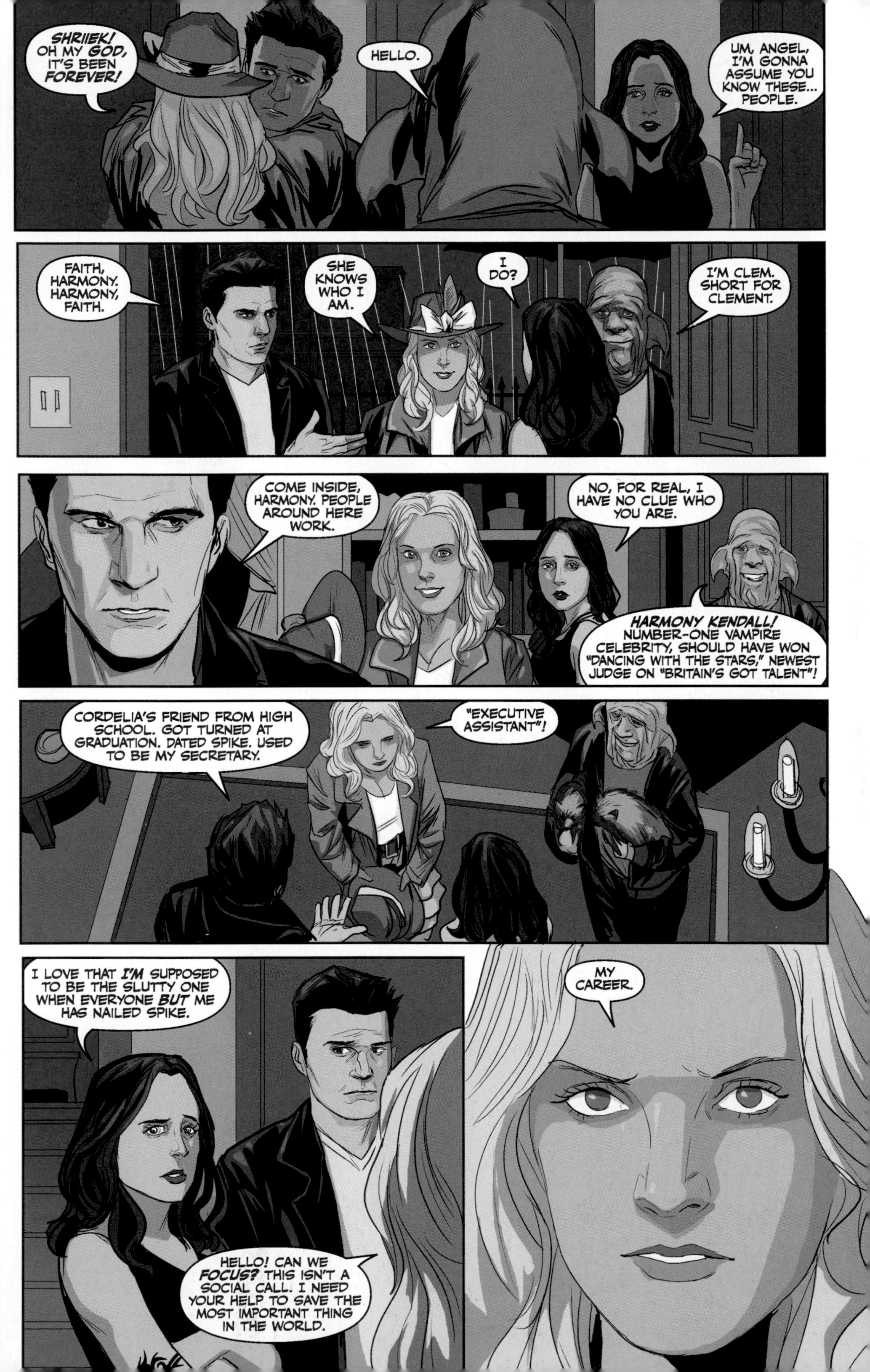
SHRIIEK! OH MY GOD, IT'S BEEN FOREVER!
HELLO.
UM, ANGEL, I'M GONNA ASSUME YOU KNOW THESE... PEOPLE.
FAITH, HARMONY. HARMONY, FAITH.
SHE KNOWS WHO I AM.
I DO?
I'M CLEM. SHORT FOR CLEMENT.
COME INSIDE, HARMONY. PEOPLE AROUND HERE WORK.
NO, FOR REAL, I HAVE NO CLUE WHO YOU ARE.
HARMONY KENDALL! NUMBER-ONE VAMPIRE CELEBRITY, SHOULD HAVE WON "DANCING WITH THE STARS," NEWEST JUDGE ON "BRITAIN'S GOT TALENT"!
CORDELIA'S FRIEND FROM HIGH SCHOOL. GOT TURNED AT GRADUATION. DATED SPIKE. USED TO BE MY SECRETARY.
"EXECUTIVE ASSISTANT"!
I LOVE THAT I'M SUPPOSED TO BE THE SLUTTY ONE WHEN EVERYONE BUT ME HAS NAILED SPIKE.
HELLO! CAN WE FOCUS? THIS ISN'T A SOCIAL CALL. I NEED YOUR HELP TO SAVE THE MOST IMPORTANT THING IN THE WORLD.
MY CAREER.

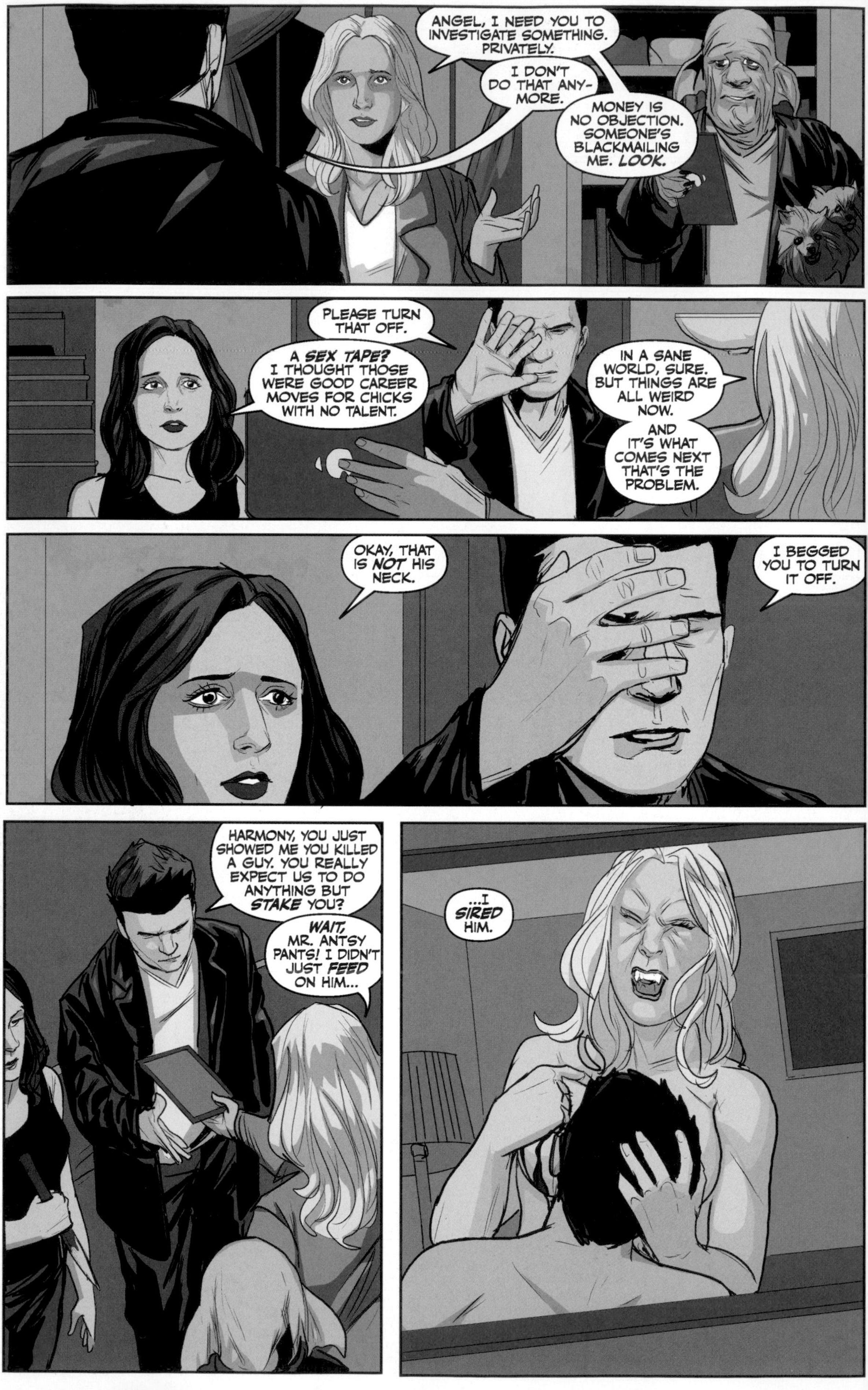
ANGEL, I NEED YOU TO INVESTIGATE SOMETHING. PRIVATELY.
I DON'T DO THAT ANY-MORE.
MONEY IS NO OBJECTION. SOMEONE'S BLACKMAILING ME. *LOOK.*
PLEASE TURN THAT OFF.
A *SEX TAPE?* I THOUGHT THOSE WERE GOOD CAREER MOVES FOR CHICKS WITH NO TALENT.
IN A SANE WORLD, SURE. BUT THINGS ARE ALL WEIRD NOW.
AND IT'S WHAT COMES NEXT THAT'S THE PROBLEM.
OKAY, THAT IS *NOT* HIS NECK.
I BEGGED YOU TO TURN IT OFF.
HARMONY, YOU JUST SHOWED ME YOU KILLED A GUY. YOU REALLY EXPECT US TO DO ANYTHING BUT *STAKE* YOU?
WAIT, MR. ANTSY PANTS! I DIDN'T JUST *FEED* ON HIM...
...I *SIRED* HIM.

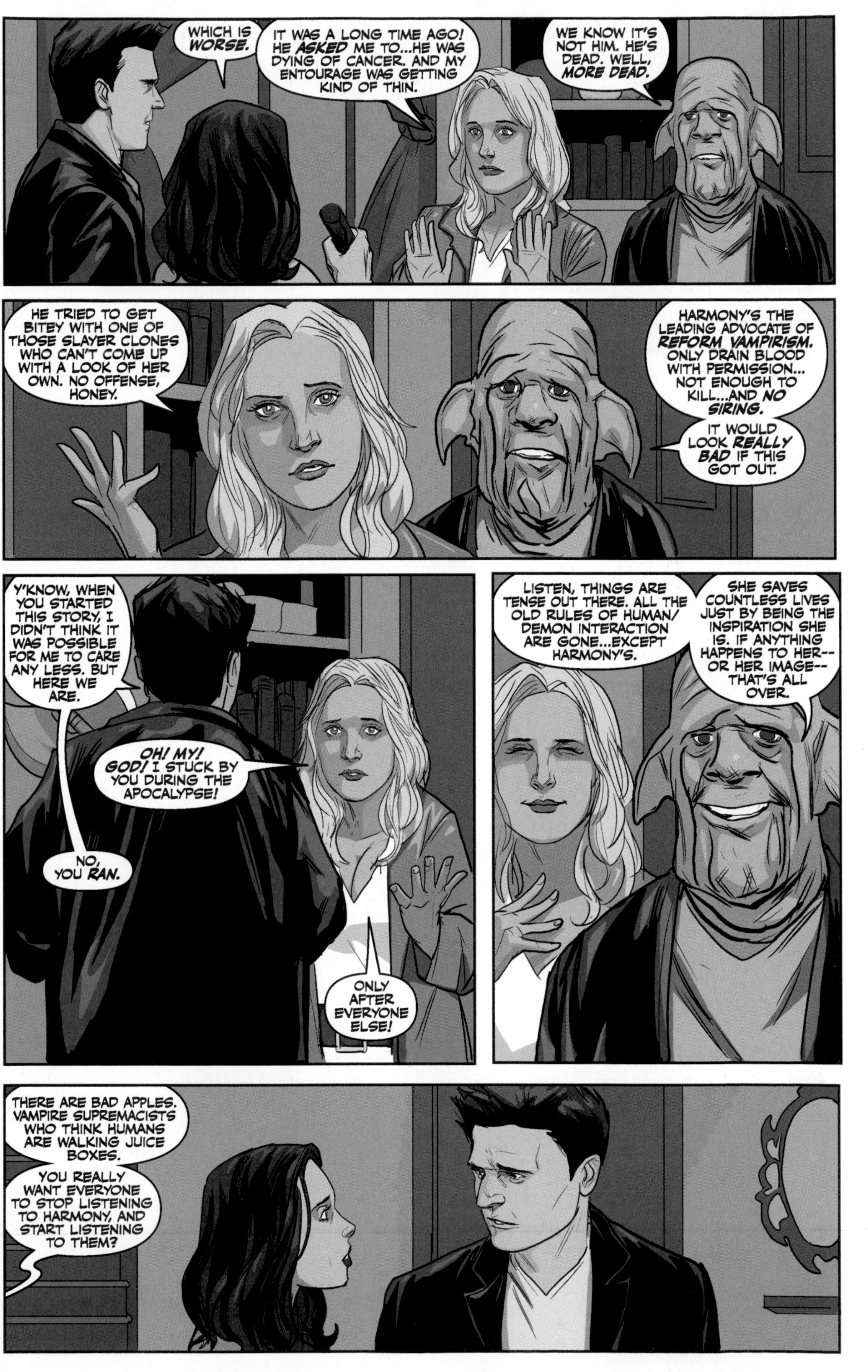
WHICH IS WORSE.
IT WAS A LONG TIME AGO! HE ASKED ME TO...HE WAS DYING OF CANCER. AND MY ENTOURAGE WAS GETTING KIND OF THIN.
WE KNOW IT'S NOT HIM. HE'S DEAD. WELL, MORE DEAD.
HE TRIED TO GET BITEY WITH ONE OF THOSE SLAYER CLONES WHO CAN'T COME UP WITH A LOOK OF HER OWN. NO OFFENSE, HONEY.
HARMONY'S THE LEADING ADVOCATE OF REFORM VAMPIRISM. ONLY DRAIN BLOOD WITH PERMISSION... NOT ENOUGH TO KILL...AND NO SIRING.
IT WOULD LOOK REALLY BAD IF THIS GOT OUT.
Y'KNOW, WHEN YOU STARTED THIS STORY, I DIDN'T THINK IT WAS POSSIBLE FOR ME TO CARE ANY LESS. BUT HERE WE ARE.
OH! MY! GOD! I STUCK BY YOU DURING THE APOCALYPSE!
NO, YOU RAN.
ONLY AFTER EVERYONE ELSE!
LISTEN, THINGS ARE TENSE OUT THERE. ALL THE OLD RULES OF HUMAN/ DEMON INTERACTION ARE GONE...EXCEPT HARMONY'S.
SHE SAVES COUNTLESS LIVES JUST BY BEING THE INSPIRATION SHE IS. IF ANYTHING HAPPENS TO HER-- OR HER IMAGE-- THAT'S ALL OVER.
THERE ARE BAD APPLES. VAMPIRE SUPREMACISTS WHO THINK HUMANS ARE WALKING JUICE BOXES.
YOU REALLY WANT EVERYONE TO STOP LISTENING TO HARMONY, AND START LISTENING TO THEM?

KENSINGTON. CASA DE HARMONY.

IT CAME IN THIS ENVELOPE.

NO POSTMARK...THEY'RE LOCAL. DID THIS GUY YOU SIRED HAVE FRIENDS, FAMILY...ANYONE WHO MIGHT GET THEIR HANDS ON HIS VIDEOTAPES?

IT CAME ON A *FLASH DRIVE*, GRANDPA.

AND IT'S NOT HIS, IT'S MINE. IT WAS WHEN MY REALITY SHOW GOT CANCELED...I THOUGHT I MIGHT NEED A GOOD SCANDAL TO STAY IN THE ZEITGEIST.

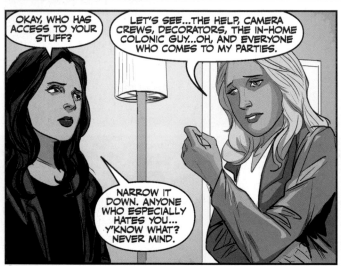

OKAY, WHO HAS ACCESS TO YOUR STUFF?

LET'S SEE...THE HELP, CAMERA CREWS, DECORATORS, THE IN-HOME COLONIC GUY...OH, AND EVERYONE WHO COMES TO MY PARTIES.

NARROW IT DOWN. ANYONE WHO ESPECIALLY HATES YOU... Y'KNOW WHAT? NEVER MIND.

LET'S CONSIDER WHO BENEFITS. CLEM MAY HAVE BEEN ON TO SOMETHING WHEN HE MENTIONED VAMPIRE SUPREMACISTS. THEY CONSIDER HER A TRAITOR.

IF YOU SQUEEZE HER FOR CASH AND RELEASE THE TAPE ANYWAY, YOU KILL TWO BIRDS.

I LOVE WATCHING YOU GUYS WORK. YOU'RE LIKE OLIVIA AND ELLIOT ON *S.V.U.* CALL ME A ROMANTIC, BUT I ALWAYS THOUGHT THOSE TWO SHOULD END UP TOGETHER.

HARM GETS A LOT OF HATE MAIL. I SAVE IT, JUST IN CASE... HERE.

SAME KIND OF ENVELOPE. NO POSTMARK.

AND THESE DAYS, VAMPIRES WHO STILL SIRE PEOPLE AREN'T HARD TO TRACK DOWN.

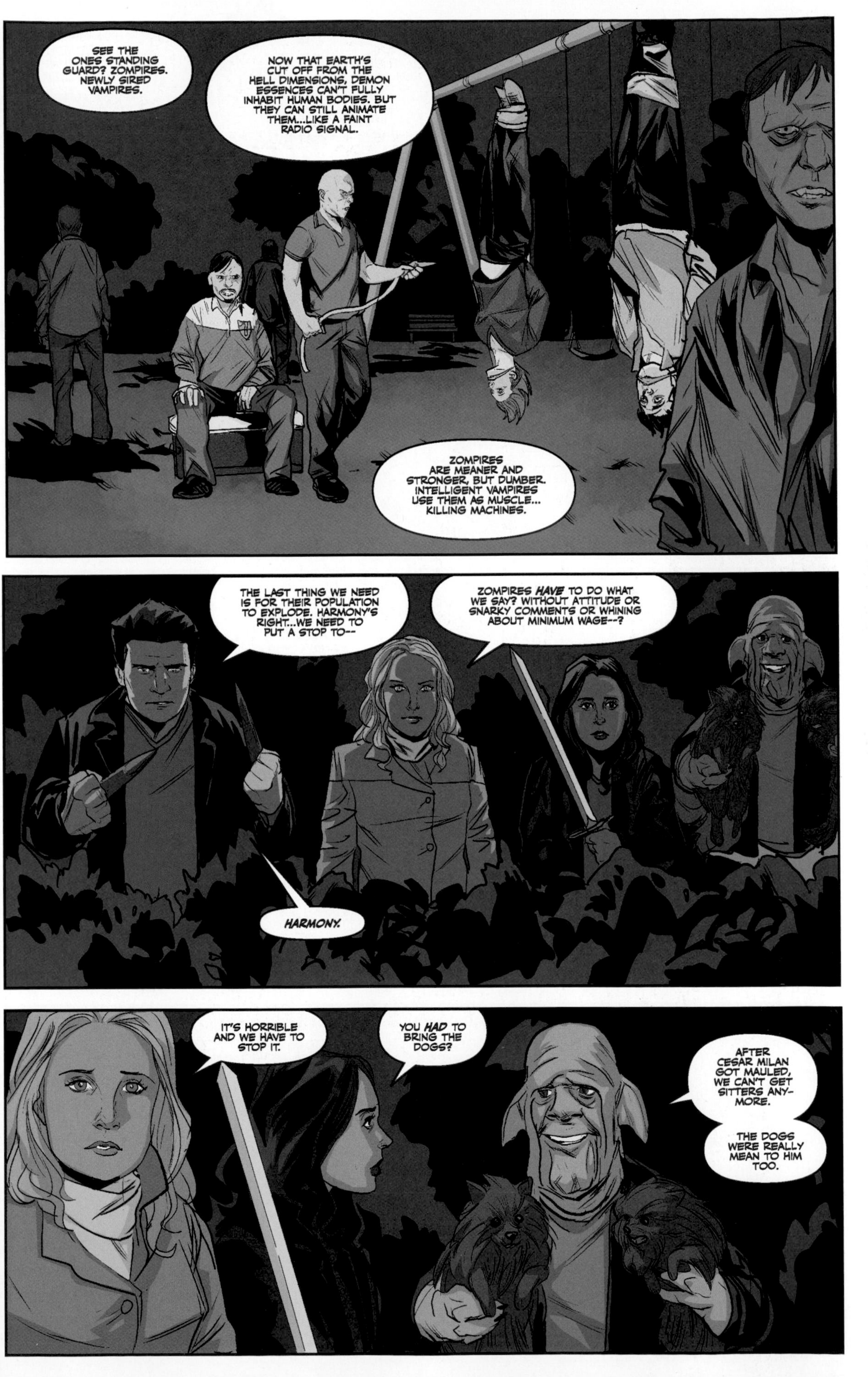
SEE THE ONES STANDING GUARD? ZOMPIRES. NEWLY SIRED VAMPIRES.
NOW THAT EARTH'S CUT OFF FROM THE HELL DIMENSIONS, DEMON ESSENCES CAN'T FULLY INHABIT HUMAN BODIES. BUT THEY CAN STILL ANIMATE THEM...LIKE A FAINT RADIO SIGNAL.
ZOMPIRES ARE MEANER AND STRONGER, BUT DUMBER. INTELLIGENT VAMPIRES USE THEM AS MUSCLE... KILLING MACHINES.
THE LAST THING WE NEED IS FOR THEIR POPULATION TO EXPLODE. HARMONY'S RIGHT...WE NEED TO PUT A STOP TO--
ZOMPIRES *HAVE* TO DO WHAT WE SAY? WITHOUT ATTITUDE OR SNARKY COMMENTS OR WHINING ABOUT MINIMUM WAGE--?
HARMONY.
IT'S HORRIBLE AND WE HAVE TO STOP IT.
YOU *HAD* TO BRING THE DOGS?
AFTER CESAR MILAN GOT MAULED, WE CAN'T GET SITTERS ANY-MORE.
THE DOGS WERE REALLY MEAN TO HIM TOO.

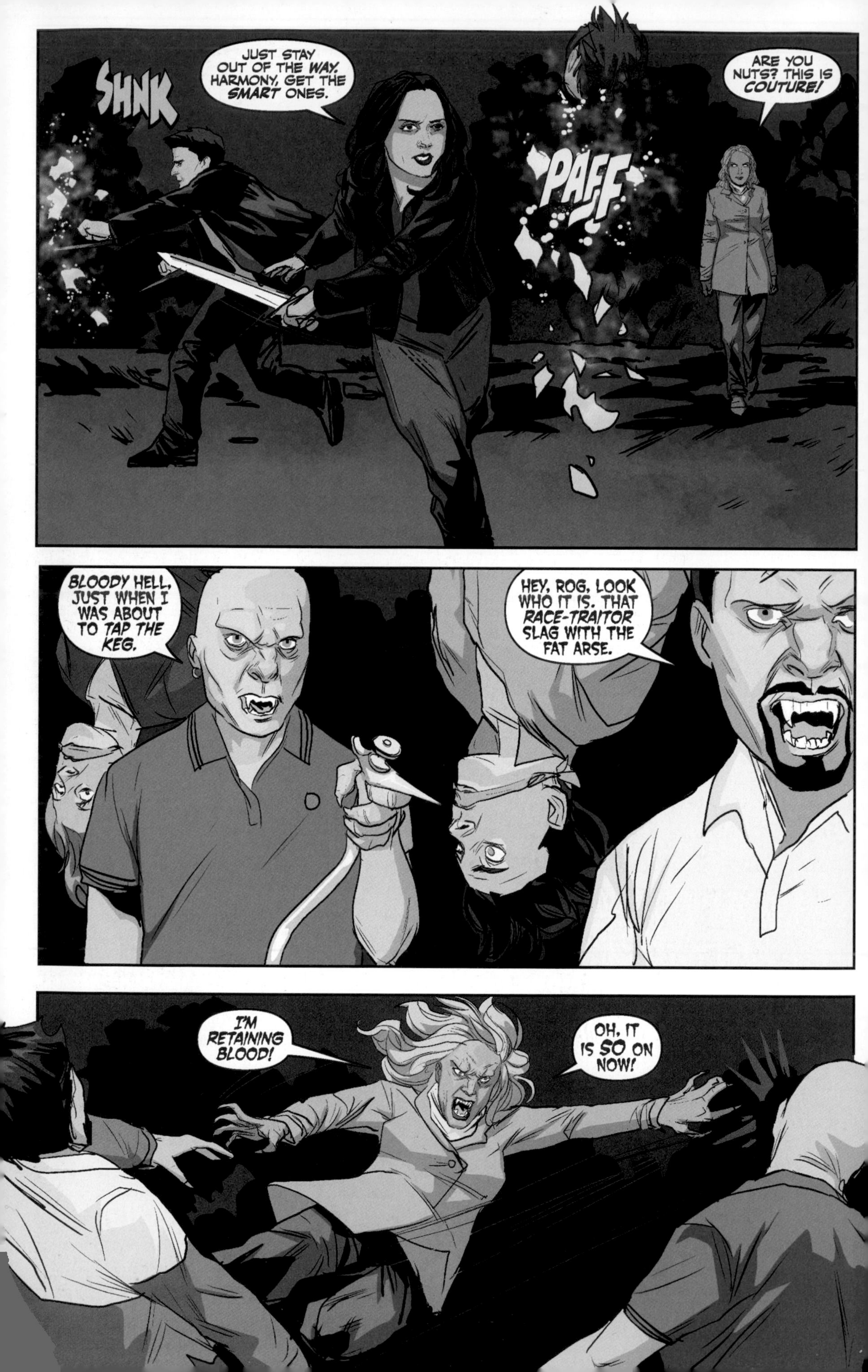
SHNK
JUST STAY OUT OF THE WAY. HARMONY, GET THE SMART ONES.
ARE YOU NUTS? THIS IS COUTURE!
PAFF
BLOODY HELL, JUST WHEN I WAS ABOUT TO TAP THE KEG.
HEY, ROG, LOOK WHO IT IS. THAT RACE-TRAITOR SLAG WITH THE FAT ARSE.
I'M RETAINING BLOOD!
OH, IT IS SO ON NOW!

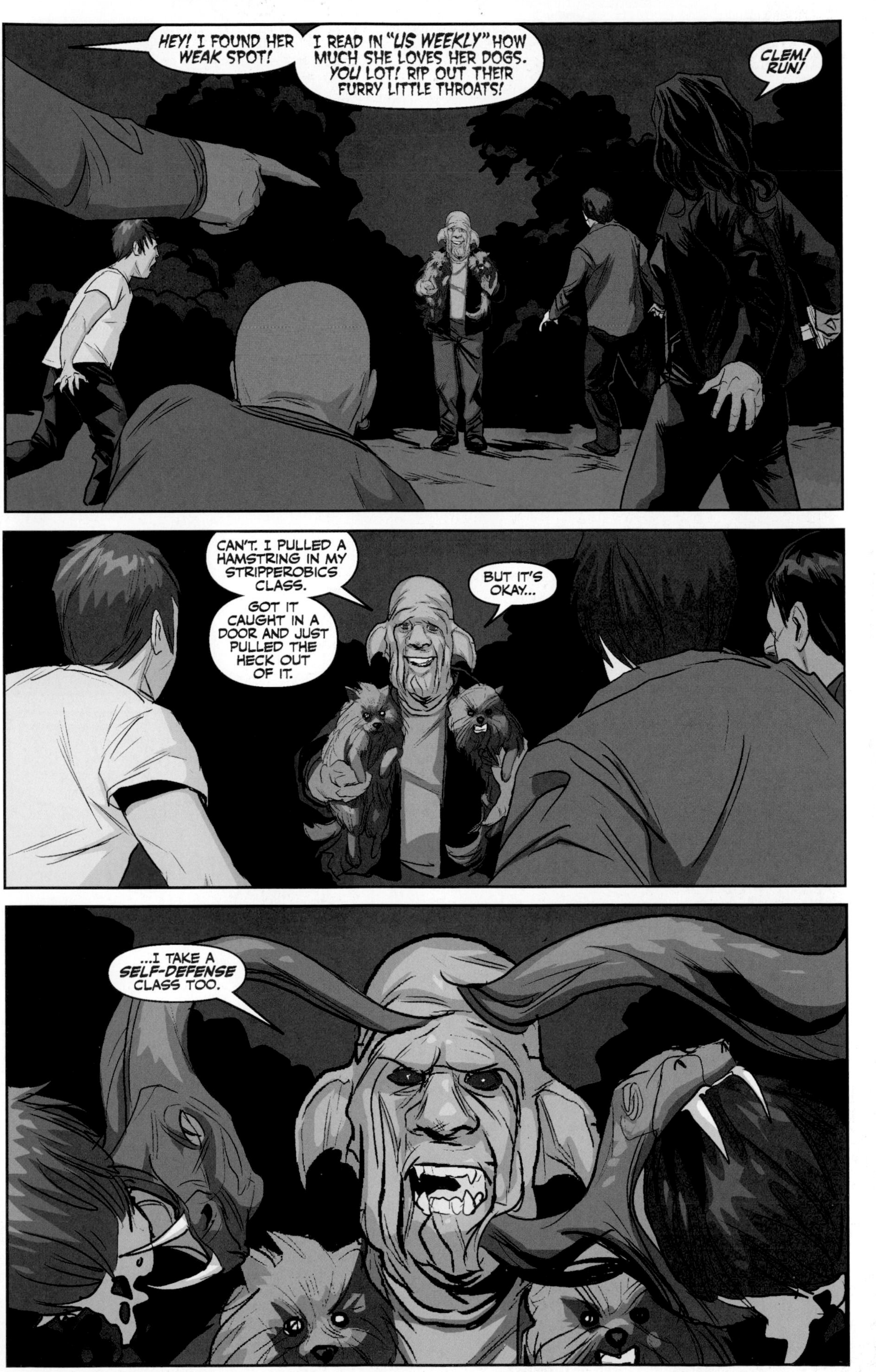
HEY! I FOUND HER WEAK SPOT!
I READ IN "US WEEKLY" HOW MUCH SHE LOVES HER DOGS. YOU LOT! RIP OUT THEIR FURRY LITTLE THROATS!
CLEM! RUN!
CAN'T. I PULLED A HAMSTRING IN MY STRIPPEROBICS CLASS.
GOT IT CAUGHT IN A DOOR AND JUST PULLED THE HECK OUT OF IT.
BUT IT'S OKAY...
...I TAKE A SELF-DEFENSE CLASS TOO.

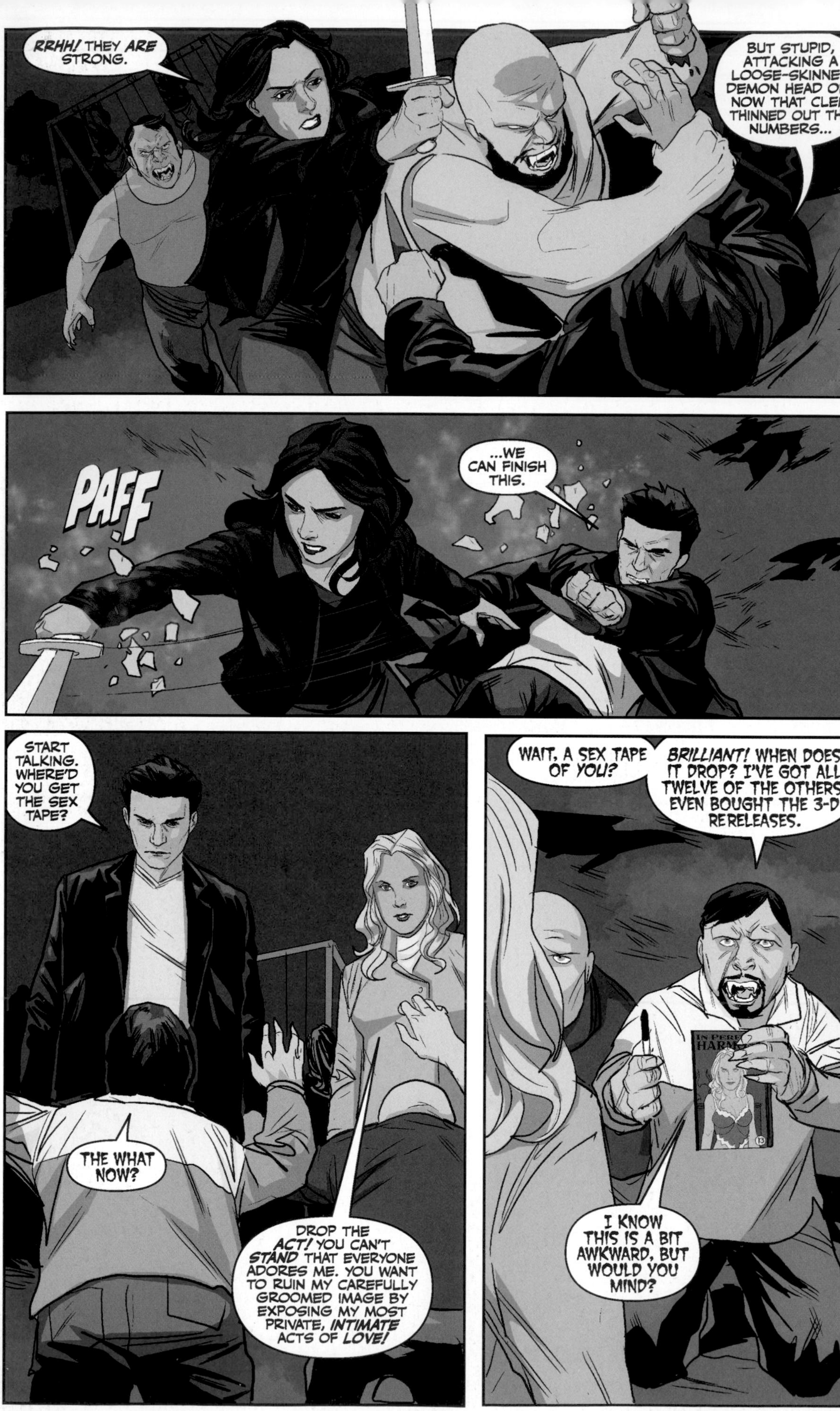
RRHH! THEY ARE STRONG.
BUT STUPID, ATTACKING A LOOSE-SKINNED DEMON HEAD ON. NOW THAT CLEM THINNED OUT THE NUMBERS...
PAFF
...WE CAN FINISH THIS.
START TALKING. WHERE'D YOU GET THE SEX TAPE?
THE WHAT NOW?
DROP THE ACT! YOU CAN'T STAND THAT EVERYONE ADORES ME. YOU WANT TO RUIN MY CAREFULLY GROOMED IMAGE BY EXPOSING MY MOST PRIVATE, INTIMATE ACTS OF LOVE!
WAIT, A SEX TAPE OF YOU?
BRILLIANT! WHEN DOES IT DROP? I'VE GOT ALL TWELVE OF THE OTHERS. EVEN BOUGHT THE 3-D RERELEASES.
I KNOW THIS IS A BIT AWKWARD, BUT WOULD YOU MIND?

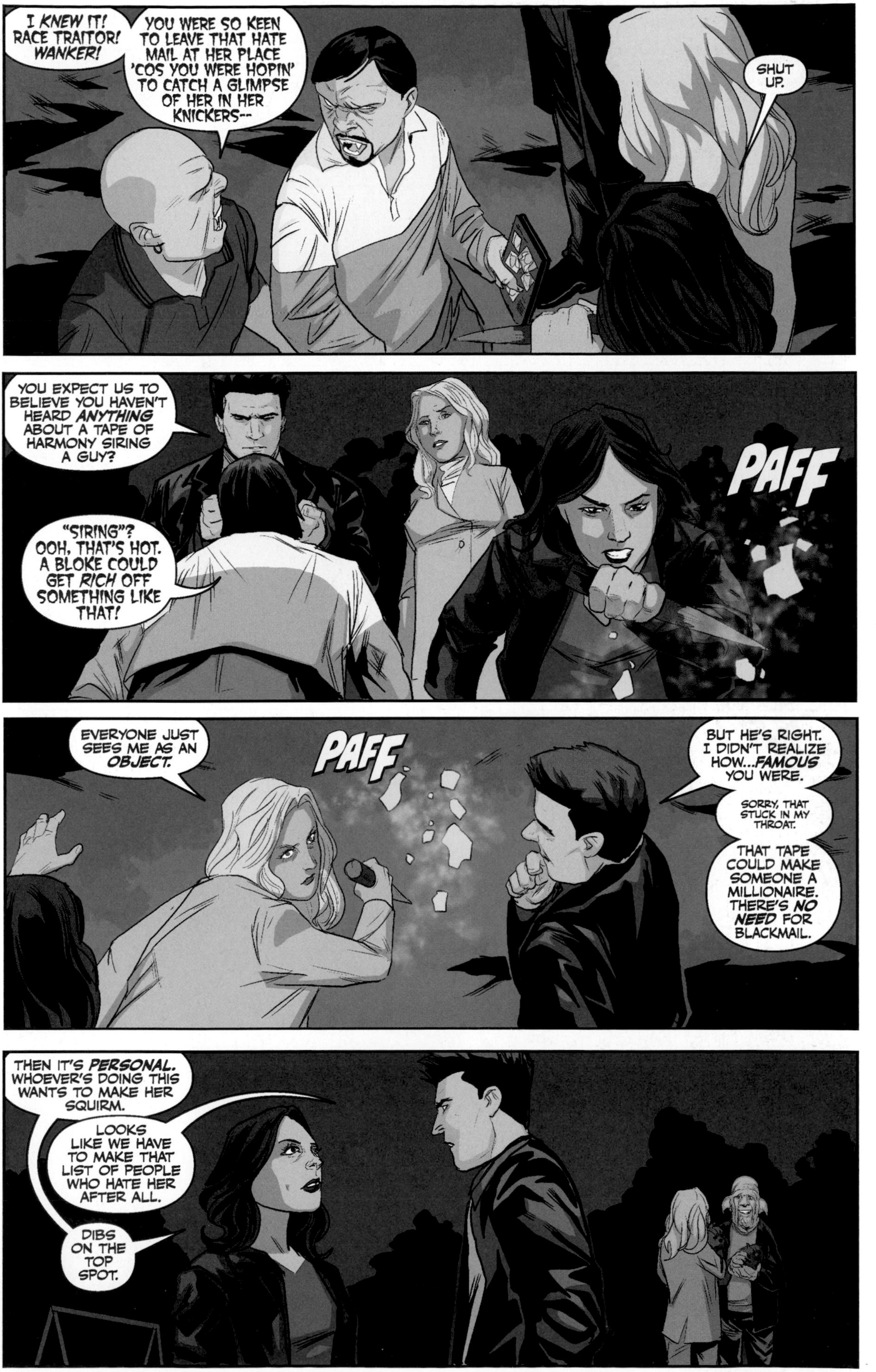
I KNEW IT! RACE TRAITOR! WANKER!
YOU WERE SO KEEN TO LEAVE THAT HATE MAIL AT HER PLACE 'COS YOU WERE HOPIN' TO CATCH A GLIMPSE OF HER IN HER KNICKERS--
SHUT UP.
YOU EXPECT US TO BELIEVE YOU HAVEN'T HEARD ANYTHING ABOUT A TAPE OF HARMONY SIRING A GUY?
"SIRING"? OOH, THAT'S HOT. A BLOKE COULD GET RICH OFF SOMETHING LIKE THAT!
PAFF
EVERYONE JUST SEES ME AS AN OBJECT.
PAFF
BUT HE'S RIGHT. I DIDN'T REALIZE HOW...FAMOUS YOU WERE.
SORRY, THAT STUCK IN MY THROAT.
THAT TAPE COULD MAKE SOMEONE A MILLIONAIRE. THERE'S NO NEED FOR BLACKMAIL.
THEN IT'S PERSONAL. WHOEVER'S DOING THIS WANTS TO MAKE HER SQUIRM.
LOOKS LIKE WE HAVE TO MAKE THAT LIST OF PEOPLE WHO HATE HER AFTER ALL.
DIBS ON THE TOP SPOT.

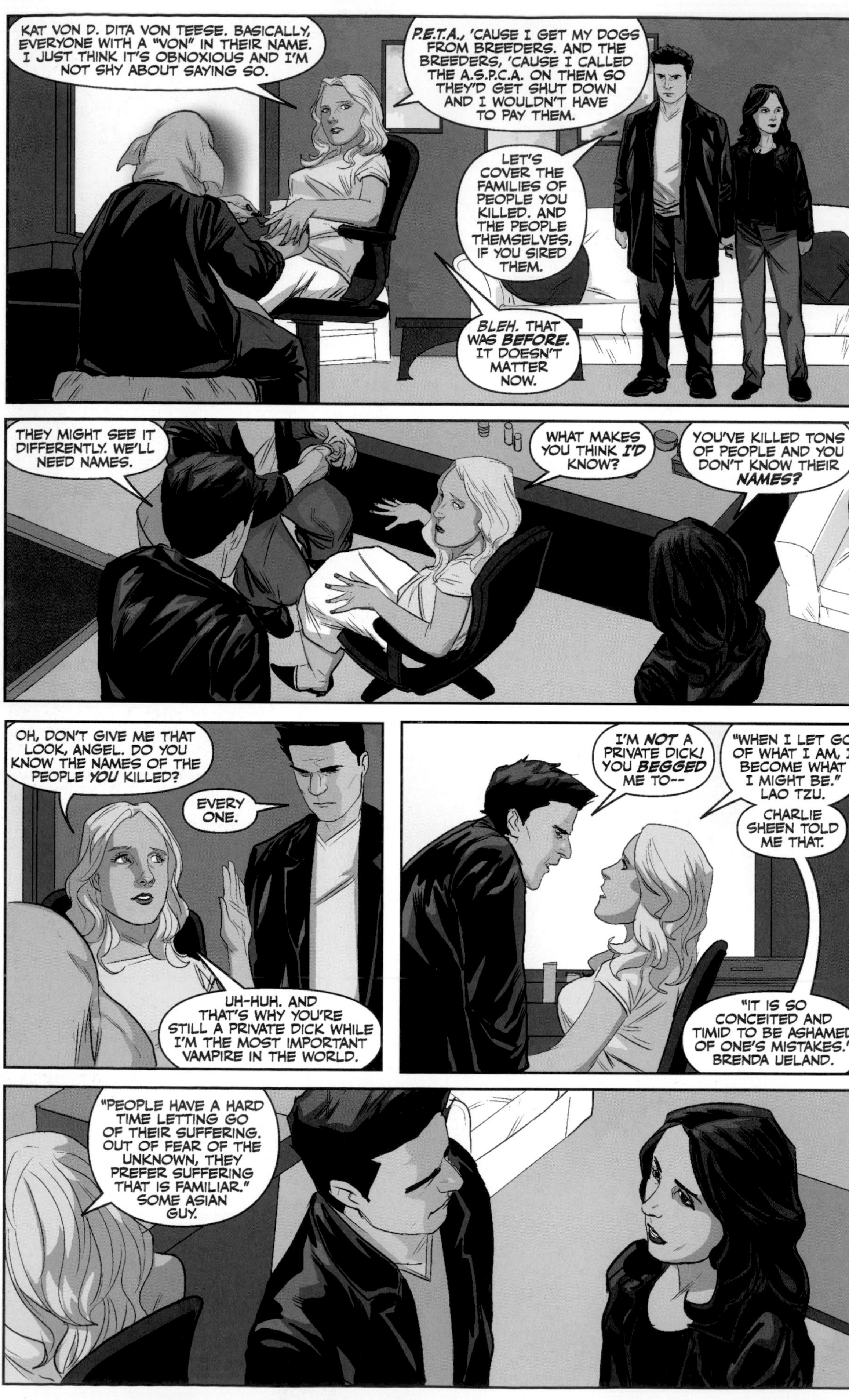
KAT VON D. DITA VON TEESE. BASICALLY, EVERYONE WITH A "VON" IN THEIR NAME. I JUST THINK IT'S OBNOXIOUS AND I'M NOT SHY ABOUT SAYING SO.
P.E.T.A., 'CAUSE I GET MY DOGS FROM BREEDERS. AND THE BREEDERS, 'CAUSE I CALLED THE A.S.P.C.A. ON THEM SO THEY'D GET SHUT DOWN AND I WOULDN'T HAVE TO PAY THEM.
LET'S COVER THE FAMILIES OF PEOPLE YOU KILLED. AND THE PEOPLE THEMSELVES, IF YOU SIRED THEM.
BLEH. THAT WAS BEFORE. IT DOESN'T MATTER NOW.
THEY MIGHT SEE IT DIFFERENTLY. WE'LL NEED NAMES.
WHAT MAKES YOU THINK I'D KNOW?
YOU'VE KILLED TONS OF PEOPLE AND YOU DON'T KNOW THEIR NAMES?
OH, DON'T GIVE ME THAT LOOK, ANGEL. DO YOU KNOW THE NAMES OF THE PEOPLE YOU KILLED?
EVERY ONE.
UH-HUH. AND THAT'S WHY YOU'RE STILL A PRIVATE DICK WHILE I'M THE MOST IMPORTANT VAMPIRE IN THE WORLD.
I'M NOT A PRIVATE DICK! YOU BEGGED ME TO--
"WHEN I LET GO OF WHAT I AM, I BECOME WHAT I MIGHT BE." LAO TZU.
CHARLIE SHEEN TOLD ME THAT.
"IT IS SO CONCEITED AND TIMID TO BE ASHAMED OF ONE'S MISTAKES." BRENDA UELAND.
"PEOPLE HAVE A HARD TIME LETTING GO OF THEIR SUFFERING. OUT OF FEAR OF THE UNKNOWN, THEY PREFER SUFFERING THAT IS FAMILIAR." SOME ASIAN GUY.

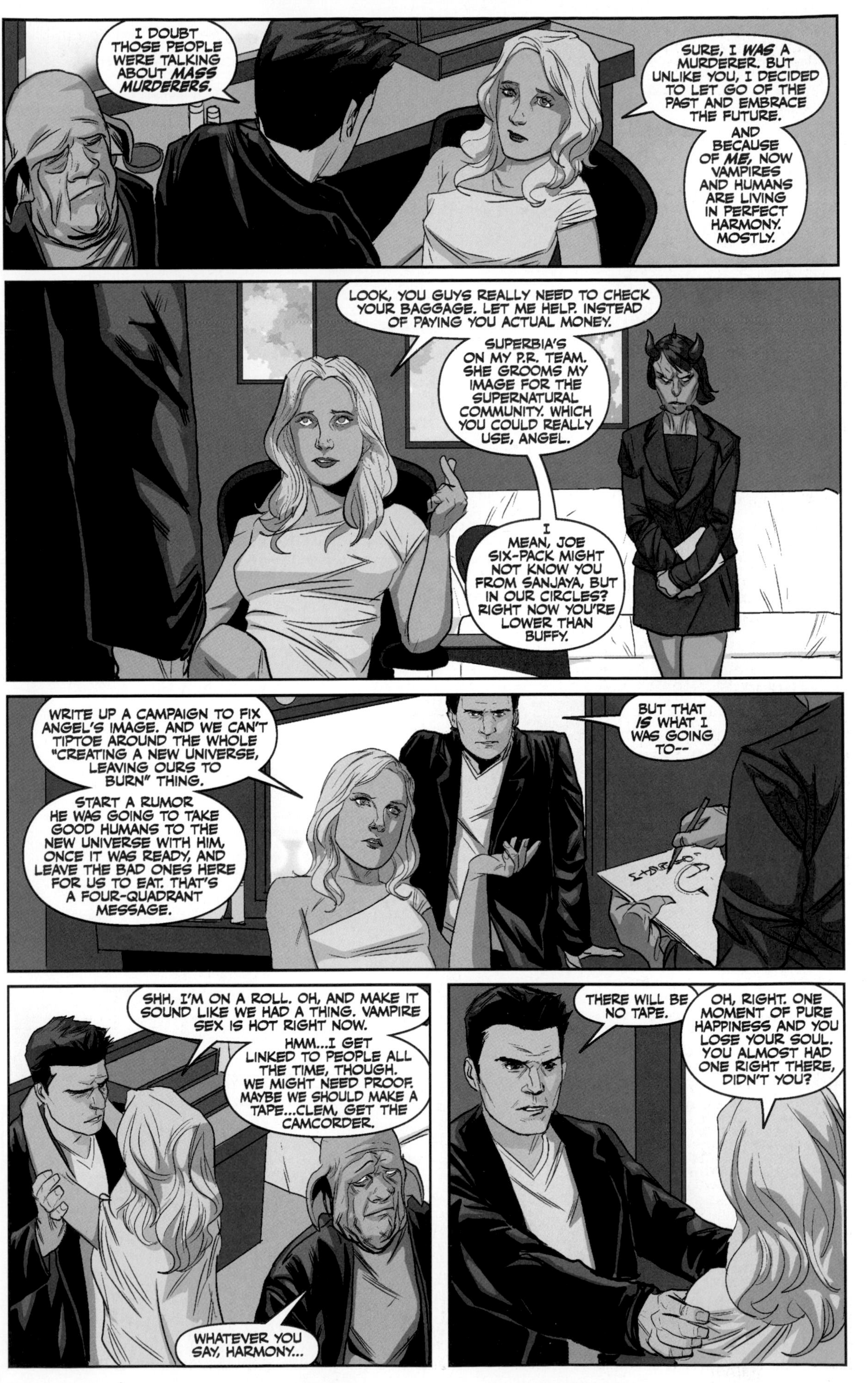
I DOUBT THOSE PEOPLE WERE TALKING ABOUT MASS MURDERERS.
SURE, I WAS A MURDERER. BUT UNLIKE YOU, I DECIDED TO LET GO OF THE PAST AND EMBRACE THE FUTURE.
AND BECAUSE OF ME, NOW VAMPIRES AND HUMANS ARE LIVING IN PERFECT HARMONY. MOSTLY.
LOOK, YOU GUYS REALLY NEED TO CHECK YOUR BAGGAGE. LET ME HELP. INSTEAD OF PAYING YOU ACTUAL MONEY.
SUPERBIA'S ON MY P.R. TEAM. SHE GROOMS MY IMAGE FOR THE SUPERNATURAL COMMUNITY. WHICH YOU COULD REALLY USE, ANGEL.
I MEAN, JOE SIX-PACK MIGHT NOT KNOW YOU FROM SANJAYA, BUT IN OUR CIRCLES? RIGHT NOW YOU'RE LOWER THAN BUFFY.
WRITE UP A CAMPAIGN TO FIX ANGEL'S IMAGE. AND WE CAN'T TIPTOE AROUND THE WHOLE "CREATING A NEW UNIVERSE, LEAVING OURS TO BURN" THING.
START A RUMOR HE WAS GOING TO TAKE GOOD HUMANS TO THE NEW UNIVERSE WITH HIM, ONCE IT WAS READY, AND LEAVE THE BAD ONES HERE FOR US TO EAT. THAT'S A FOUR-QUADRANT MESSAGE.
BUT THAT IS WHAT I WAS GOING TO--
SHH, I'M ON A ROLL. OH, AND MAKE IT SOUND LIKE WE HAD A THING. VAMPIRE SEX IS HOT RIGHT NOW.
HMM...I GET LINKED TO PEOPLE ALL THE TIME, THOUGH. WE MIGHT NEED PROOF. MAYBE WE SHOULD MAKE A TAPE...CLEM, GET THE CAMCORDER.
WHATEVER YOU SAY, HARMONY...
THERE WILL BE NO TAPE.
OH, RIGHT. ONE MOMENT OF PURE HAPPINESS AND YOU LOSE YOUR SOUL. YOU ALMOST HAD ONE RIGHT THERE, DIDN'T YOU?

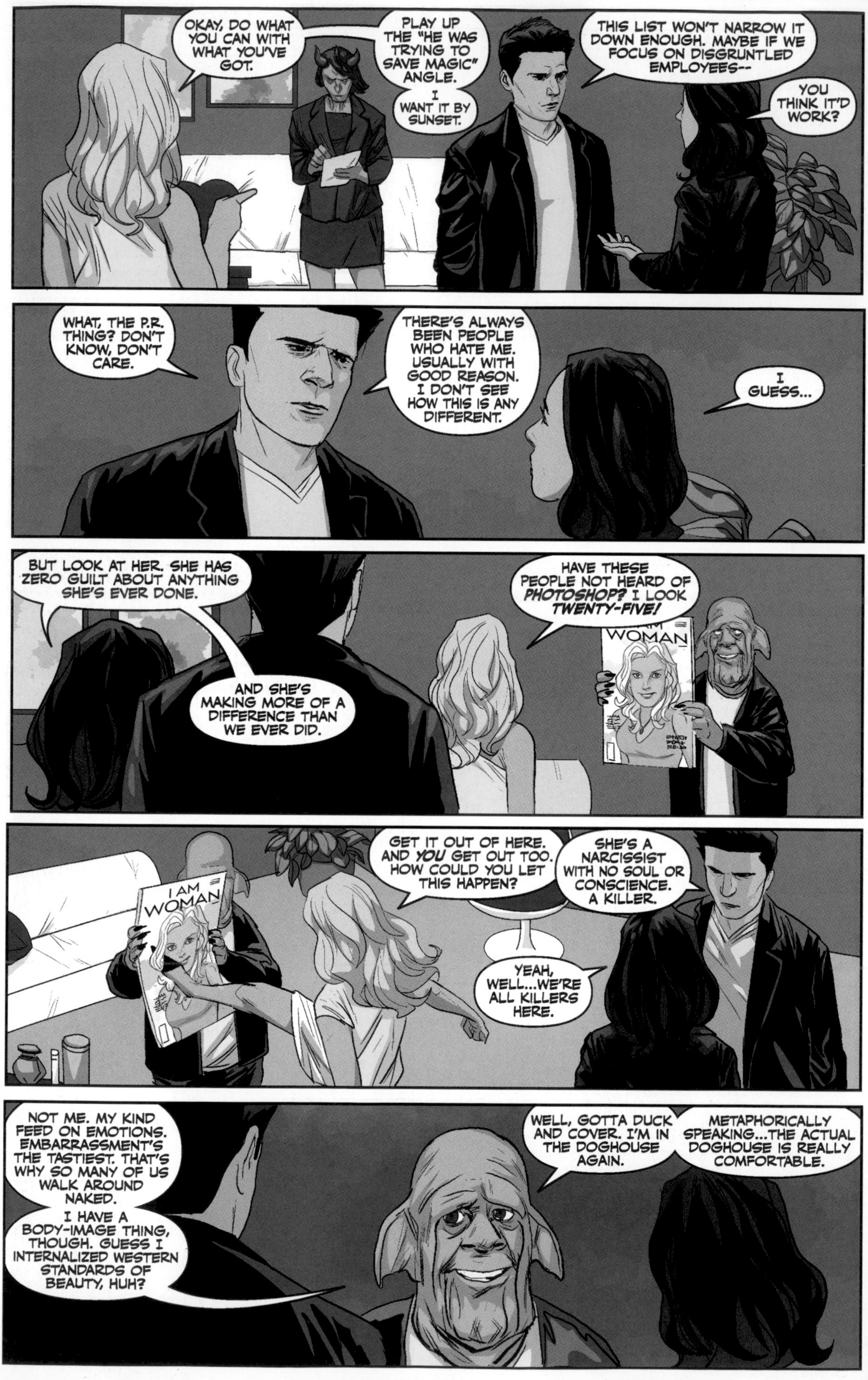
OKAY, DO WHAT YOU CAN WITH WHAT YOU'VE GOT.
PLAY UP THE "HE WAS TRYING TO SAVE MAGIC" ANGLE.
I WANT IT BY SUNSET.
THIS LIST WON'T NARROW IT DOWN ENOUGH. MAYBE IF WE FOCUS ON DISGRUNTLED EMPLOYEES--
YOU THINK IT'D WORK?
WHAT, THE P.R. THING? DON'T KNOW, DON'T CARE.
THERE'S ALWAYS BEEN PEOPLE WHO HATE ME. USUALLY WITH GOOD REASON. I DON'T SEE HOW THIS IS ANY DIFFERENT.
I GUESS...
BUT LOOK AT HER. SHE HAS ZERO GUILT ABOUT ANYTHING SHE'S EVER DONE.
AND SHE'S MAKING MORE OF A DIFFERENCE THAN WE EVER DID.
HAVE THESE PEOPLE NOT HEARD OF *PHOTOSHOP?* I LOOK ***TWENTY-FIVE!***
I AM WOMAN
GET IT OUT OF HERE. AND *YOU* GET OUT TOO. HOW COULD YOU LET THIS HAPPEN?
SHE'S A NARCISSIST WITH NO SOUL OR CONSCIENCE. A KILLER.
YEAH, WELL...WE'RE ALL KILLERS HERE.
NOT ME. MY KIND FEED ON EMOTIONS. EMBARRASSMENT'S THE TASTIEST. THAT'S WHY SO MANY OF US WALK AROUND NAKED.
I HAVE A BODY-IMAGE THING, THOUGH. GUESS I INTERNALIZED WESTERN STANDARDS OF BEAUTY, HUH?
WELL, GOTTA DUCK AND COVER. I'M IN THE DOGHOUSE AGAIN.
METAPHORICALLY SPEAKING...THE ACTUAL DOGHOUSE IS REALLY COMFORTABLE.

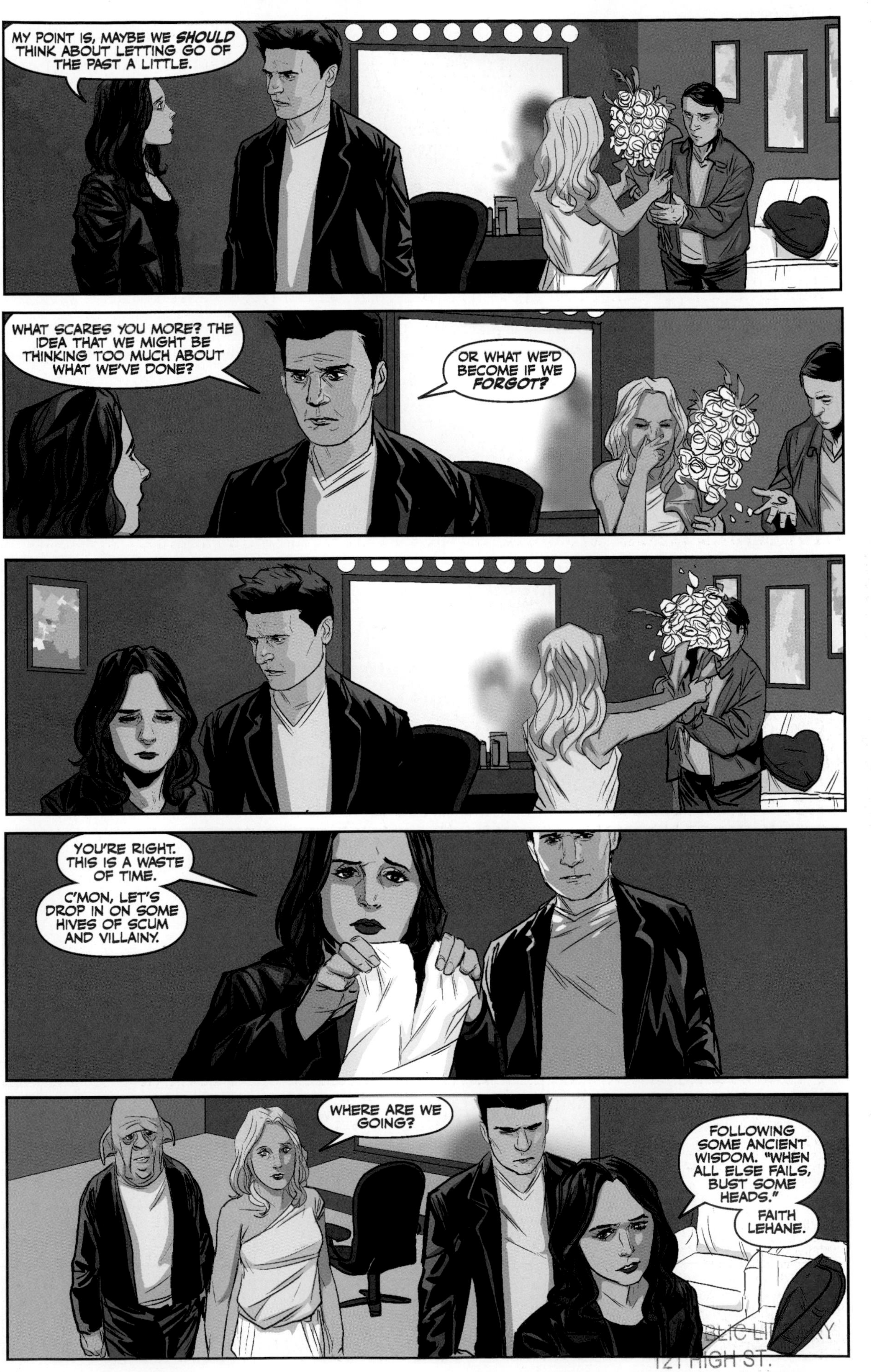
MY POINT IS, MAYBE WE *SHOULD* THINK ABOUT LETTING GO OF THE PAST A LITTLE.
WHAT SCARES YOU MORE? THE IDEA THAT WE MIGHT BE THINKING TOO MUCH ABOUT WHAT WE'VE DONE?
OR WHAT WE'D BECOME IF WE *FORGOT?*
YOU'RE RIGHT. THIS IS A WASTE OF TIME.
C'MON, LET'S DROP IN ON SOME HIVES OF SCUM AND VILLAINY.
WHERE ARE WE GOING?
FOLLOWING SOME ANCIENT WISDOM. "WHEN ALL ELSE FAILS, BUST SOME HEADS."
FAITH LEHANE.

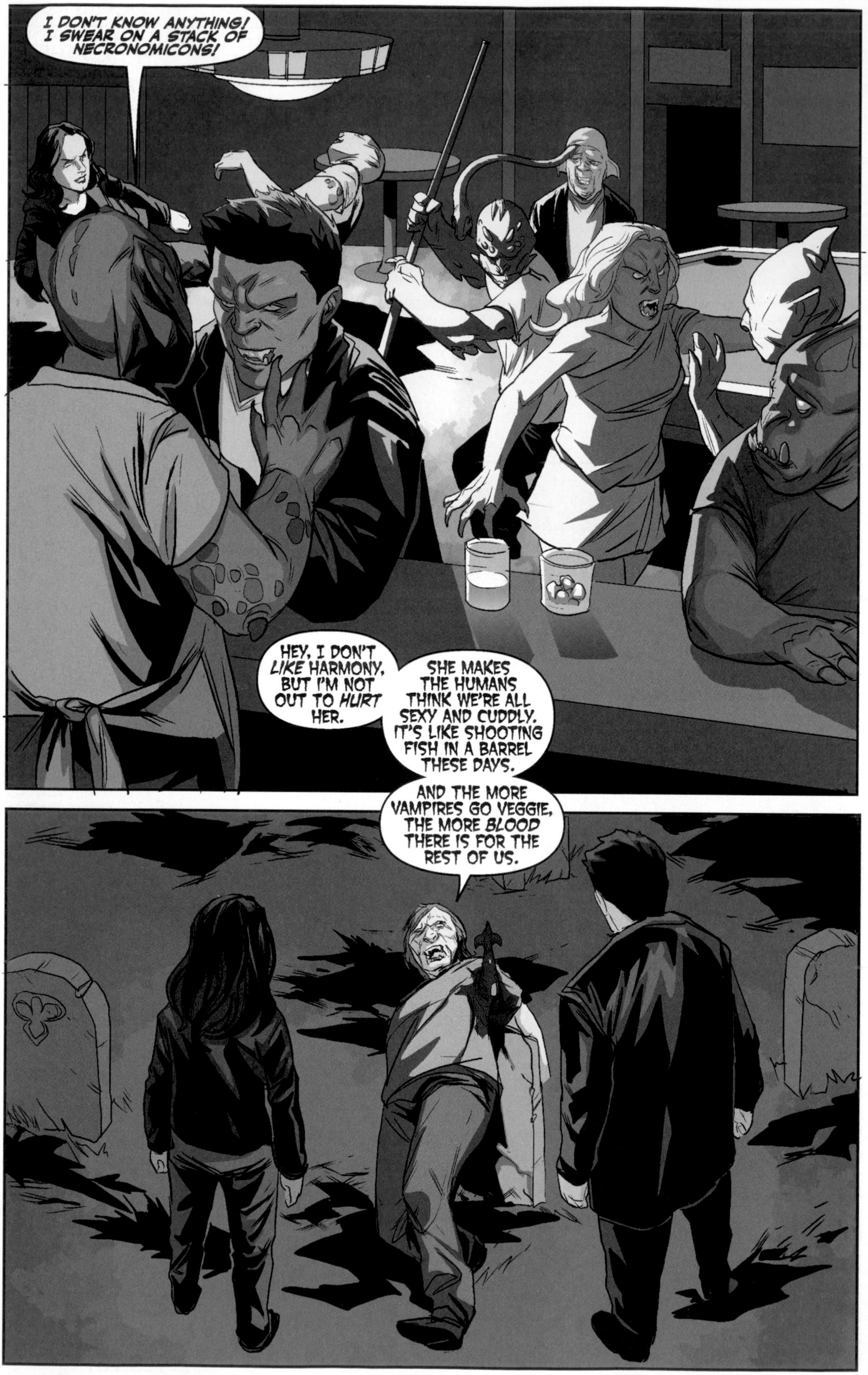
I DON'T KNOW ANYTHING! I SWEAR ON A STACK OF NECRONOMICONS!
HEY, I DON'T *LIKE* HARMONY, BUT I'M NOT OUT TO *HURT* HER.
SHE MAKES THE HUMANS THINK WE'RE ALL SEXY AND CUDDLY. IT'S LIKE SHOOTING FISH IN A BARREL THESE DAYS.
AND THE MORE VAMPIRES GO VEGGIE, THE MORE *BLOOD* THERE IS FOR THE REST OF US.

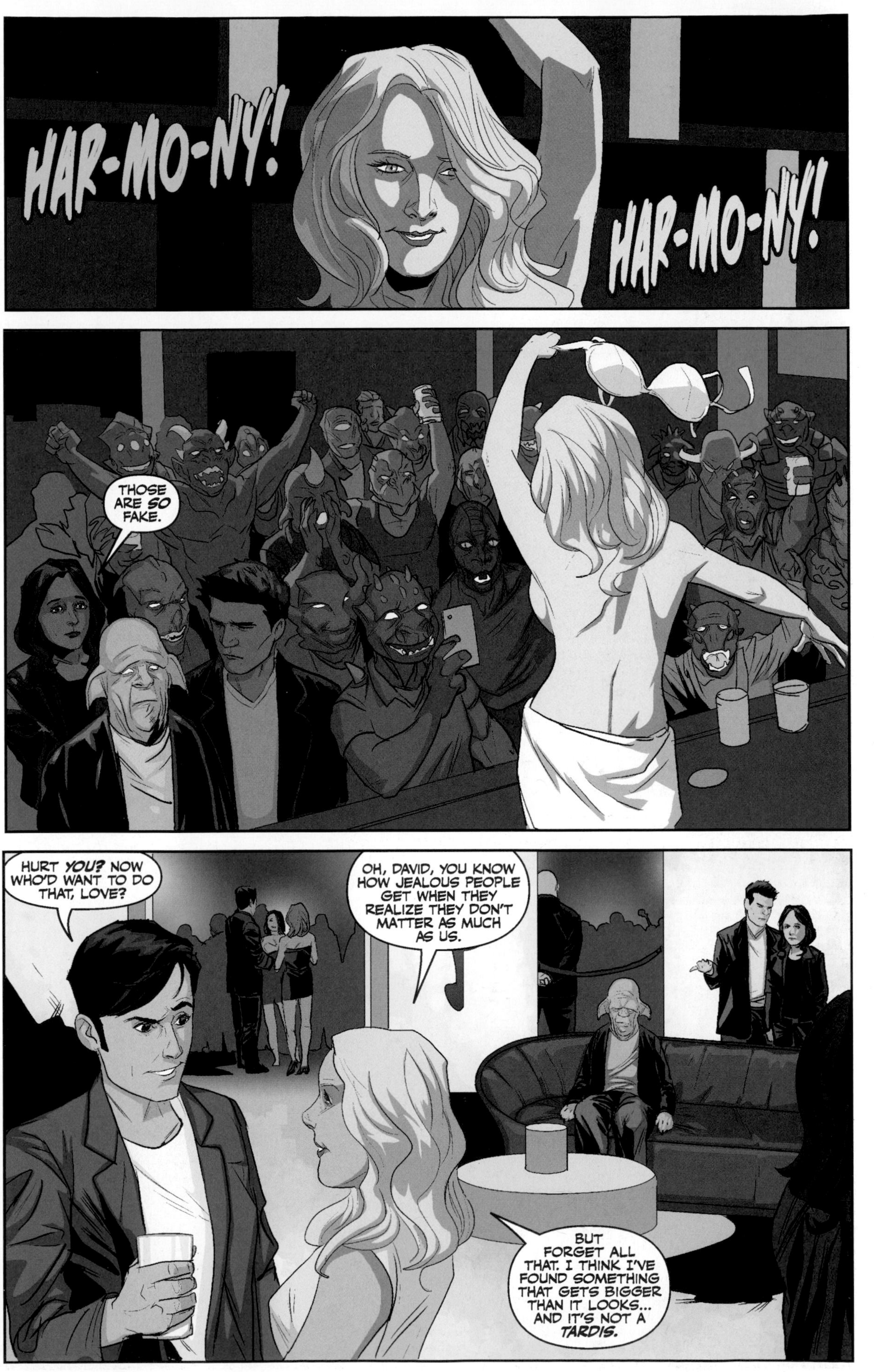
HAR-MO-NY!
HAR-MO-NY!
THOSE ARE *SO* FAKE.
HURT *YOU?* NOW WHO'D WANT TO DO THAT, LOVE?
OH, DAVID, YOU KNOW HOW JEALOUS PEOPLE GET WHEN THEY REALIZE THEY DON'T MATTER AS MUCH AS US.
BUT FORGET ALL THAT. I THINK I'VE FOUND SOMETHING THAT GETS BIGGER THAN IT LOOKS... AND IT'S NOT A *TARDIS.*

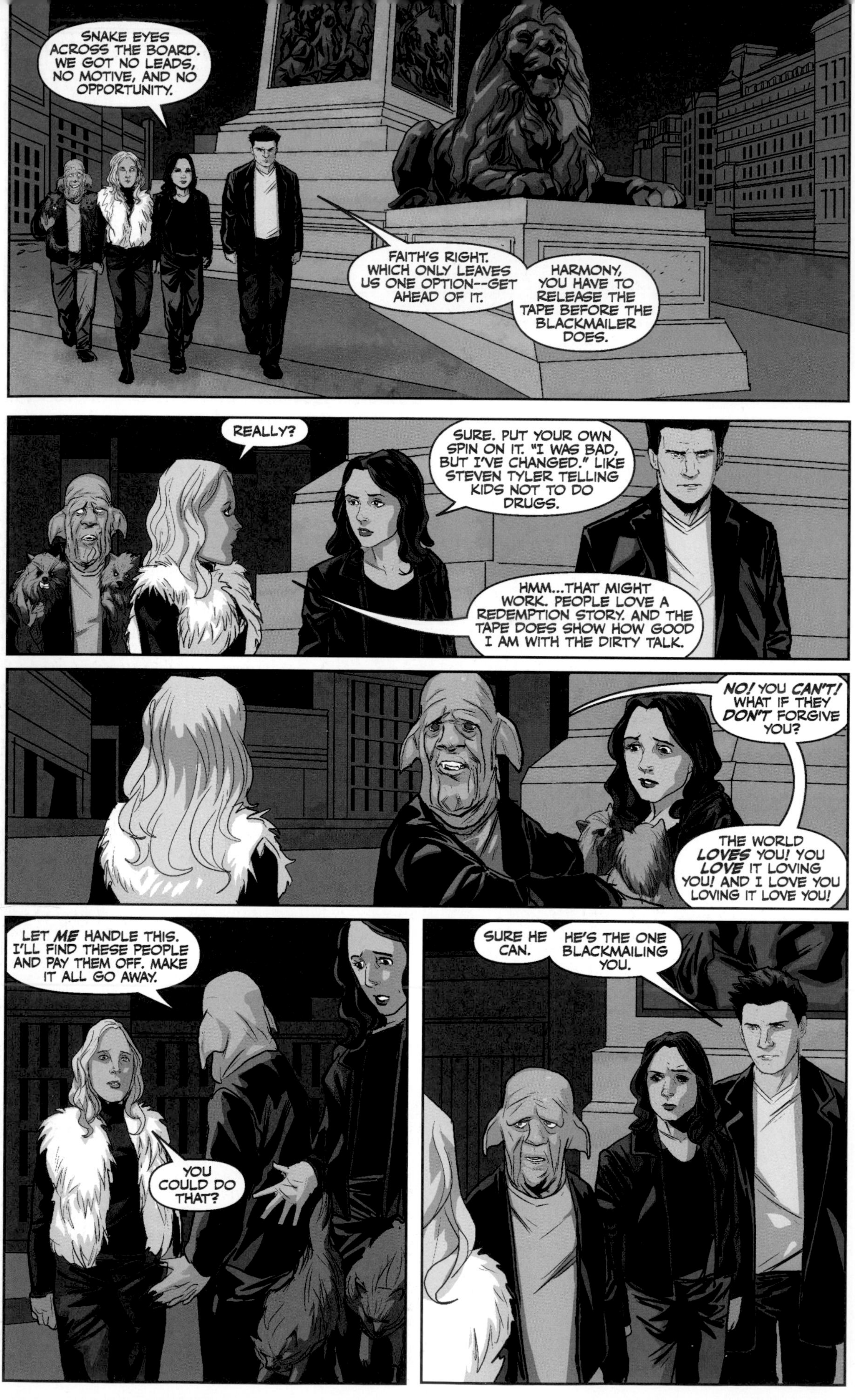
SNAKE EYES ACROSS THE BOARD. WE GOT NO LEADS, NO MOTIVE, AND NO OPPORTUNITY.
FAITH'S RIGHT. WHICH ONLY LEAVES US ONE OPTION--GET AHEAD OF IT.
HARMONY, YOU HAVE TO RELEASE THE TAPE BEFORE THE BLACKMAILER DOES.
REALLY?
SURE. PUT YOUR OWN SPIN ON IT. "I WAS BAD, BUT I'VE CHANGED." LIKE STEVEN TYLER TELLING KIDS NOT TO DO DRUGS.
HMM...THAT MIGHT WORK. PEOPLE LOVE A REDEMPTION STORY. AND THE TAPE DOES SHOW HOW GOOD I AM WITH THE DIRTY TALK.
NO! YOU CAN'T! WHAT IF THEY DON'T FORGIVE YOU?
THE WORLD LOVES YOU! YOU LOVE IT LOVING YOU! AND I LOVE YOU LOVING IT LOVE YOU!
LET ME HANDLE THIS. I'LL FIND THESE PEOPLE AND PAY THEM OFF. MAKE IT ALL GO AWAY.
YOU COULD DO THAT?
SURE HE CAN.
HE'S THE ONE BLACKMAILING YOU.

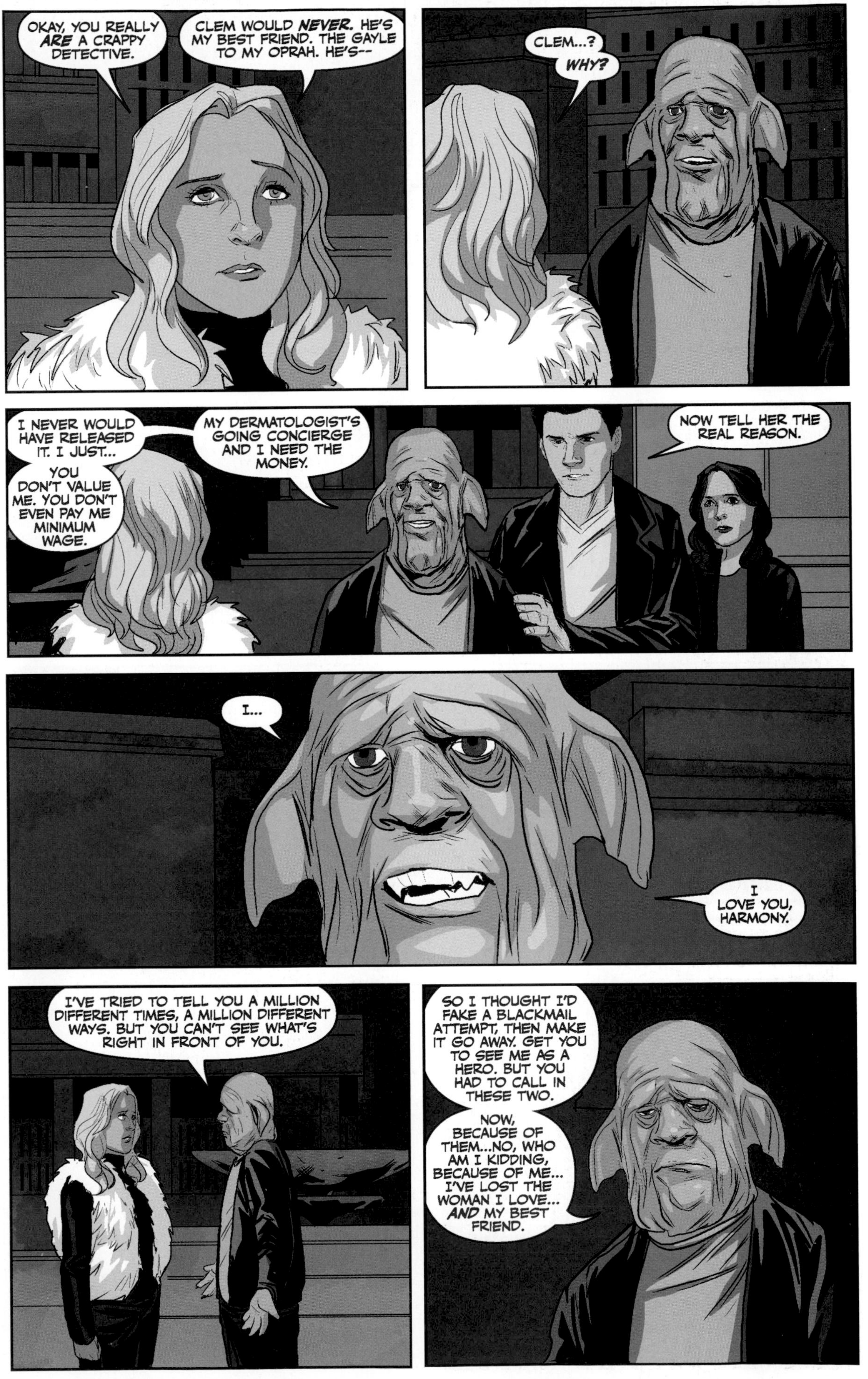
OKAY, YOU REALLY ARE A CRAPPY DETECTIVE.
CLEM WOULD NEVER. HE'S MY BEST FRIEND. THE GAYLE TO MY OPRAH. HE'S--
CLEM...? WHY?
I NEVER WOULD HAVE RELEASED IT. I JUST...
YOU DON'T VALUE ME. YOU DON'T EVEN PAY ME MINIMUM WAGE.
MY DERMATOLOGIST'S GOING CONCIERGE AND I NEED THE MONEY.
NOW TELL HER THE REAL REASON.
I...
I LOVE YOU, HARMONY.
I'VE TRIED TO TELL YOU A MILLION DIFFERENT TIMES, A MILLION DIFFERENT WAYS. BUT YOU CAN'T SEE WHAT'S RIGHT IN FRONT OF YOU.
SO I THOUGHT I'D FAKE A BLACKMAIL ATTEMPT, THEN MAKE IT GO AWAY. GET YOU TO SEE ME AS A HERO. BUT YOU HAD TO CALL IN THESE TWO.
NOW, BECAUSE OF THEM...NO, WHO AM I KIDDING, BECAUSE OF ME... I'VE LOST THE WOMAN I LOVE... AND MY BEST FRIEND.

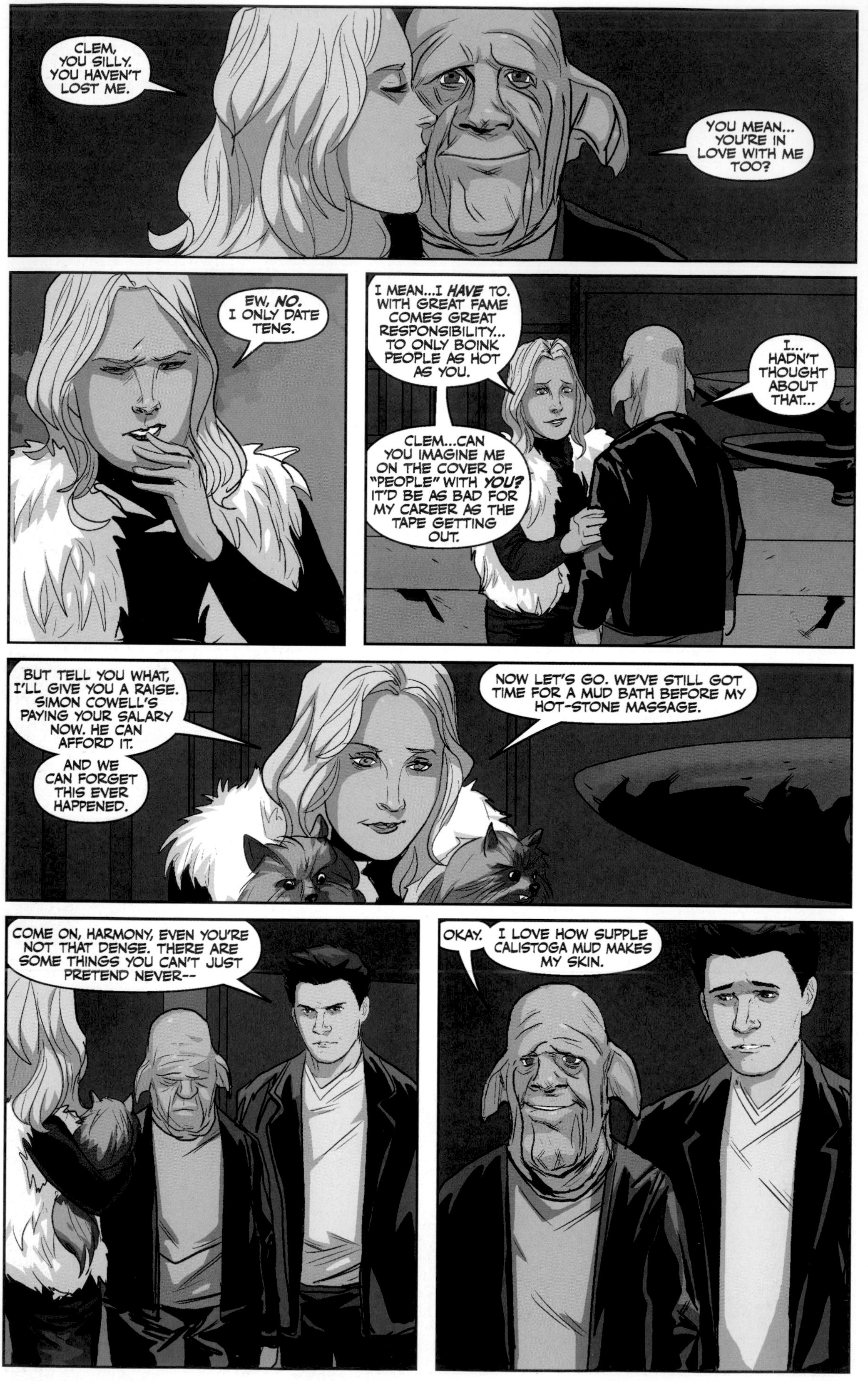
CLEM, YOU SILLY. YOU HAVEN'T LOST ME.
YOU MEAN... YOU'RE IN LOVE WITH ME TOO?
EW, NO. I ONLY DATE TENS.
I MEAN...I HAVE TO. WITH GREAT FAME COMES GREAT RESPONSIBILITY... TO ONLY BOINK PEOPLE AS HOT AS YOU.
I... HADN'T THOUGHT ABOUT THAT...
CLEM...CAN YOU IMAGINE ME ON THE COVER OF "PEOPLE" WITH YOU? IT'D BE AS BAD FOR MY CAREER AS THE TAPE GETTING OUT.
BUT TELL YOU WHAT, I'LL GIVE YOU A RAISE. SIMON COWELL'S PAYING YOUR SALARY NOW. HE CAN AFFORD IT.
AND WE CAN FORGET THIS EVER HAPPENED.
NOW LET'S GO. WE'VE STILL GOT TIME FOR A MUD BATH BEFORE MY HOT-STONE MASSAGE.
COME ON, HARMONY, EVEN YOU'RE NOT THAT DENSE. THERE ARE SOME THINGS YOU CAN'T JUST PRETEND NEVER--
OKAY.
I LOVE HOW SUPPLE CALISTOGA MUD MAKES MY SKIN.

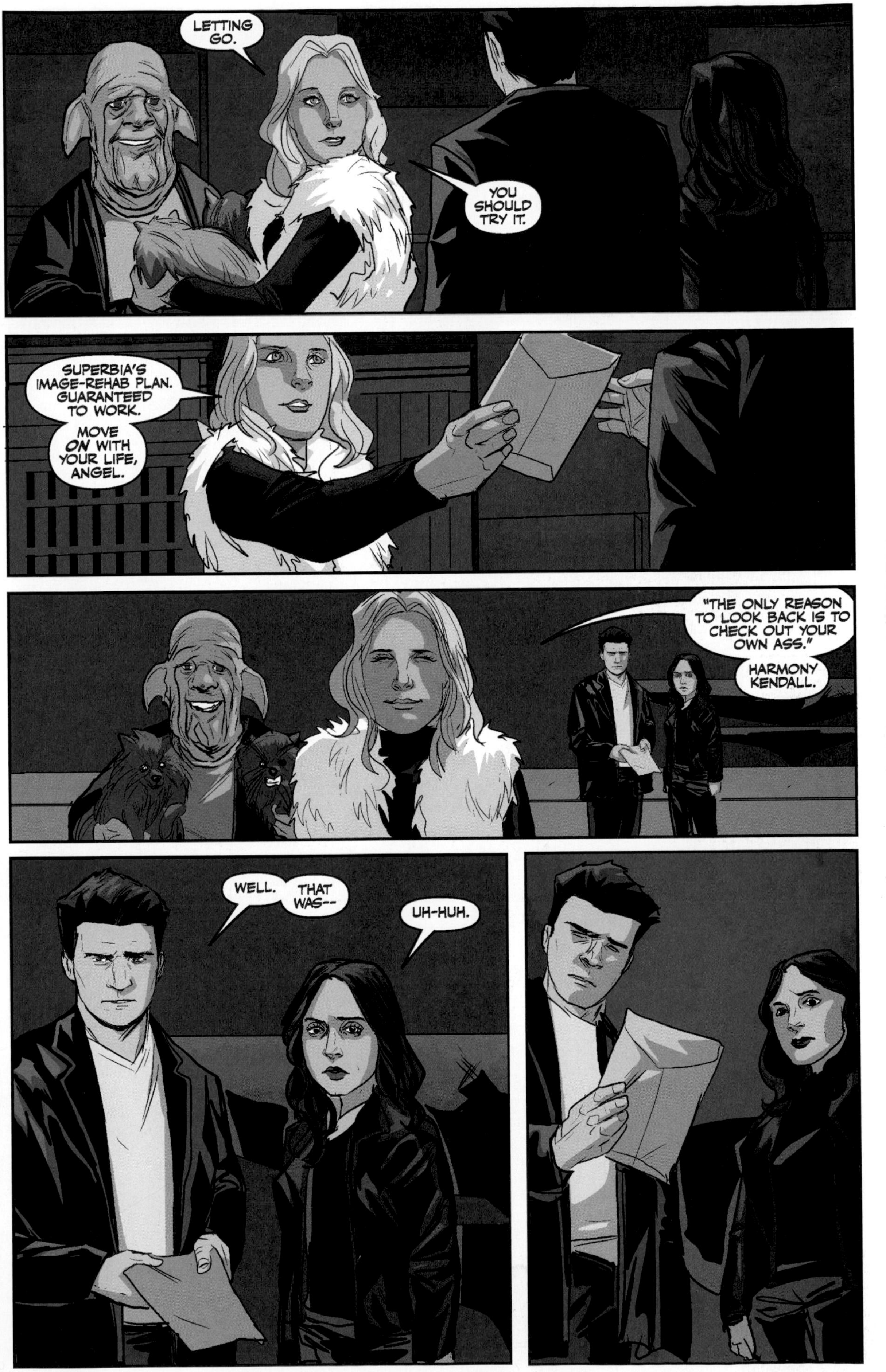
LETTING GO.
YOU SHOULD TRY IT.
SUPERBIA'S IMAGE-REHAB PLAN. GUARANTEED TO WORK.
MOVE *ON* WITH YOUR LIFE, ANGEL.
"THE ONLY REASON TO LOOK BACK IS TO CHECK OUT YOUR OWN ASS."
HARMONY KENDALL.
WELL.
THAT WAS--
UH-HUH.

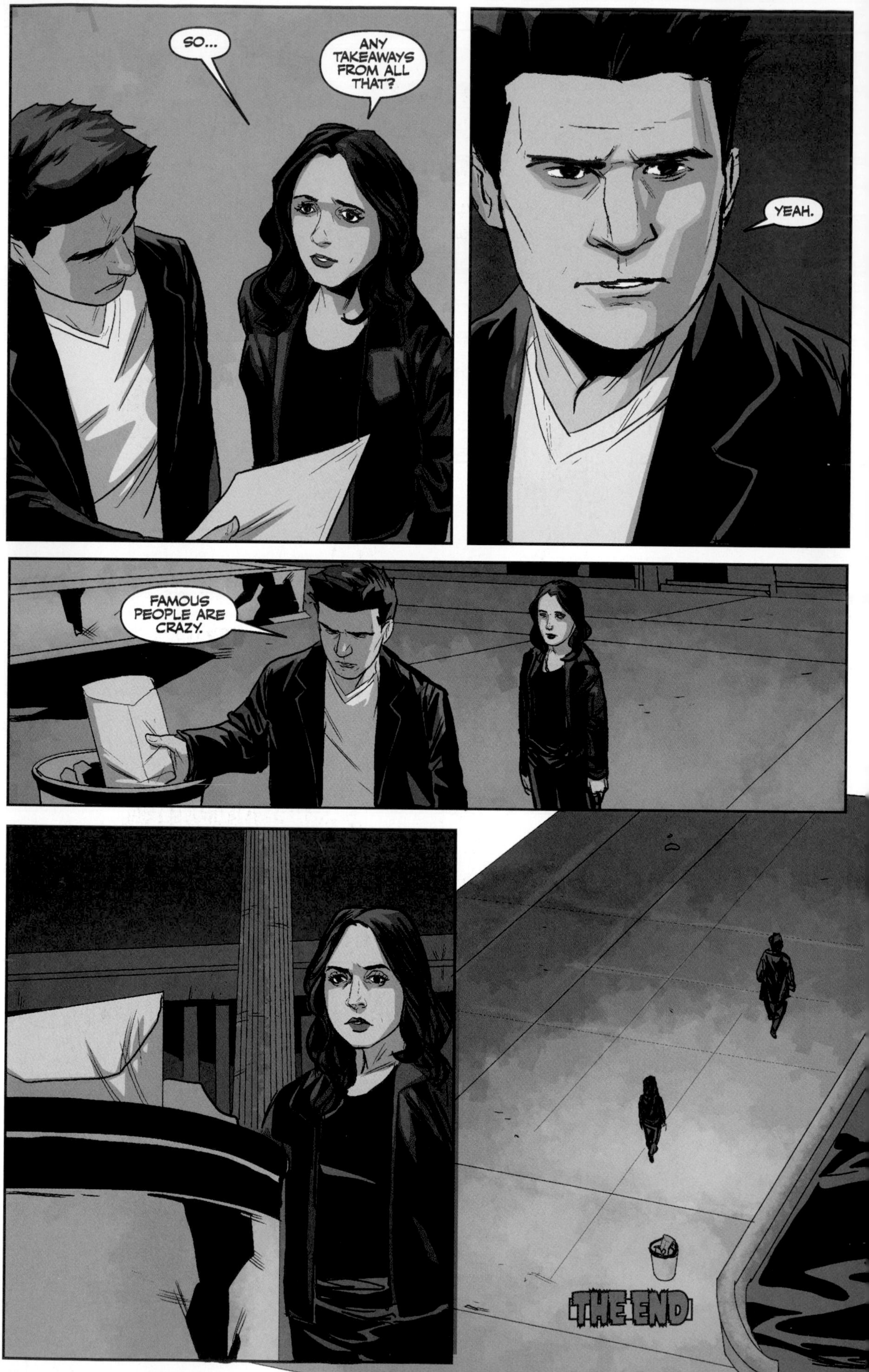
SO...
ANY TAKEAWAYS FROM ALL THAT?
YEAH.
FAMOUS PEOPLE ARE CRAZY.
THE END

ANGEL & FAITH COVER GALLERY AND SKETCHBOOK

WITH NOTES FROM
REBEKAH ISAACS

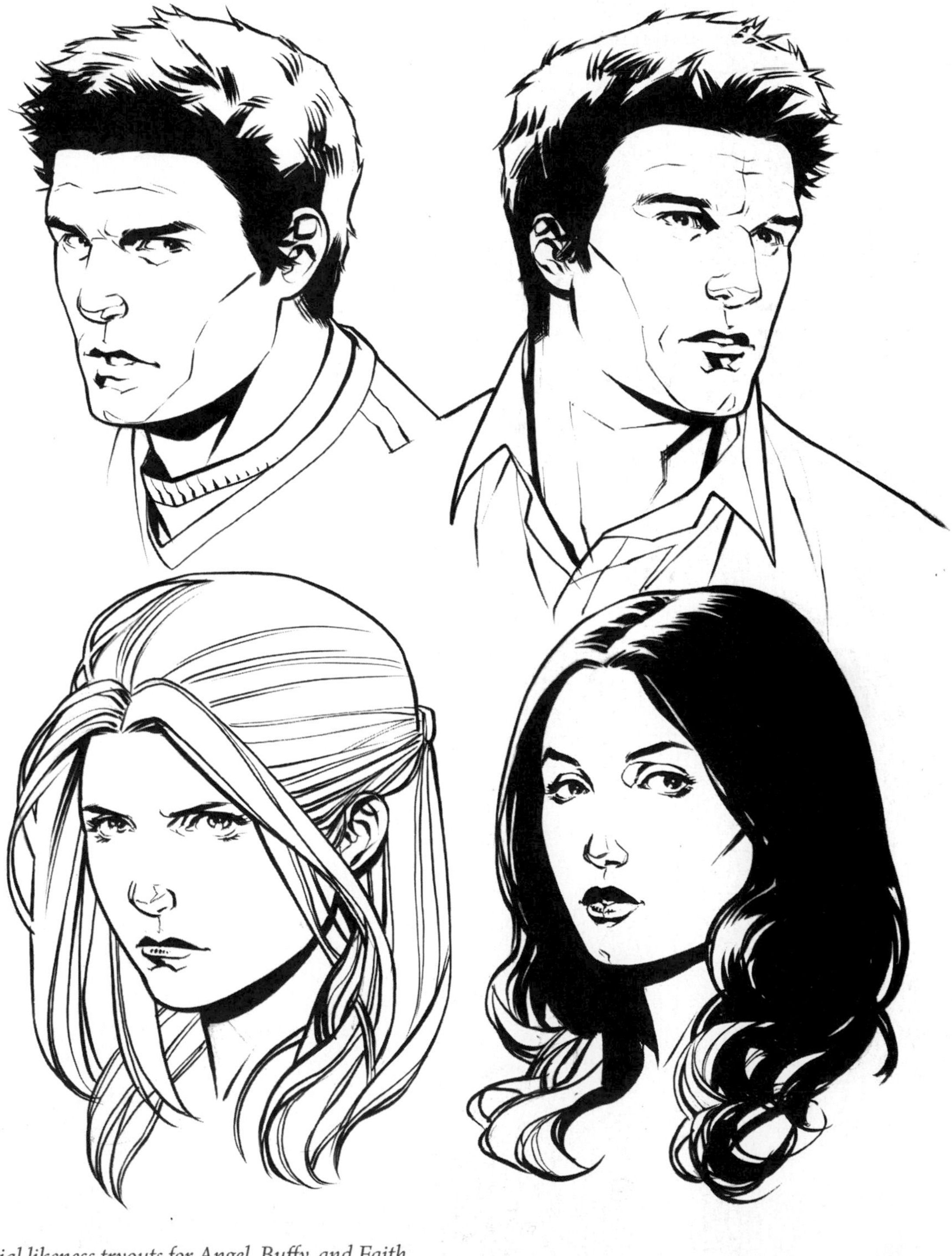

Initial likeness tryouts for Angel, Buffy, and Faith.

This cover was commissioned for a New England signing tour for Angel & Faith #1, for the NECRA retailer group. I think it stands to reason that Faith would be a huge Sox fan! International readers may not be familiar with the Red Sox/Yankees rivalry—it can get very intense. I looked around online for the most ridiculous anti-Boston slogan I could find, and finally ran across a T-shirt that read Redsux Nation. Its hilarious boneheadedness, combined with the vampire perpetrator, made it the perfect choice for the graffiti on the wall. Angel might just be more of a Phillies fan, but on this night he's along for the ride with Faith. Colors by Dan Jackson.

The Dark Horse Comics twenty-fifth anniversary special cover art for Angel & Faith #1: pencils by Georges Jeanty, inks by Dexter Vines, colors by JD Mettler.

Opposite: *Various early likeness warm-ups of Giles for the flashback sequences, and the original concept drawing for Giles's great-aunts, Lavinia and Sophronia, who appeared on the last page of issue #1—foreshadowing their surprise appearance in issue #10.*

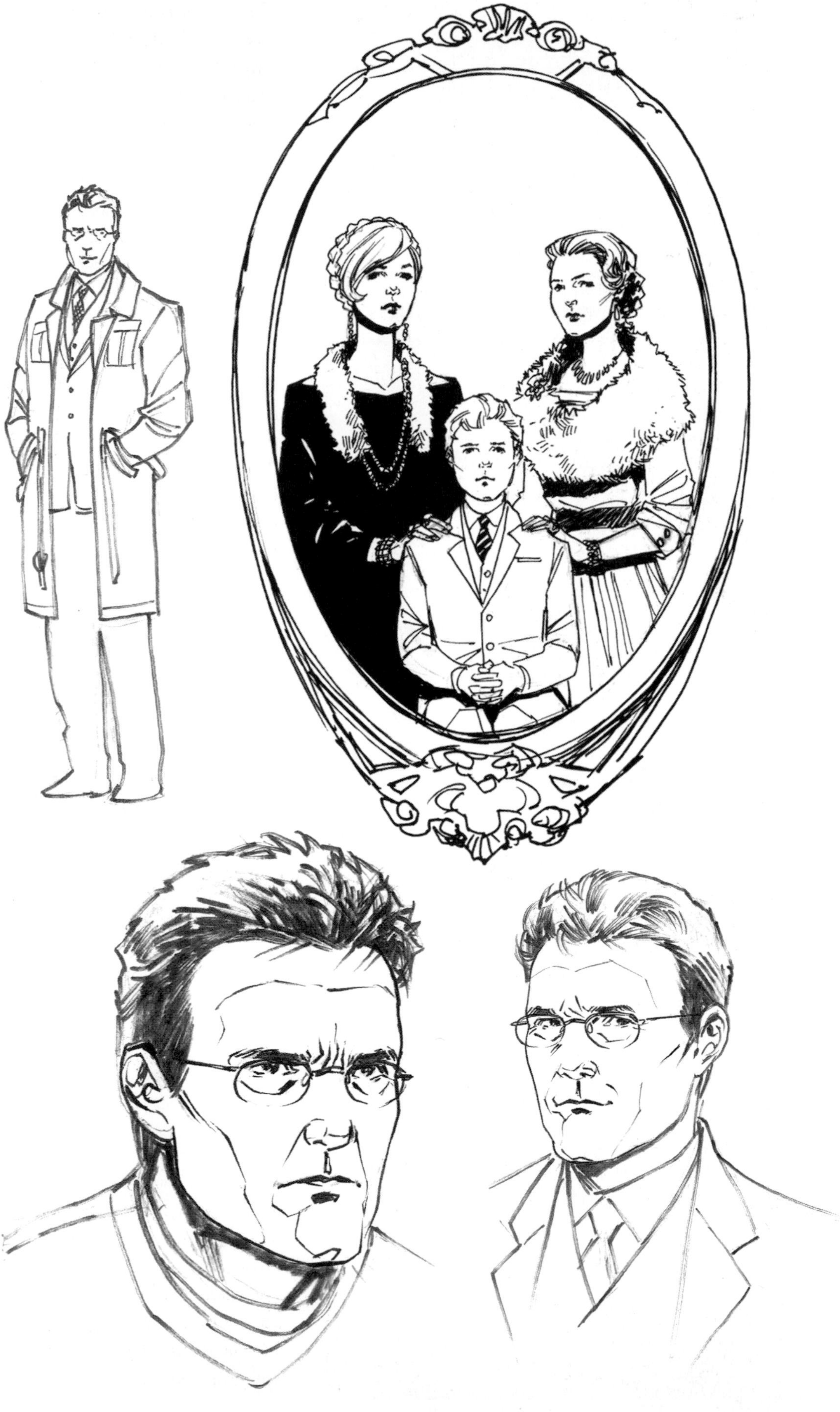

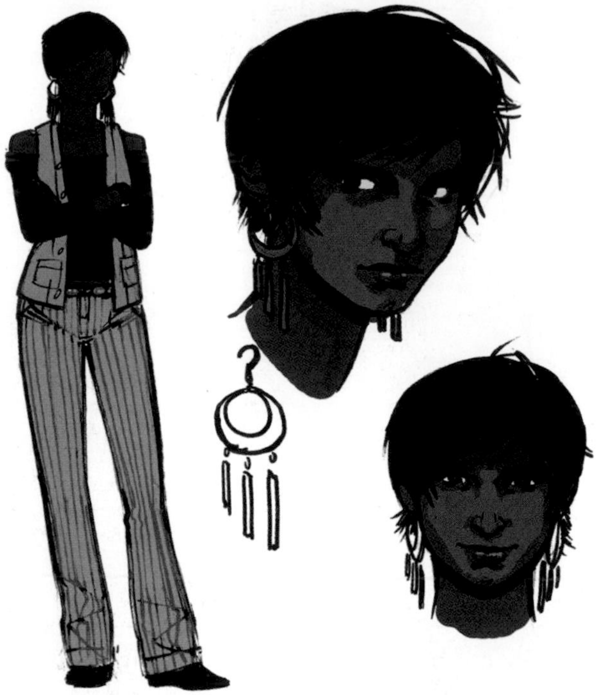

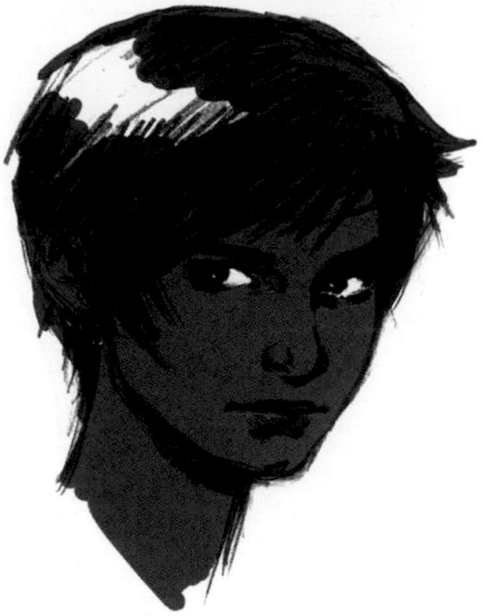

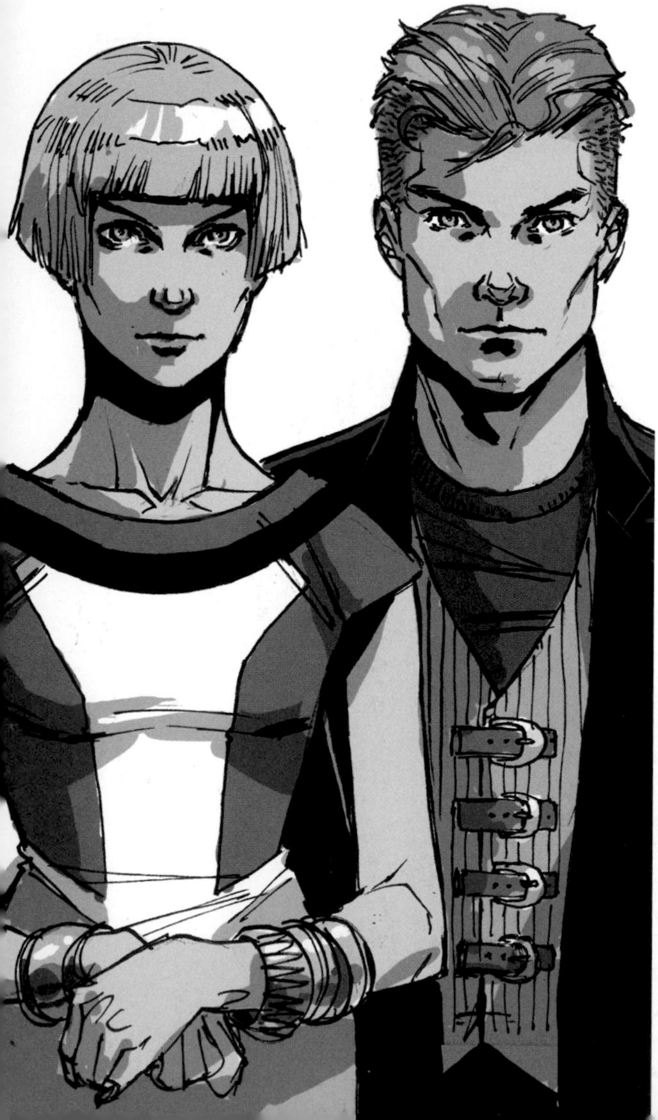

NADIRA

Smart and stylish, but tough as nails. I think the usual idea for a brooding, angry, ticking time bomb of a character would be dark clothes, more of a goth sensibility. Instead I imagined she'd overcompensate with flashy clothes while going out on the town with her new Slayers, a scenario which doubtless makes her a bit uncomfortable. But at heart she is in full fight mode at all times, so I gave her a more tomboyish haircut and a very intense demeanor.

BAD GUYS

Like most evildoers, Pearl and Nash (left) *feel they're owed the world, and they take whatever they want, whenever they want. I figured that would extend to rampaging through designer showrooms to stock their closets, enhancing their intended image as some sort of demon royalty. To make them beautiful in an other-worldly way, I kept Lady Gaga and Thin White Duke Bowie in mind.*

Opposite: *The great thing about the* Buffy *and* Angel *comics is that we're not limited by makeup, prosthetics, or FX budgets, so I was asked to design demons that wouldn't have been possible on the shows. These were a blast to draw, and the icy void in the middle of the Baphon's chest still kinda creeps me out. But it was still really fun to design Kurth, more of a classic "guy with some horns and makeup" from the* Angel *TV series.*

Following pages: *Covers to* Angel & Faith *#2 and #3. Inks for #2 by Andy Owens.*

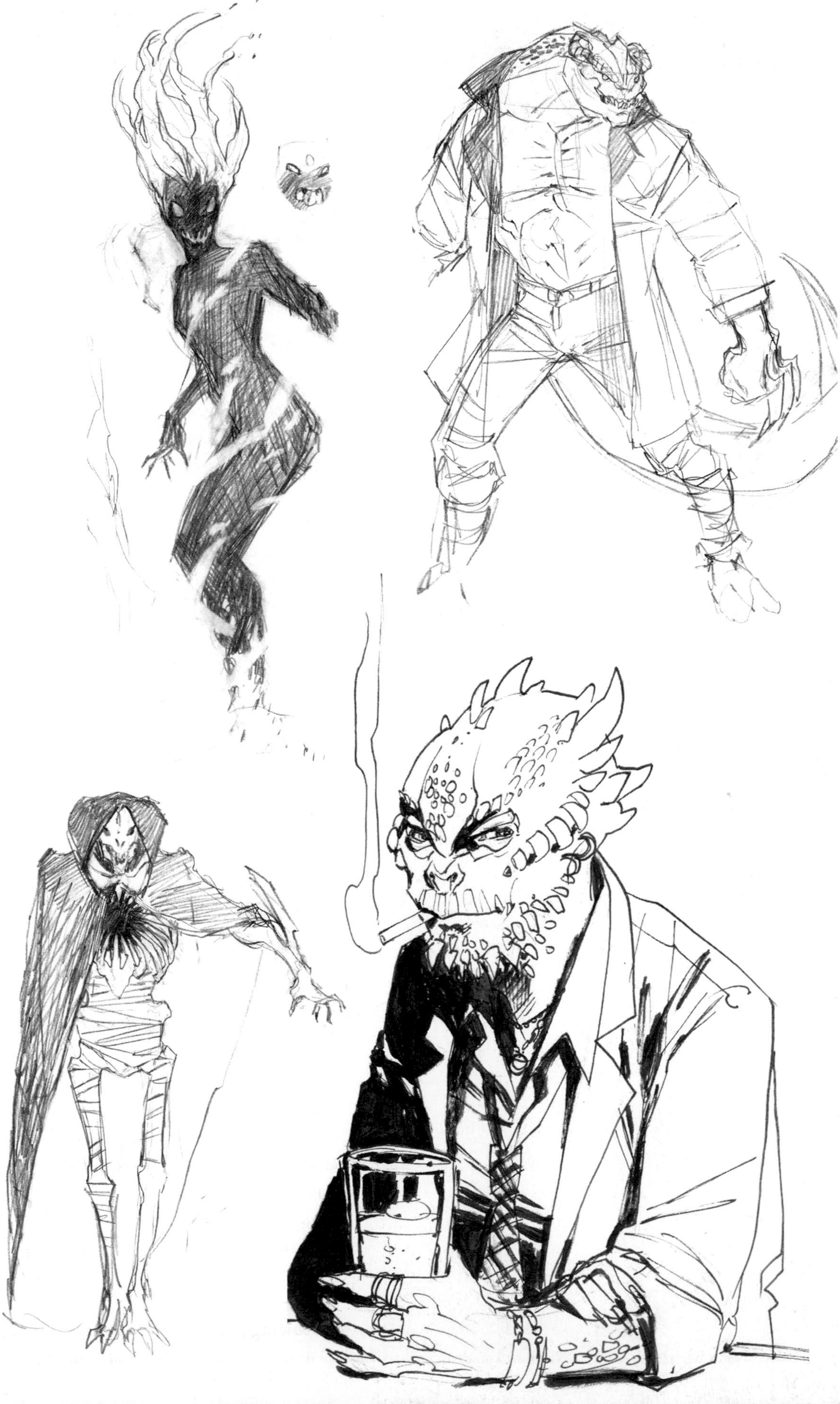

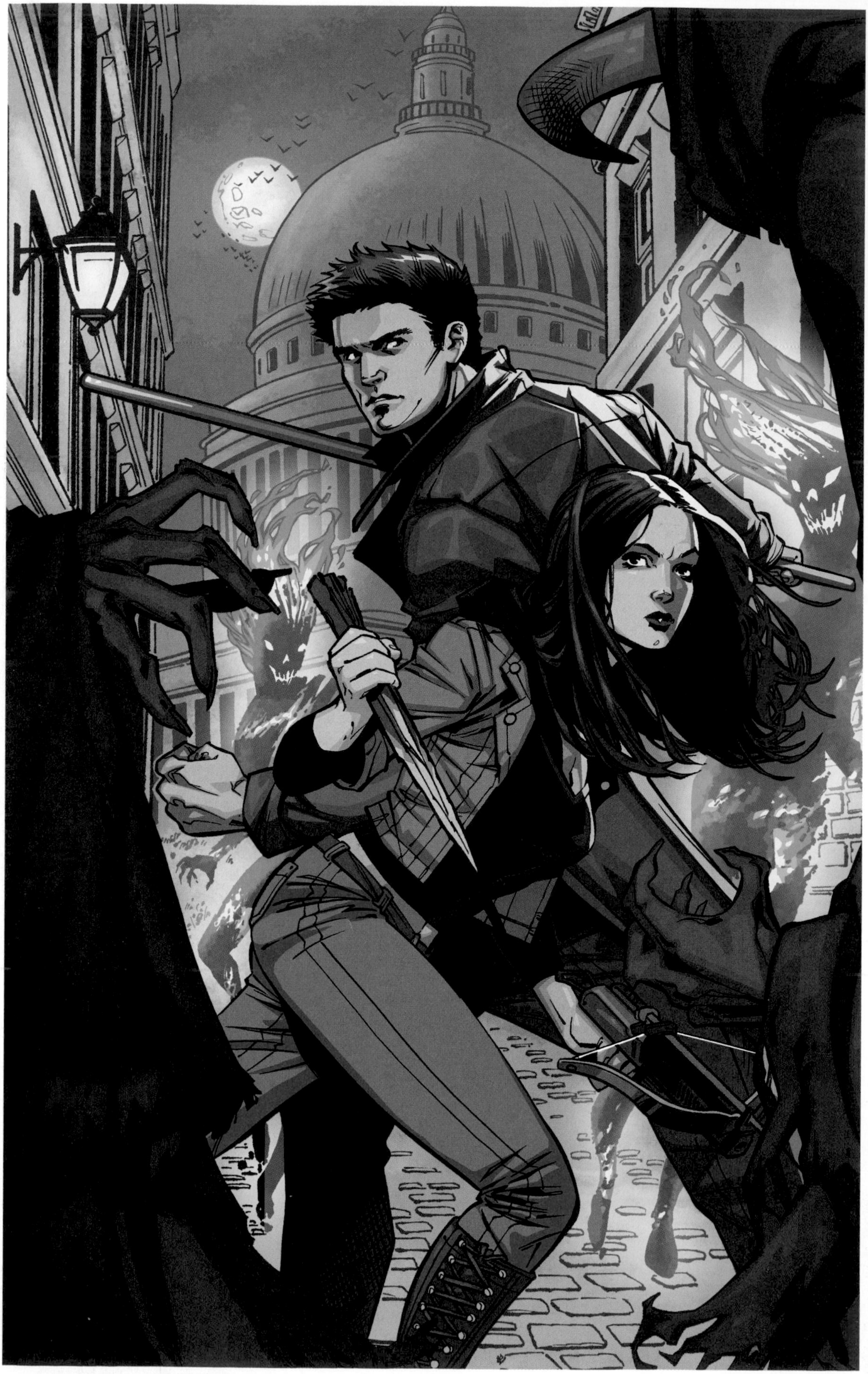

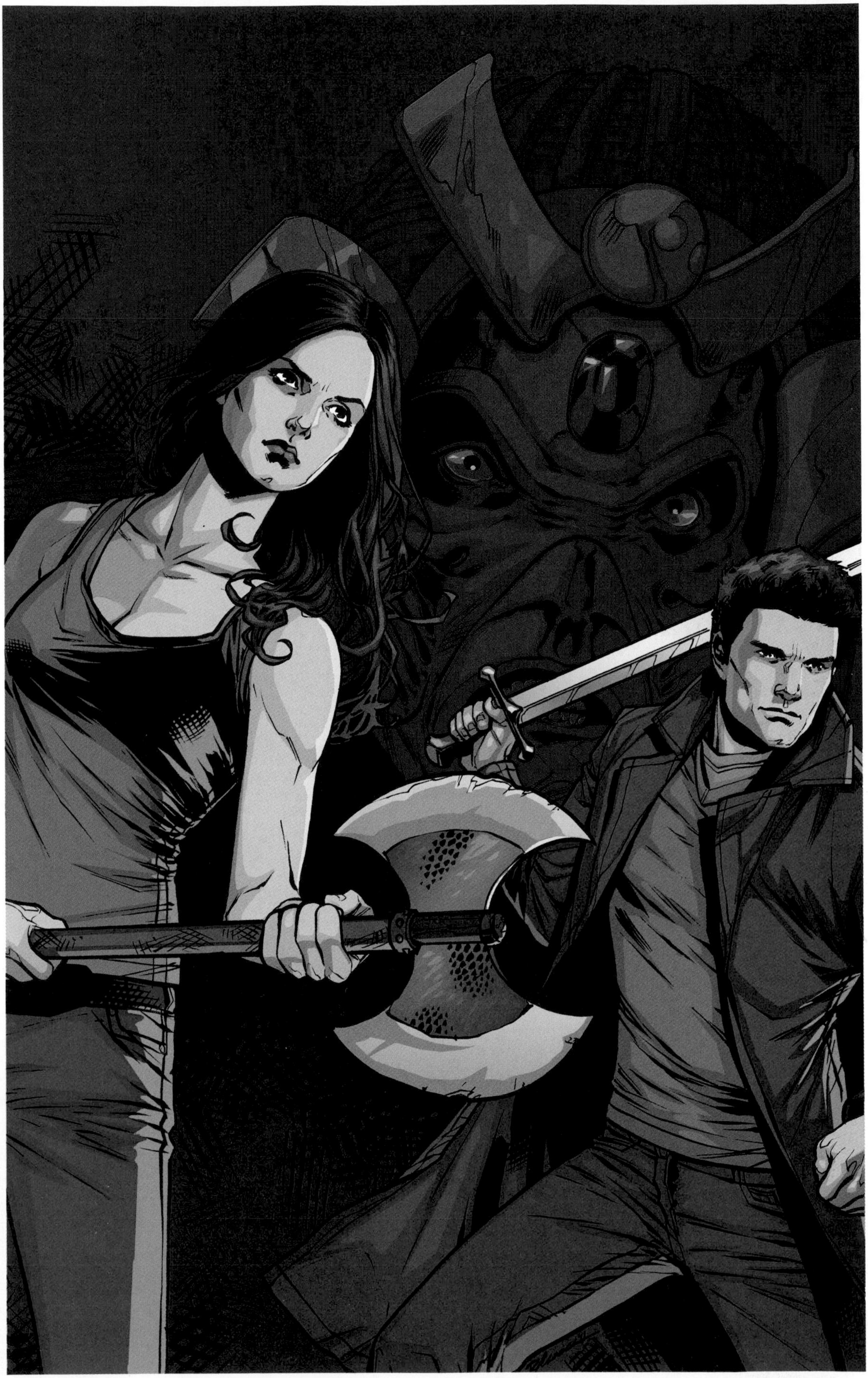

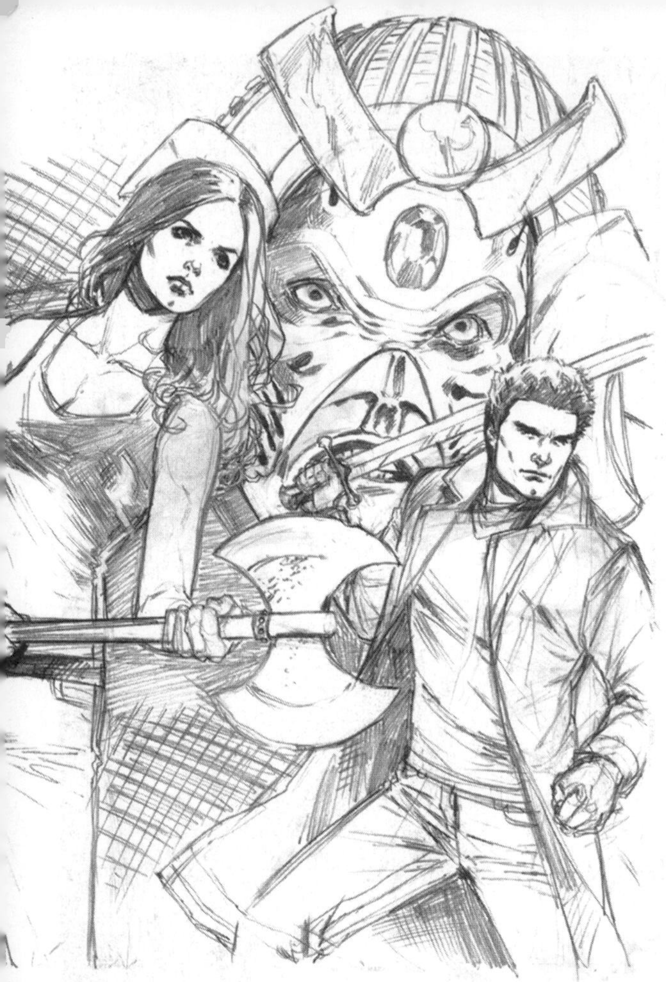

Left: *Cover pencils for* Angel & Faith #3.

COVER PROCESS

First, the editorial team and Christos will send me a concept or two. Like most comics covers, the concepts usually cover the general feeling or themes of an issue, not a specific moment from the story. I'll send between three and five different thumbnails, and after everyone dukes it out over their choice, and ideas are exchanged on what to add or remove, the dust settles and one thumbnail emerges victorious. Because I ink my own work, I like to keep my thumbnailing process very loose and do most of my design work in the pencils stage. Hence the stand-in anonymous baddies in the #2 cover sketches (below, A–E), *which were fleshed out in their demon forms during the pencils stage. Then on to inks and Dan's magical colors. The last three sketches below were for my cover to* Angel & Faith #4 (final art, facing).

Following page: Angel & Faith #5 *cover.*

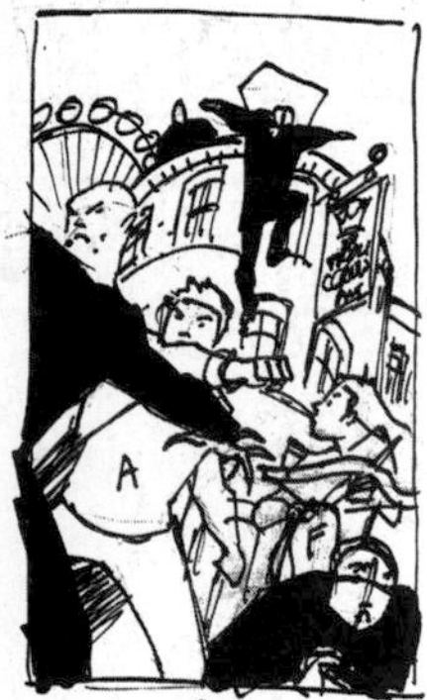
A
A
F

A

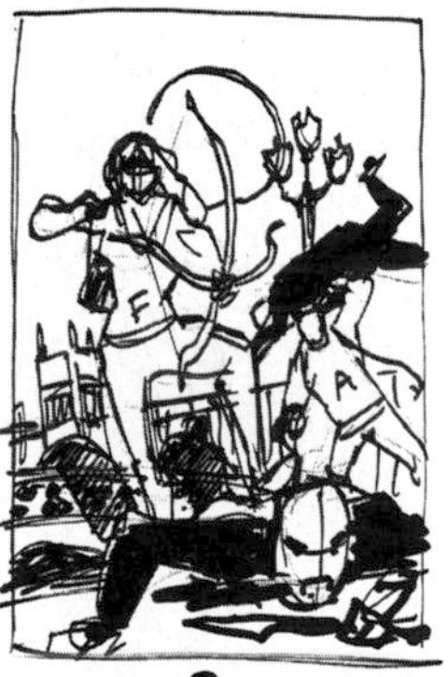
F
A

B

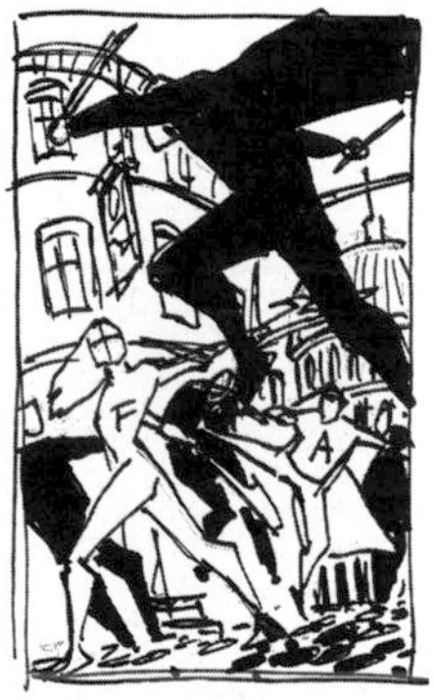
F
A

C

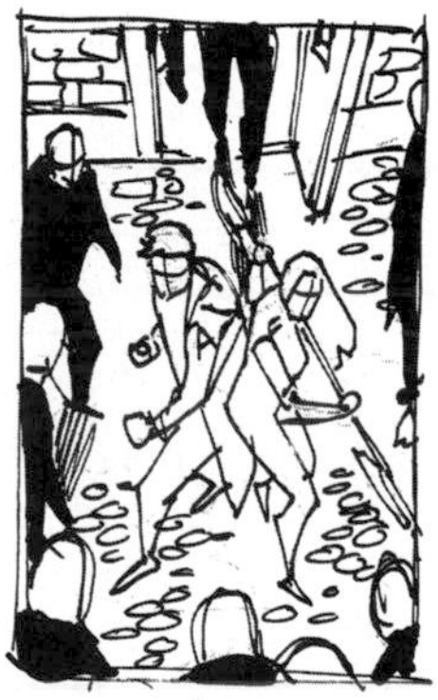
A
F

D

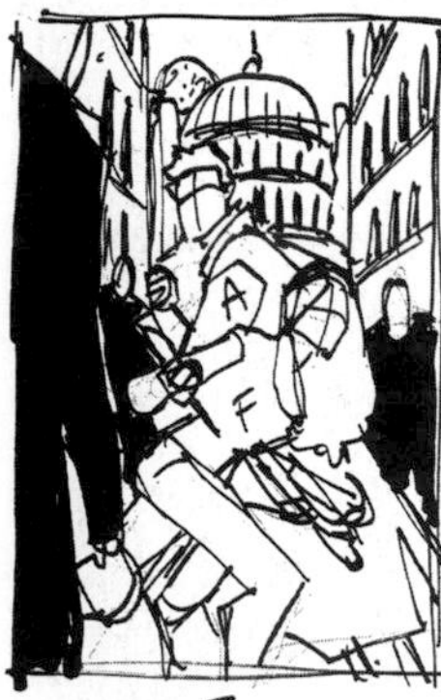
A
F

E

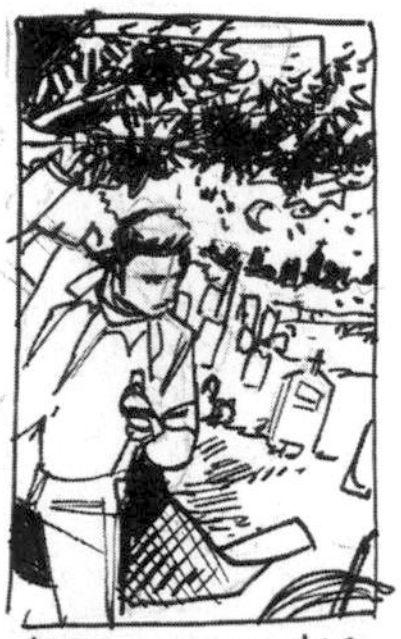

Angel approaching grave w/ vial of Mohra blood

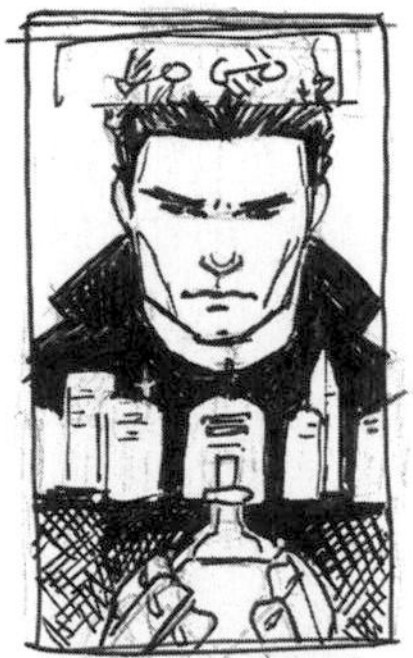

Angel w/ vial w/ design element of graves (only Giles's tombstone's inscription is legible front and center)

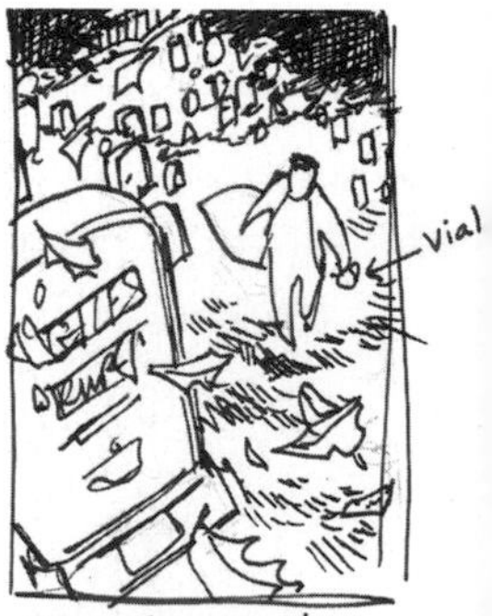
vial

Here I've placed Giles's gravestone on a hill within the graveyard

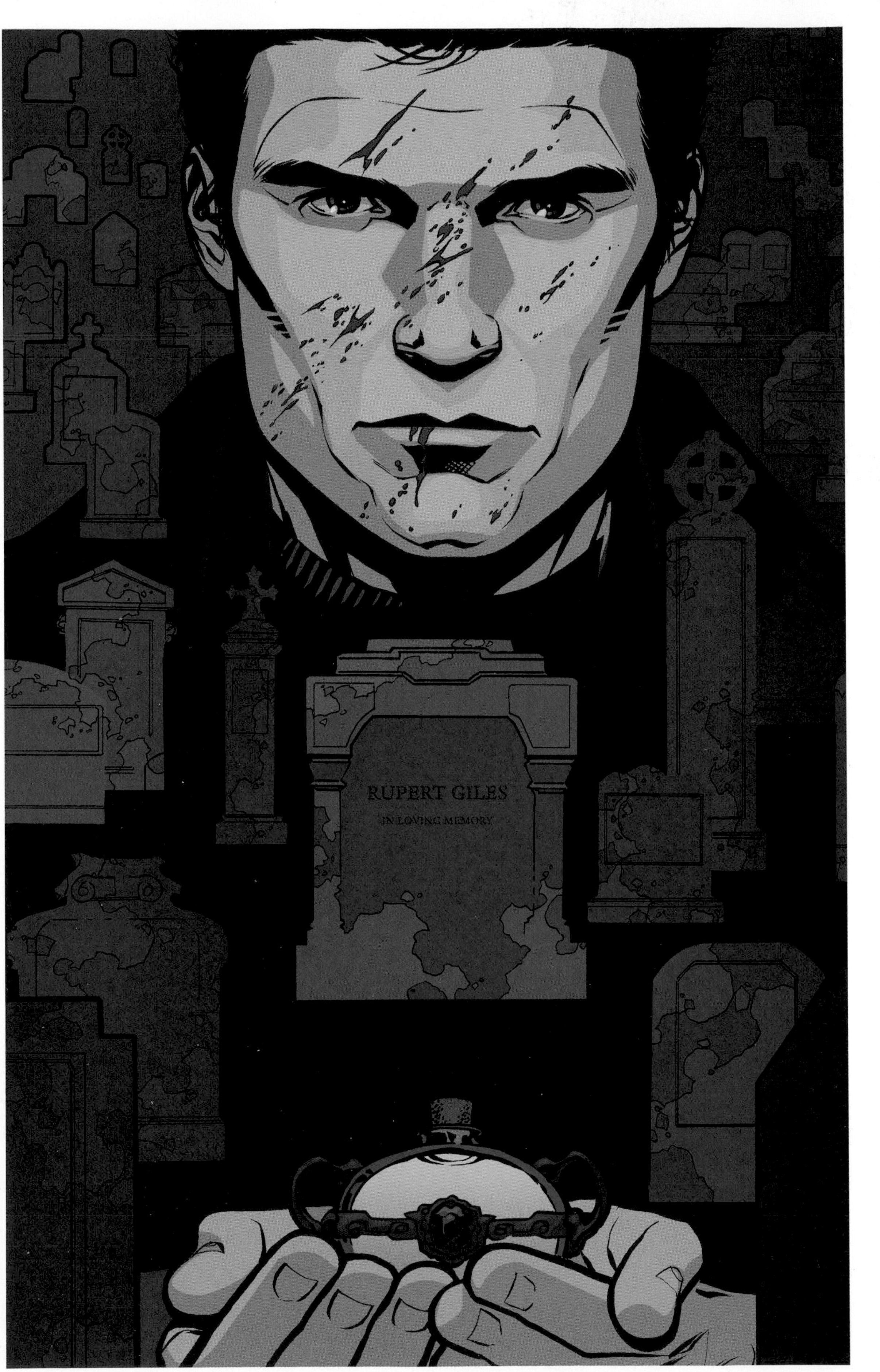
RUPERT GILES
IN LOVING MEMORY

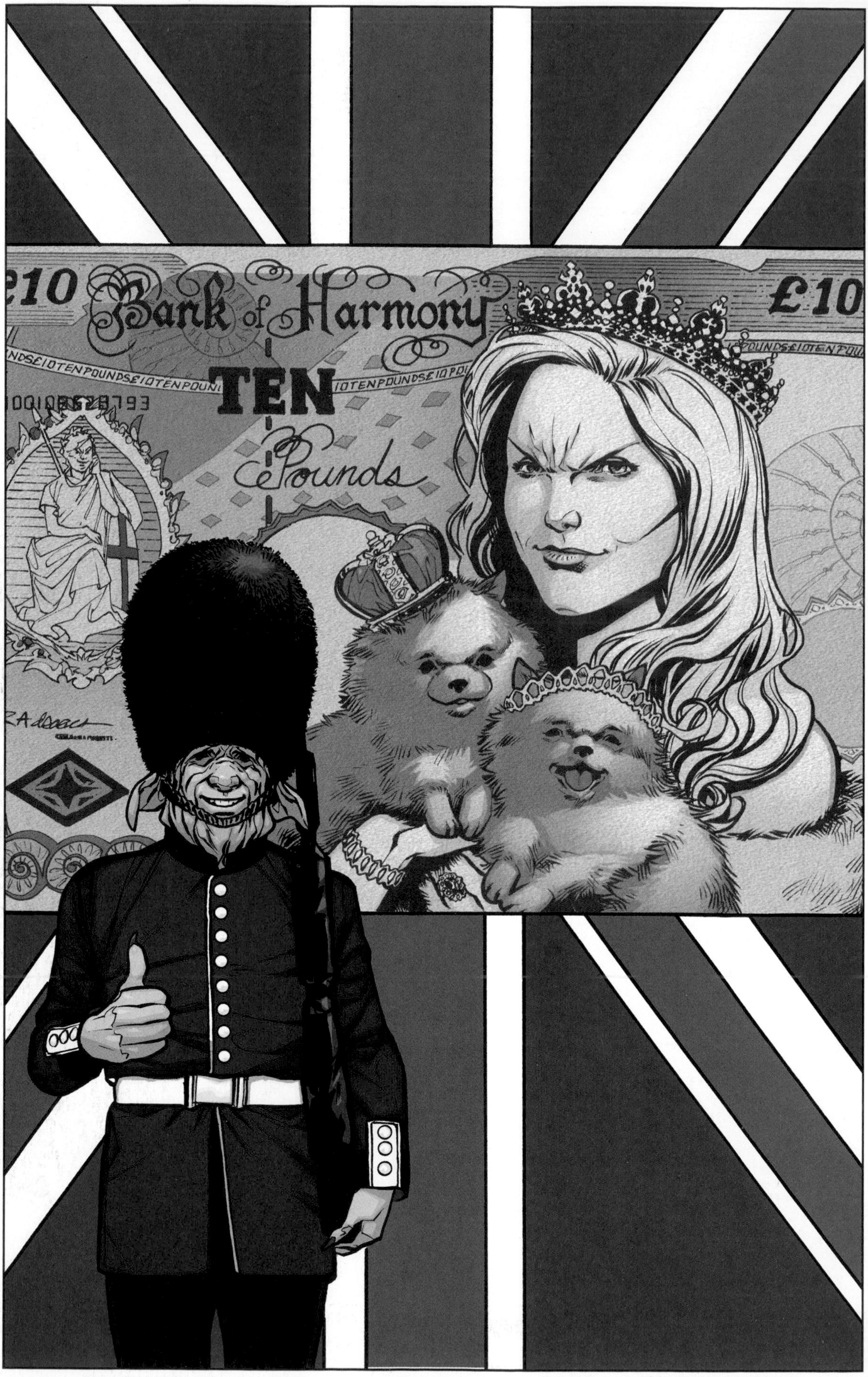
£10
Bank of Harmony
TEN
Pounds
£10

FROM JOSS WHEDON

BUFFY THE VAMPIRE SLAYER SEASON 8
VOLUME 1: THE LONG WAY HOME
Joss Whedon and Georges Jeanty
ISBN 978-1-59307-822-5 | $15.99

VOLUME 2: NO FUTURE FOR YOU
Brian K. Vaughan, Georges Jeanty, and Joss Whedon
ISBN 978-1-59307-963-5 | $15.99

VOLUME 3: WOLVES AT THE GATE
Drew Goddard, Georges Jeanty, and Joss Whedon
ISBN 978-1-59582-165-2 | $15.99

VOLUME 4: TIME OF YOUR LIFE
Joss Whedon, Jeph Loeb, Georges Jeanty, and others
ISBN 978-1-59582-310-6 | $15.99

VOLUME 5: PREDATORS AND PREY
Joss Whedon, Jane Espenson, Cliff Richards, Georges Jeanty, and others
ISBN 978-1-59582-342-7 | $15.99

VOLUME 6: RETREAT
Joss Whedon, Jane Espenson, Cliff Richards, Georges Jeanty, and others
ISBN 978-1-59582-415-8 | $15.99

VOLUME 7: TWILIGHT
Joss Whedon, Brad Meltzer, and Georges Jeanty
ISBN 978-1-59582-558-2 | $16.99

VOLUME 8: LAST GLEAMING
Joss Whedon, Scott Allie, and Georges Jeanty
ISBN 978-1-59582-610-7 | $16.99

BUFFY THE VAMPIRE SLAYER SEASON 9
VOLUME 1: FREEFALL
Joss Whedon, Andrew Chambliss, Cliff Richards, Georges Jeanty, and others
ISBN 978-1-59582-922-1 | $17.99

TALES OF THE SLAYERS
Joss Whedon, Amber Benson, Gene Colan, P. Craig Russell, Tim Sale, and others
ISBN 978-1-56971-605-2 | $14.99

TALES OF THE VAMPIRES
Joss Whedon, Brett Matthews, Cameron Stewart, and others
ISBN 978-1-56971-749-3 | $15.99

BUFFY THE VAMPIRE SLAYER: TALES
ISBN 978-1-59582-644-2 | $29.99

FRAY: FUTURE SLAYER
Joss Whedon and Karl Moline
ISBN 978-1-56971-751-6 | $19.99

ALSO FROM DARK HORSE...
BUFFY THE VAMPIRE SLAYER OMNIBUS

VOLUME 1
ISBN 978-1-59307-784-6 | $24.99

VOLUME 2
ISBN 978-1-59307-826-3 | $24.99

VOLUME 3
ISBN 978-1-59307-885-0 | $24.99

VOLUME 4
ISBN 978-1-59307-968-0 | $24.99

VOLUME 5
ISBN 978-1-59582-225-3 | $24.99

VOLUME 6
ISBN 978-1-59582-242-0 | $24.99

VOLUME 7
ISBN 978-1-59582-331-1 | $24.99

ANGEL OMNIBUS
Christopher Golden, Eric Powell, and others
ISBN 978-1-59582-706-7 | $24.99

ANGEL & FAITH VOLUME 1: LIVE THROUGH THIS
Christos Gage, Rebekah Isaacs, Phil Noto, and others
ISBN 978-1-59582-887-3 | $17.99

BUFFY THE VAMPIRE SLAYER: PANEL TO PANEL
ISBN 978-1-59307-836-2 | $19.99

ALSO FROM JOSS WHEDON

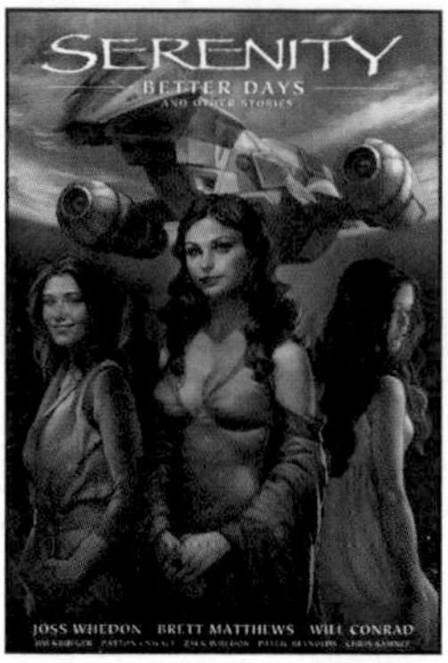
SERENITY
BETTER DAYS
JOSS WHEDON BRETT MATTHEWS WILL CONRAD

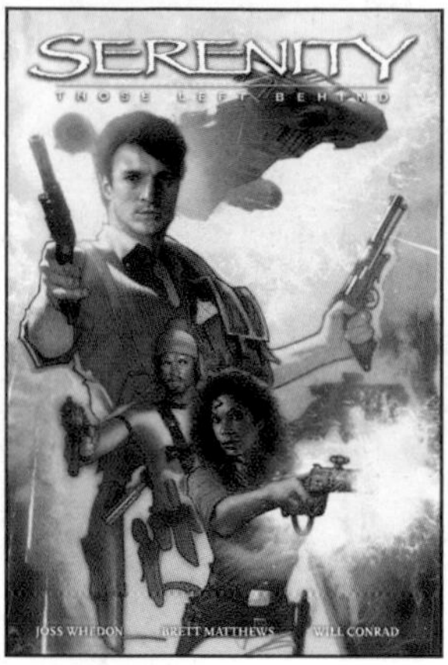
SERENITY
THOSE LEFT BEHIND
JOSS WHEDON BRETT MATTHEWS WILL CONRAD

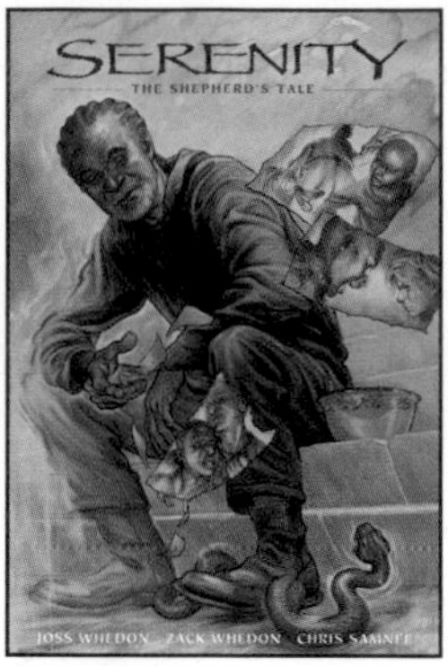
SERENITY
THE SHEPHERD'S TALE
JOSS WHEDON ZACK WHEDON CHRIS SAMNEE

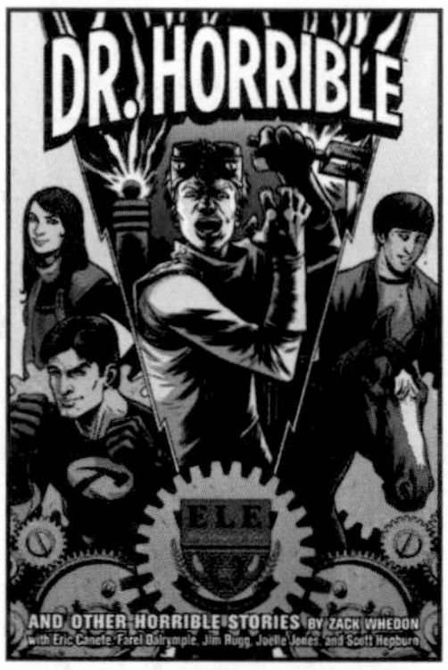
DR. HORRIBLE
E.L.E.
AND OTHER HORRIBLE STORIES BY ZACK WHEDON
with Eric Canete, Farel Dalrymple, Jim Rugg, Joëlle Jones, and Scott Hepburn

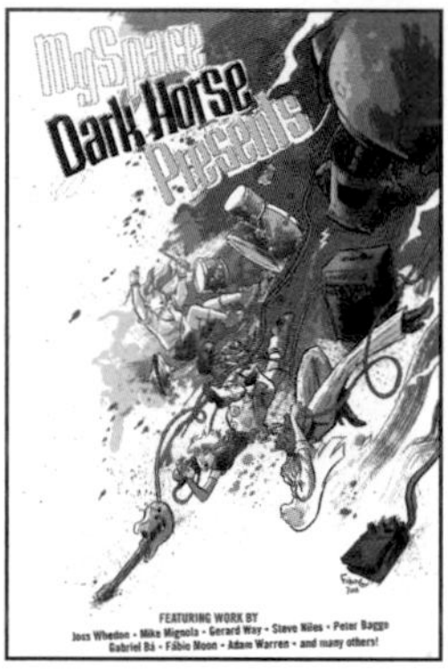
MySpace
Dark Horse
Presents
FEATURING WORK BY

SERENITY VOLUME 1: THOSE LEFT BEHIND SECOND EDITION HARDCOVER
Joss Whedon, Brett Matthews, and Will Conrad
ISBN 978-1-59307-846-1 $17.99

SERENITY VOLUME 2: BETTER DAYS AND OTHER STORIES HARDCOVER
Joss Whedon, Patton Oswalt, Zack Whedon, Patric Reynolds and others
ISBN 978-1-59582-739-5 $19.99

SERENITY VOLUME 3: THE SHEPHERD'S TALE HARDCOVER
Joss Whedon, Zack Whedon, and Chris Samnee
ISBN 978-1-59582-561-2 $14.99

DR. HORRIBLE AND OTHER HORRIBLE STORIES
Joss Whedon, Zack Whedon, Joëlle Jones, and others
ISBN 978-1-59582-577-3 $9.99

MYSPACE DARK HORSE PRESENTS VOLUME 1
Featuring Sugarshock *by Joss Whedon and Fábio Moon*
ISBN 978-1-59307-998-7 $19.99

DOLLHOUSE VOLUME 1: EPITAPHS
Andrew Chambliss, Jed Whedon, Maurissa Tancharoen, and Cliff Richards
ISBN 978-1-59582-863-7 $18.99

DARK HORSE BOOKS
DarkHorse.com

AVAILABLE AT YOUR LOCAL COMICS SHOP OR BOOKSTORE!
TO FIND A COMICS SHOP IN YOUR AREA, CALL 1-888-266-4226.
For more information or to order direct visit DarkHorse.com or call 1-800-862-0052 Mon.–Fri. 9 AM to 5 PM Pacific Time.